Entertaining the Citizen

Recent Titles in the Series
Harold Innis
    Paul Heyer
Toward a Political Economy of Culture: Capitalism and Communication in the Twenty-First Century
    Edited by Andrew Calabrese and Colin Sparks
Many Voices, One World: Towards a New, More Just, and More Efficient World Information and Communication Order
    The MacBride Commission
Changing Concepts of Time
    Harold A. Innis
Mass Communication and American Social Thought: Key Texts, 1919–1968
    Edited by John Durham Peters and Peter Simonson
Entertaining the Citizen: When Politics and Popular Culture Converge
    Liesbet van Zoonen

Forthcoming
A Fatal Attraction: Public Television and Politics in Italy
    Cinzia Padovani
Global Electioneering
    Gerald Sussman
The Blame Game: Why Television Is Not Our Fault
    Eileen R. Meehan
Film Industries and Cultures in Transition
    Dina Iordanova
Raymond Williams
    Alan O'Connor

Entertaining the Citizen

When Politics and
Popular Culture Converge

Liesbet van Zoonen

ROWMAN & LITTLEFIELD PUBLISHERS, INC.
Lanham • Boulder • New York • Toronto • Oxford

ROWMAN & LITTLEFIELD PUBLISHERS, INC.

Published in the United States of America
by Rowman & Littlefield Publishers, Inc.
A wholly owned subsidiary of The Rowman & Littlefield Publishing Group, Inc.
4501 Forbes Boulevard, Suite 200, Lanham, MD 20706
www.rowmanlittlefield.com

P.O. Box 317, Oxford OX2 9RU, UK

British Library Cataloguing in Publication Information Available

Library of Congress Cataloging-in-Publication Data
Zoonen, Liesbet van, 1959–
  Entertaining the citizen : when politics and popular culture converge / Liesbet
van Zoonen.
    p. cm. — (Critical media studies series)
  Includes bibliographical references and index.
  ISBN 0-7425-2906-1 (cloth : alk. paper) — ISBN 0-7425-2907-X (pbk. : alk. paper)
  1. Popular culture—Political aspects—United States. 2. Mass media—Political
aspects—United States. 3. Politics and culture—United States. 4. United
States—Politics and government—1989– 5. United States—Politics and government—1945–1989. I. Title. II. Series: Critical media studies
  E169.12 .Z655 2005
  306.2'0973—dc22
                                                                    2004010653

Printed in the United States of America

⊗ ™ The paper used in this publication meets the minimum requirements of
American National Standard for Information Sciences—Permanence of Paper for
Printed Library Materials, ANSI/NISO Z39.48-1992.

Contents

Preface

One day, while researching for this book, I came across an excited text from an American student who had to watch *The West Wing*, an American television series about life and politics at the White House, for her political science class. Did I envy her! I remember reading *All the President's Men* and watching the movie in the Netherlands in the mid-seventies, when I was in my teens. I found it electrifying; what an amazing arrogance of the Nixon administration, what a daring investigation by the *Washington Post* journalists, what a right and proper outcome of the democratic process. How exhilarating politics could be! I don't really remember whether the book and the movie made me go to university to study political science, but I do recall my surprise and frustration in my first year that politics could be made so tiresome. We did not get movies at my Dutch university, but there were lots of readings, endless theorizing, enigmatic statistical logics, and discussion—always more discussion. On only a few occasions did a teacher manage to convey some of the passion and vitality that motivates people to become involved in politics or to study political science. More often I found myself struggling with the abstract concepts of "the state," "ideology," and "the public sphere." I found out only later that my bewilderment as an eighteen-year-old (Where is this public sphere exactly?) was a running gag among scholars working with the concept. Had they told me then, I may not have ended up with such a love-hate relationship with politics and political science; much of which also had to do, as I understood again much later, with being one of the few women to study this peculiar discipline.

After my first disappointing year, I turned away and focused on research methodology and media studies. These proved to be much more concrete and fun; apparently I was not cut out for the intense and solemn business of politics and political science. Some two decades later I have managed to shrug off my inevitable sense of failure and turn the issue around. I started to wonder if there was a deficiency in politics and political science itself. Perhaps my difficulties with the discipline were not the result of my frivolity but a consequence of how politics and the belonging discipline framed itself. It seemed likely that I was not the only one who was terribly bored; after all, political interest and student numbers seemed to be declining, at least in the late nineties in the Netherlands.

Obviously, age, experience, and position enabled me to ask the questions that I thought were trivial when I was eighteen. This book is the result. It is meant as an agenda to think about entertaining politics, instead of simply discarding it as irrelevant and dangerous to citizenship and the democratic project. It is meant as a starting point for debate, and it is meant to stimulate and entertain students and all others reading it.

Others have stimulated and entertained me in writing it. First I would like to thank my Ph.D. students and postdocs at the Centre for Popular Culture of the University of Amsterdam. Chris Aalberts, Joost de Bruin, Vincent Crone, Marc Deuze, Linda Duits, Jeroen de Kloet, Juul Mulder, Stijn Reijnders, Frank Schaap, Eugenia Siapera, and Mirjam Vosmeer invariably produced the most critical and constructive of the comments that I received. Femke Bilderbeek has assisted most helpfully in collecting material and literature for this book. My colleagues—John Corner, Jeroen Jansz, Dick Pels, and John Street—have offered valuable suggestions and assured me of being on the right track. I am especially grateful to Gary Carter, my favorite twin brother, who read and commented on all chapters. The book is for my incredible family: my unfailing parents, Arie and Jannie van Zoonen-Zielman, my wonderful sons, Tom and Bram, and my indescribable husband, Jaap Schoufour.

1

⊰⊱

Distinctions

QUESTIONS

Can politics be combined with entertainment? Can political involvement and participation be fun? Can citizenship be pleasurable? These and similar questions have forced themselves upon us again and again in the past years: they were, for instance, raised by Arnold Schwarzenegger's election as governor of California. They were implicit in the meetings between U2 lead singer Bono and world leaders, which concerned Third World debts. They were behind the outcry that greeted the proposal, by American cable network FX, to run a televised political popularity contest in the vein of *American Idol*, with the purpose of selecting presidential candidates. They were inherent in the acclaim for the award-winning television series *The West Wing*, a fictional portrayal of day-to-day political processes in the White House. They were heightened in the dispute about the portrayal of Ronald and Nancy Reagan in the 2003 television series *The Reagans*, which made CBS decide not to air the show on network television.

But these questions were not only raised as a result of our contemporary entertainment societies. Ronald Reagan, of course, preceded Arnold Schwarzenegger in the 1980s; musicians have cast their fate with politicians from the advent of popular music and before; and Hollywood was already producing political melodrama prior to World War II. Going further back in history, the famous nineteenth-century Lincoln-Douglas debates, upheld in many a textbook as the quintessential political confrontation capturing audiences on the basis of

1

substantial oratory, were simultaneously entertaining social events crowded by popular artists, magicians, and quacks (Schudson, 1998).

Historical treatments of these wide-ranging articulations of politics and entertainment are scarce. A few titles come to mind, such as Ronald Brownstein's *The Power and the Glitter* (1992), about the twentieth-century connections between Hollywood and Washington. However, a systematic search in relevant academic databases such as the Web of Science, or the American Library of Congress, produces only a small number of titles.[1] This lack of historical analysis of the manifold connections between entertainment and politics has not prevented scientists and philosophers from condemning such connections outright. Chief among them was Neil Postman, whose vilification of entertainment in *Amusing Ourselves to Death* (1985) sold 200,000 copies and was translated into eight languages (McCain, 2003). On the long list are other great names, such as the French sociologist Pierre Bourdieu, German philosopher Jürgen Habermas, and—if one digs even deeper—the Greek philosopher Plato, who had no place for poetic diversion in his ideal state unless it served a higher educational purpose. I will discuss these authors and their views in more detail later in this chapter. Let us say for the moment that we are faced with a phenomenon—the enduring encounters between entertainment and politics—about which there is little knowledge but much opinion.

This book will not offer another onslaught on the coupling of politics and entertainment. Surely, there are enough books about the political flaws of the sound-bite society, media torrents, or video malaise, and they are likely to keep coming. They unanimously seem to long for a period without television (some authors have gone as far as to recommend the *elimination* of television altogether; see Mander, 1977) and for a political discourse and practice that is purely informational, rational, and deliberative. There is, of course, nothing wrong with these desires, but they are rather limited and remarkably out of touch with current political challenges. Notwithstanding the continuous lamentation over the role of entertainment in politics, its presence and relevance have only intensified. This is not a surprise: most people have to "do" politics in their leisure time, and leisure is a highly competitive sector. Keeping up with politics by reading the newspaper has to be secured from other reading: from other parts of the newspaper, magazines, books, or comics. Keeping up with politics by watching the relevant television programs is in competition with sports, comedies, or quiz shows. Visiting a political demonstration is in conflict with going to a simultaneously scheduled classic car fair, whereas participating in political meetings has to be a better way to spend one's scarce free evening than going to the gym or out bowling with friends (although television critics suggest that doesn't happen anymore; see Putnam, 2000). Politics thus has to compete with a large offer of diversion—mediated and unmediated—to gain people's attention, interest, and involvement. Even natural cultural allies of politics, such as literature and the arts, are increasingly molded in entertaining formats; they position their creators as celebrities and construct exhibitions as engaging experiences in which all senses are involved (see Gitlin, 2002, p. 115, for a more extensive, somewhat despairing treatment of the "Sensurround pleasure dome of everyday life").

The average critic of entertainment in politics does not disagree with this analysis of the current cultural climate, but argues that politics should be kept "clean." Neil Postman (1985) had nothing against entertainment per se, but hated its invasion of politics. However, to set politics apart from the rest of culture is not a feasible option for the maintenance of citizenship: not only will it not survive the competition for spare time, but more importantly it will also be separated, different, and distant from everyday life. Stephen Coleman, a British political scientist, has discussed the lessons that politics could learn from the immensely popular television reality program *Big Brother* (Coleman, 2003). Comparing the representative qualities of the Big Brother House and the House of Commons, Coleman concludes that the fans of the program consider *Big Brother* candidates as much more representative than politicians because the candidates are like the fans themselves. Such a reflection is, however, but one meaning of representation. In most democratic theory, the more common meaning is the delegation of one's opinion and interests to democratically elected politicians. Representation in that sense fails ordinary people, not only because most politicians are not very well connected to the people—as Coleman claims—but also because their mode of representation is "abstruse and beguiling," "opaque," "complacent," and "incestuous": "Politicians are seen as talking *at* rather than talking *to*, preaching rather than sharing. This does not feel like representation" (2003, p. 33). In both senses of representation, then—resemblance and delegation—too big a distance between the representers and the represented is a breeding ground for a crisis that goes much further than straightforward political conflict. Politics has to be connected to the everyday culture of its citizens; otherwise it becomes an alien sphere, occupied by strangers no one cares and bothers about.

A proper treatment of the role of entertainment in politics, therefore, cannot settle for denunciation, however intricately elaborated; nor can it advocate the isolation of politics or the abolition of entertainment, or simply propose the education of citizens to "higher" standards. These measures are profoundly out of touch with everyday experience in the entertainment society. These are well-trod roads but they lead backward, in a nostalgic yearning for supposedly better times (to which I will come back later in this chapter). Nevertheless, the opposite journey, toward celebration, is not in order either. Popular means of political communication, celebrity politics, or populist rhetoric—to mention only a few cases of entertainment in politics—are not simply valuable because they are up to date, savvy, and in touch with the experience of ordinary people, although they are an important sign that politics is part of everyday culture and not above it. Entertainment in politics comes in various formats and qualities that need to be analyzed in their particular contexts, with their particular features and their particular effects on the democratic project, before they can be denounced, cheered, or blissfully ignored. Only by such situated analyses will we know whether, when, and how entertainment functions to *entertain the citizen* in the triple sense of the word: does entertainment provide a context to contemplate the concept of citizenship, does it provide an environment in which citizenship can flourish, and does it make citizenship pleasurable? These are the questions that guide this book. In the following chapters, articulations of politics with soap opera, popular music, fandom, talk shows, gossip, romantic genres, movies, and other television series will be reviewed. To keep this assortment together in one relatively consistent academic project, a few more notes on the key concepts and key arguments are necessary.

CONCEPTS

I have used various terms rather loosely. Politics, citizenship, representation, and the democratic project have come up together. Entertainment has appeared in conjunction with pleasure and fun. Terms with a long definitional history such as political information, involvement, or participation have not yet been explicated. The overall concepts in this book are politics, citizenship, and entertainment, notions that in themselves have been contested regarding what they mean and to what they refer, and which in triangulation become a vast terrain rather than a clearly delineated object. Nevertheless, some limits need to be drawn, first around politics.

Politics

A journalist calls a senator and asks him for an interview. The senator is hesitant:

"I have nothing to say."

"I know," says the journalist, "so let's start."

Jokes like these abound and seem to express a common knowledge about what politics is and what its deficiencies are (Dor and Federman,

1964). Politicians have a bad name and are regularly accused of being ignorant, greedy, and corrupt. They are among the least trusted groups in society, and their ranking seems to be going down. Their reputation is beaten only by journalists (Dalton, 1996). In fact, they have such a sorry reputation that people who participate in activities that are considered political by most standards refuse to label their pursuits as such (Eliasoph, 1998). But politics is not just what politicians do, although that is by far the easiest meaning and in essence not so far from the understanding that I will be using here. Politics is also a "field" that exists independently from its practitioners and that accommodates the continuous struggle about power relations in society.

According to Bourdieu (1991), who developed this notion of politics as a field that coexists with other fields such as the arts and science, the field is structured according to a system of differences between what could be called left and right, progressive and conservative, change and stability, or libertarian and authoritarian. The relation of these oppositions to existing social demands and conflicts is variable, says Bourdieu. For instance, in pre–World War II France and Germany, the environment as a political issue was part of a conservative agenda, whereas it nowadays signifies a progressive perspective. The structure of the field as a system of differences requires that politicians and parties define their positions *internally* in competition with each other as much as *externally* in relation to their constituencies. The inevitable internal orientation of the field necessitates a thorough knowledge of its history and its discourse, a practical competence in positioning oneself politically and rhetorically as dissimilar from others, and a desire to invest in the field and submit to its historical rules and routines. Those have become such enormous requirements that specific education, training, and socialization have come on top of the considerable amount of available time and cultural capital necessary to develop the political habitus that enables one to participate in the field. The effect is restriction of the people who can participate and of the ideas that can be expressed.

> This means that the political field in fact produces an effect of censorship by limiting the universe of political discourse, and thereby the universe of what is politically thinkable, to the finite space of discourses capable of being produced or reproduced within the limits of the political *problematic*, understood as a space of stances effectively adopted within the field—i.e. stances that are socio-logically possible given the laws that determine entry into the field. (Bourdieu, 1991, p. 172)

The beauty of Bourdieu's analysis is that it explains the commonsense idea of politics as an ivory tower populated by people only talking to themselves as a structural sociological phenomenon and not, as populists would claim, as arising from the deranged narcissism of politicians, or, as elitists would say, as a result of the moronic apathy of ordinary people. In fact, Bourdieu considers popular antipolitical attitudes a revolt against the monopoly of professional politicians over politics. Such a legitimate antipolitics can take the form of jokes, satire, cynicism, and apathy, and, paradoxically, a political struggle about politics. Parts of the disputes activated by the new social movements of the 1960s were indeed about the sheer definition of politics and the particular discourse in which political problems could be legitimately expressed. The feminist slogan "the personal is political" was a claim to open up the political field to issues formerly considered private, such as violence against women and children in the family. It was also a call to consider the social and personal conflicts taking place outside of the political field as battles against—among other things—white, patriarchal, heterosexual power. Insofar as these conflicts could not be articulated within the political field—because they concerned, for instance, equality between heterosexual partners, the legitimacy of particular cultural tastes, or the acknowledgment of emotional experience as social knowledge—they have become part of the arguments around cultural citizenship, about which I will say more shortly.

The current political situation has parallels to the initial stages of new social movement politics that emerged in the mid-1960s, because there seems to be a similar sense of crisis of representation. Under the label of a "gap" between politics and citizens, it is claimed that the political field and its different actors have again become so internally focused that their *external* mobilizing potential has faded. The appearance of right-wing populist parties throughout western Europe is as much an expression of sentiments excluded from the political field demanding and wanting to get in as the appearance of the new social movements was (e.g., Melucci, 1988). In Bourdieu's structuralist understanding, such assaults on the self-absorption of politics are part of an inevitable cycle of the field, a position that is—for that matter—very much in line with classic republican thought, although there inevitable corruption of politicians was held responsible instead of the structure of the field itself. Gradual or violent renovation would follow, and then the whole cycle would start all over.

What is behind the present gap between politics and citizens is a matter of dispute. Chantal Mouffe (2000) argues that current theorizing about deliberative democracy and its practical translations in Third Way politics has eradicated antagonism and confrontation from politics in a suffocating evocation of unifiable incompatible interests. In the denial of the fundamental differences that structure the field, internal consensus overwhelms external relevance and puts citizens at a dangerous distance. It follows that political interest and involvement would pick up when conflicts and oppositions were stronger and more explicit. Corner and

Pels (2003, p. 2) add that struggles themselves are not enough; they need a sense of drama: "Political interest and electoral enthusiasm have generally picked up wherever politics has attained a high level of drama, offering spectacular storylines and flamboyant personalities rather than ideological standoffs or partisan bickering." Observations like these have brought critics into a fit about "drama democracy," "spectator democracy," or other supposed perversions of democracy (Elchardus, 2002; Manin, 1997). But there is nothing controversial about the observation that politics needs to be communicated in order to acquire the interest and involvement of its external referents, the average citizens. Nor is there anything extraordinary about the thought that historical modes of political communication have their basis in the particular culture of their time. Kathleen Hall Jamieson (1988), for instance, has examined how political eloquence has changed through the centuries, from the belligerent language of fire and sword to the intimate discourse of personal disclosure and companionship. That politics needs drama, story lines, and personalities is therefore not the issue: the issue is the forms into which they are molded by historical cultural requirements. Our contemporary case invites the question as to what kind of political drama, story lines, and personalities are produced by the dominant cultural mode of entertainment, and whether and how they enable a closure of the estrangement between politics and citizens.

Citizenship

Certainly the outcome of the above discussion is a narrow understanding of politics and citizenship, wherein politics is curbed within the confines of an institutionalized field in and toward which people can articulate their rights and obligations—around which, in other words, they can achieve and perform citizenship. In T. H. Marshall's (1950) classic tripartition of citizenship, this is what is meant by political citizenship: the rights and duties of citizens to participate in the formation and decisions of government. It was these rights that were fought for by the nineteenth-century emancipation movements of workers and women. In Marshall's historical phase model, they came on top of "civil" citizenship: the rights and obligations toward the law that emanated from the democratic revolutions of the eighteenth century. Marshall's final development in citizenship developed with the materialization of the welfare state in the twentieth century, which guaranteed the economic minimum for people to be full citizens.

Marshall's historical phase model suggests that new types of citizenship have occurred only after the older one has been fully realized. However, the new social movements of the 1960s demonstrated how basic civil, political, and social rights, supposedly all accomplished in previous decades and centuries, were withheld from African Americans, Native Americans, other ethnic minorities, women, gays, and other groups deviating from the male white Anglo-Saxon Protestant average (see Freeman, 1983). On top of their struggle for equal rights, which was fought in and against the political field, the goals and activities of social movements produced a new arena of citizenship: that of culture. The women's movement, for instance, began to dispute stereotypical and confining cultural definitions of women and femininity and developed an alternative culture that consisted of—among other things—journalism, literature, cinema, health care, therapy, dress style, and everything else that makes a counterculture (Cohen, 1988). Here, the slogan "the personal is political" developed yet another meaning. Likewise, the civil rights movement has exposed dominant culture as profoundly white, as stereotyping blacks and black culture, and as ignoring black history and knowledge. In response, a black public culture has come about "whose violent birth and diasporic conditions of life provide a counter narrative to the exclusionary national narratives of Europe, the United States, the Caribbean and Africa" (Black Public Sphere Collective, 1995, p. 1). New social movements are not the single sources that have made "culture" a battleground where demands for rights and duties are fiercely asserted and denied. Migration and religion, in combination with the demise of the nation-state and the ubiquitous and still-growing presence of mass media and communication technologies, are other factors mentioned in the literature (e.g., Turner, 1993). At stake is *cultural citizenship*, a condition that has not been well defined but that, according to many authors, minimally implies "being included" in culture (Dahlgren, 1995, p. 136; see also Stevenson, 2001). That seemingly nominal requirement is behind intense confrontations about national and minority languages or religions; about the validity and legitimacy of particular kinds of knowledge; about cultural heritage and protectionism; and about lifestyles, identities, norms, values, decency, and good and bad taste.

Civil, social, political, and cultural citizenship have been examined extensively. Lately, an additional notion of "corporate citizenship" has popped up as a shortcut to the responsibilities corporations have toward society and their employees (Simon, 2001). From feminist and queer activism come claims to "sexual" citizenship, conceptualized as sexual rights and, more generally, access to rights regardless of sexuality (Richardson, 2001). Michael Schudson (1998) therefore speaks of a widening web of citizenship in which "ideals of equality, due process, and rights" (p. 265) come to bear on an ever-larger set of domains, among which are the home, the workplace, lower and higher education, the professions, and the political process itself.

In the context of this book, such an all-embracing notion of citizenship would result in a rather indistinct question of how rights and obligations of individuals and groups (not to forget corporations) in each domain of life are articulated in and through entertainment. Studies of the portrayal of particular disadvantaged groups in the media could be seen as part of such an overall project, as could studies with titles like *The Politics of Pictures* (Hartley, 1992), *The Politics of Television and Cultural Change* (Wayne, 1998), or *The Politics of Entertainment* (Parenti, 1998). "Politics" in these works refers to social conflict and change that occurs outside of the political field and implies a broad rather than a narrow understanding of politics. A broad focus like that is not my intention. My concern here is with political citizenship, with the rights and duties of citizens vis-à-vis the political process, with matters of government, and more generally with the democratic project. The reason for this particular focus is that politics seems to be the area that is most contested when it comes to the inroads that entertainment has been making. While the advance of entertainment in journalism, public broadcasting, public education, government communication, and the arts has been denounced as well, the disgust for entertainment in politics seems unrivaled. Every year a new book that speaks against it seems to appear, invariably receiving approving media attention: great philosophers, scientists, and world leaders alike have joined in rejecting it. There is, therefore, an impinging urgency to come to a more situated and practical understanding of the articulations between entertainment and *political* citizenship. That doesn't mean that the debates on cultural citizenship are irrelevant to the book; on the contrary, they have unmistakably asserted the *cultural dimensions* of political citizenship. They have identified and undermined the partial language, epistemology, aesthetics, rituals, and pleasures of politics (e.g., Corner and Pels, 2003) and have impelled the central question of this book: whether there are articulations of entertainment and politics that are beneficial to citizenship.

Entertainment

Until now I have used the term "entertainment" as a catchall term that indicates specific industries, genres, and products, as well as an overall cultural condition. This does not exhaust the meanings of entertainment: a significant school of media scholars has identified entertainment in terms of media effects rather than genres: "It is most meaningful to treat the entertainment experience as an effect. It is, in fact, *the* effect of entertainment consumption" (Zillman and Bryant, 1994, p. 415). An unexamined by-product of this conception of entertainment is that genres and fields usually considered its quintessential opposite—information, journalism, and politics—can be seen as entertainment as well, since they too can provide gratification and enjoyment. Plato, for instance, had a *hedonistic* notion of political activity, because he thought that it should serve human pleasure and happiness. His road to pleasure, however, went through the cerebral contemplation of the good society (cf. de Vos, 1978). The contemporary political habitus includes an appreciation of the run-of-the-mill political process as "drama and excitement," as many a political biography testifies (see, for instance, Baker, 1993).

Yet the entertaining effects of present-day politics are unmistakably limited to a handful of professional practitioners and observers; otherwise the omnipresent efforts of campaigners and spin doctors to make politics compelling for a wider group of people would not have been necessary. We can therefore safely reject a definition of entertainment as an *effect* of political communication and keep an understanding of entertainment as located in particular cultural genres and products. Politics has its own entertainment genre in the form of satire (e.g., Keighron, 1998), but my interest is wider than that and extends to entertainment as an important, if not the main, ingredient of popular culture. John Street (1997, p. 7) also links entertainment to popular culture when he says: "Popular culture is a form of entertainment that is mass produced or is made available to large numbers of people (for example, on television)." Nevertheless, the terms "entertainment" and "popular culture" are not simply interchangeable. Their use, for instance, signals different disciplinary traditions, with popular culture "belonging" to history, sociology, and cultural studies, and entertainment more commonly "owned" by the various strands of psychology. Thus entertainment has been studied often at the microlevel of individual media effects (Bryant and Thompson, 2002), whereas popular culture has been more regularly examined at the mesolevel of discourse and everyday life (e.g., Miller and McHoul, 1998). Entertainment is easily associated with escape from social conflict and concerns, whereas popular culture has a history of opposition to elite affairs and politics (e.g., Burke, 1978). These differences resonate in this book: both entertainment and popular culture provide the shortcut term to the popular genres and features discussed in this book, but my angle on the articulation of politics with popular entertainment is very much one inspired by the popular culture tradition. Thus, my interest in the relation between entertainment and politics does not directly lie with the psychological question of whether it makes individual citizens more politically interested and involved, or whether it provides them with undesirable means to escape political realities. Rather, I look at the way in which the concept of (political) citizenship is entertained through popular genres and means: How does popular culture reflect on citizenship, and what kind of joy does it connect to citizenship? These questions are located at the plane of culture and discourse rather than at the level of individual meanings and under-standings.

ARGUMENTS

The common complaint about entertainment in relation to politics is di-rected at a particular medium and a particular genre. Television has re-peatedly been identified as the scapegoat, supposedly being a medium that is suited for entertainment alone. Television journalism would thus be an inevitable contradiction in terms. Sound bites, immediacy, symbolism, emotions, face, personality, celebrity, "deep reads," sensationalism, and what have you are alleged to guide television journalism. They are con-sidered unmistakable evidence that television provides infotainment in-stead of the serious information, reasonable debate, and sound opinions that citizens require to make sense of politics. The undesirable outcome is claimed to be a citizenry that is uninformed, misguided, and manipulated but nevertheless completely confident about its own judgment and choices. For political scientists, therefore, says William Gamson (1992, p. 5), "the mystery is . . . how people manage to have opinions about so many matters about which they lack the most elementary understanding."

The empirical accuracy of this television malaise thesis (see Bennett et al., 1999) has been questioned from various angles. One main strand of criticism is that the misery would be an American phenomenon in partic-ular, which does not hold outside of the United States. Brants (1998), for instance, has suggested that European television journalism is by and large serious and deliberative, and has also found that European politi-cians have not overwhelmingly surrendered to television logic. Never-theless, other European authors keep expressing concerns about Ameri-canization and the alleged dumbing down of television journalism and political communication (Blumler, 1999). Another counterargument says that, regardless of national particularities, there is no empirical support for the thesis that citizens become less informed and apathetic *because* of television and infotainment (Norris, 2000). Related to that position is the more general argument that television malaise authors grossly overstate the influence of television, especially in comparison with other everyday influences on citizens, such as the family, peers, education, and work (Newton, 2003). Such empirical refutations notwithstanding, "television malaise" remains *the* dominant academic, political, and journalistic dis-course to look at contemporary political communication both in the United States and Europe.[2] That persistent popularity suggests the ques-tions of how the argument that such a malaise exists is constructed, why it is so popular, and what it achieves.

By and large, television malaise arguments are essentialist contentions: politics *proper* is said to have changed for the worse because of the fundamentally antipolitical nature of television. Paradoxically, the critics have singled out different cores of politics as being endangered by different features of television. In his classic thunder against entertainment, Neil Postman (1985) claims that it is the *epistemology* of politics that television perverts. He starts from the observation that oral, written, and visual television produce different ways of knowing and understanding the world. For Postman, print culture is the prerequisite for democracy because it enables an attitude of objectivity and detachment, from which informed judgment can arise. Television epistemology has replaced this written discourse of exposition and produced a "peek-a-boo world, where now this event, now that pops into view for a moment, then vanishes again" (p. 77). Television has made entertainment the "natural format for the representation of all experience" (p. 87), and as a result politics has come to look like a commercial in which politicians appear as celebrities. Roderick Hart (1994) also declares an essential transformation of politics. His focus, however, is on *phenomenology*, or the way the experience of politics has changed. The typical television discourse of disclosure, Hart writes, has shown the rich variety of human lives and engendered intimacy and personal involvement in many areas of everyday life. Hart does not criticize the intimacy of television in itself, just as Postman does not disapprove of entertainment per se. However, the language of personal relations and the visual focus on politicians' faces encourage—according to Hart—"deep reads" of politicians and their psychological motives instead of a conversant examination of their policies. Television thus makes people *feel* informed instead of really and adroitly knowledgeable. Jeffry Scheuer (2001) sees another mainstay of politics disappear through television, namely, that of *ideological contestation*. Television, he argues, is intrinsically conservative, not merely because of its economic and regulatory structure, the political orientation of many commentators, or the New Right's resources to set up its own cable networks, but because the fabric of the medium is geared toward simplicity. Immediacy, superficiality, amnesia, passivity, and narcissism are only a few of the words that Scheuer uses to express television's minimalism. Because conservatism has a simpler message than liberalism—a difference that comes from their diverging views on the role of government—television favors conservatism: "TV has never been an effective tool for addressing the more systemic concerns of the left, such as poverty, progressive taxation, worker's rights, health care, education, children, the elderly, or (except for the dramatic confrontations over segregation) minorities" (p. 29). Scheuer attributes the dominance of the American New Right—which is ever increasing, as he sees it—primarily to the ubiquity of television in political communication. If epistemology, phenomenology, and ideologies of politics have so fundamentally changed since television came along, the question of whether politics has survived at all is only one step away. Thomas Meyer (2002) argues just that: television has colonized politics to the extent that we now live no longer in a democracy but in a mediacracy. It is a classic case of colonization, he says, where politics has unconditionally surrendered "at least in all visible, publicly accessible aspects of communication—to the logic of the media system" (p. 57). The ideal democratic situation in which the media *follow* politics—critically, supportively, neutrally, or else—has thus turned 180 degrees: politics now follows the media. Although more people than ever participate in the mediacracy, its democratic quality is questionable because of its theatrical, momentary, individualist tendencies.

The essentialism in these kinds of arguments is partly what makes them so attractive: Postman, Hart, Scheuer, and Meyer, as well as Bourdieu (1998) and Mander (1977), all identify the opposition between television and politics as the basic structure from which all current political problems transpire. Such dualism is a more general feature of everyday talk and academic social theory alike (e.g., Young, 1980). It comes in many dichotomies: nature-culture, women-men, black-white, emotional-rational, beauty-beast, us-them, personal-political, entertainment-information, and so on. However, if the abundant writing about the postmodern condition has agreed on anything, it is that these dichotomies have mostly blurred into hybridity: masculinity and femininity have lost their stable meanings, the political has become personal and vice versa, entertainment has mixed with information, intelligence now also applies to emotions, and so forth. In such an unpredictable, unsettled culture, one can live with the pleasure of continuous surprise and transgression, with the pain of a limitless and ungraspable experience, or with pleasure and pain both alternating and coexisting. What we hear from the authors of the malaise of television is the pain of lost clarity and boundaries around politics, information, and journalism. Their sense of loss betrays a desire for easier and more definite times. The popularity of the television malaise thesis suggests that such longing appeals to many people, if not always and unconditionally.

Apart from the appeal of delineating clear sides and boundaries, the television malaise authors also sustain their outlook with strong rhetorical means. Both Postman (1985) and Hart (1994), for instance, use bright historical images to evoke their ideals. Postman delves into the nineteenth-century daylong Lincoln-Douglas debates and typifies them as "pure print" (p. 49), a spoken discourse dominated by typography that demands an intellectual attitude from their audiences not based on passions and enthusiasm. That this is a mythical rather than a realistic description of history (cf. Schudson, 1998, pp. 133–143, for a more complete picture) hardly undermines its rhetorical validation of Postman's assertions about the superiority of the written word. Hart inserts a more idiosyncratic historical anecdote by relating a personal experience as a seven-year-old boy: in 1952 he saw Dwight Eisenhower's campaign motorcade pass through his street and was deeply impressed, also because his mother did not allow him to cheer for the candidate. Hart recollects it as a foundational experience that has not been replaced by any televised presidential appearance since. A different rhetorical device used to build the supposed inseparable dichotomy between television and politics is the reference to "others" who agree, especially canonical writers and philosophers. So Postman summons Orwell and Huxley to strengthen his position; Bourdieu (1998) discusses Flaubert and Gide, and feels their literary works prove him right in his strikes against television; and Mander (1977) comes up with Walter Benjamin as a supporting act.[3] Of such others, scientists are of course the best authorities to certify the claimed contradictions between television and politics. While a discussion of existing academic work is evidently part of normal science, the television malaise authors tend to limit their reviews to works that sustain their argument about the inseparable distance between politics and television. George Gerbner's research into cultural mainstreaming—which has produced controversial outcomes, according to academic experts in communication studies—comes up in most of the books discussed and seems to have been most helpful.[4] Finally, Postman and the others continuously lure their readers into compliance with their antitelevision claims through their frequent use of "we" and "us," constructing an imaginary community of readers that can hardly do anything else than agree with the author. In a typical quote, Hart (1994, p. 104) says that watching politics on television "gives *us* a sense of the state without placing responsibility upon *us* for the success of the state" (italics added). The community of like-minded readers thus construed can safely be asked to *imagine* a world in which television's detrimental influence did not yet exist (nostalgia) or one in which the injurious impact of television will have ceased (a future utopia). In a creative turnaround of this rhetorical strategy, Scheuer (2001, p. 32) asks his readers to imagine it is 1945, "and you, as a conservative, are free to chose an ideal vehicle, a 'dream medium,' to purvey your ideas. What would you want that medium to look like?" The only correct answer, of course, would be television, according to Scheuer.

   The simplicity of the arguments and the rhetorical maneuvers that promote them produce a discourse that has the added allure of elevating its authors above the ordinary crowds who rely on television for their political orientation. The authors implicitly proclaim themselves as the authorities who are able to see through the tricks television plays upon "us," and who will guide us out of the darkness. Civic education and media education are the predictable solutions of most writers in this genre, who are completely confident in pointing out "our" deficiencies as citizens. Hart (1994), for instance, argues for a new Puritanism that resists the vanity of television and teaches personal obligation. Mander (1977) literally puts himself up as "having seen the light" by imposing his personal conversion from commercial advertiser to environmental activist. In such frames, there is only room for two kinds of people: those who have recognized how bad television is, and those who have fallen prey to its manipulative pranks. The true citizen, then, has to rise above the troubles of television to be counted as a "good citizen." The television malaise thesis thus functions as a marker of good citizenship, just as "good taste" functions as a marker of cultural capital (Bourdieu, 1984). The result is the discursive (re)construction of a political elite whose members are completely different from ordinary folk. While television malaise authors are undeniably driven by a genuine fear about the vitality of democracy, in fact their arguments reproduce an authoritarian distinction between elites and masses, or at least propose that democracy will be better off if the masses think and act like elites. And thus enters, inevitably, the cry for better education, better journalism, new Puritanism, or media literacy programs.

I will not argue for the complete opposite, although there are authors who feel that true democracy lies with the masses and popular culture rather than with the elites (e.g., Fiske, 1989, 1992). I also will not deny that with the ubiquity of television in political communication, something has changed and been lost. But, as Michael Schudson (1999, p. 1) says, "Change happens," and what we need is not a rejection but an attempt "to incorporate the face of actual political life into a theory of desirable political forms." One needs to ask, therefore, not how one can eradicate entertainment from politics, but how one can entertain the citizen instead, how the current entertainment culture can be articulated with the requirements of political citizenship, and what kind of civic virtues can be evoked and maintained through popular culture. The following chapters take on different aspects of these questions.

OUTLINE

Chapters 2 and 3 will explore two entertainment genres and their articulation with politics in more detail. In chapter 2, I will take up my suggestion that the television malaise argument offers a means of distinction by analyzing the way politicians, journalists, and commentators alike use the term "soap opera" as a metaphor for everything they consider bad politics: conflict, incompetence, spin doctoring. The soap opera metaphor enables them to position themselves as superior and distant from their opponents who muddle through the petty emotional world evoked through the association with soap opera. Yet, at the same time, soap opera stars and soap opera narratives have been eagerly adopted in election campaigns, which shows recognition of the soap opera's capacities to engage and mobilize its audience. That contradiction between repugnance and incorporation, I argue, is made possible by the gendered subtext of the soap-politics equation: Soap operas provide acceptable campaign instruments because in that way they are supportive to the main business of politics. The soap metaphor, however, indicates that politics has become soap, which is another, substandard matter. The allowed presence of "soap" in politics is therefore very much like the presence of the first lady, supportive but in the background. The occurrence of popular music in politics shows a similar paradox, which I will take on in chapter 3. Here, the disparity between incorporating popular culture on the one hand and disapproving of it on the other is even stronger. Politicians of all ideological leanings have used pop music and rock stars to position themselves favorably vis-à-vis their desired constituencies. Yet, when popular music comes up with political agendas of its own, it becomes highly contested, scorned, and sometimes even censored, as, for instance, the protest music of the 1960s and the black inner-city rap of the 1990s has demonstrated. I take both popular music and the case of soap opera as evidence of the fact that politics will absorb all communicative repertoires to its own benefit, but will hear and allow only one proper political mode of expressing public concerns and conflict, which is characterized by informed judgment, impersonal reaction, and rational debate. This is the mode that the television malaise authors think we should all adjust to, despite its limited and elitist appeal. Throughout the rest of the book, I will refer to this notion of politics, deliberation, and communication as the modernist understanding of politics.

What would happen, however, if we abandoned the modernist notion of politics and took the soap opera and popular music as exemplary, as instances from which one could learn how citizens are informed, engaged, and mobilized? In chapter 4, I will argue that the behavior of fans in relation to soaps, popular music, and other entertainment genres is not fundamentally different from what is required of citizens. Fans and citizens—both taken as ideal types—come about as the result of performance: of artists on the one hand, and of politicians on the other. Both fans and citizens follow their objects intensely, promote them to outsiders, deliberate among each other, come to informed judgments, and propose alternatives. What may hold is a difference in the type of psychological relationship that fans have with artists and citizens have with politicians: affective and emotional versus cognitive and rational. Nevertheless, as I will claim, that tendency has fossilized into an absolute dualism that equally ignores the rational in fandom and the emotional in politics, and that overlooks recent developments in psychological research that have shown the inextricable ties between emotions and rationality (Damasio, 1995). I will conclude from that chapter that we can accept the mechanisms of fandom as a basis for rethinking engagement with politics. Two generic elements of popular culture evoke fandom, namely, a focus on individuals and an appreciation of narrative.

The next chapters will therefore look at "persons" and "stories" in politics and examine whether and how they enable entertaining citizenship. In chapter 5, I will show first how the general modernist understanding of politics has a particular variety in which personalization is condemned as being detrimental to making prudent sense of the requirements of citizenship. Yet such a denunciation does not help to judge the performance of politicians in entertainment culture. I propose instead to consider the contemporary politician in terms of the persona he or she manufactures from the equally important ingredients of politics and celebrity culture. These ingredients produce a fourfold typology of celebrity politicians whose success depends on the capacity to project an integrated persona on the triple stages of politics, media, and private life alike. In the next chapter, I will show that the persona of the celebrity politician is male defined, just like its antecedent in modernist politics. Political philosophy, history, politics, and celebrity culture all construct politics as incompatible with a private and family life, an incongruity that is portrayed as more problematic for women than for men. In addition, historical examples of female celebrity, mostly built on visual pleasure and the objectification of the female body, do not provide useful models for the persona of female politicians. Nevertheless, as I will show in the chapter, female politicians have entered and succeeded in politics, be it in continuous oscillation with dominant codes of femininity; the case of Hillary Clinton, the archetype of women's predicaments in celebrity politics, demonstrates this. In chapters 7 and 8, I examine what kinds of stories create entertaining citizenship. I propose that political stories, whether they are fictional representations or based on real events and politicians, are told through four basic frames. They are the quest, the soap, bureaucracy, and conspiracy. As the analysis in chapter 7 of specific popular film and TV series explains, quest and soap present a perspective on citizenship that is rooted in the individual efforts of (groups of) people; bureaucracy and conspiracy, on the other hand, are stories of dark collective forces whose workings extend beyond individual control or change. Yet the analysis of audience reactions to these stories in chapter 8 shows that all four types of stories make the performance of political citizenship possible. Contrary to modernist beliefs about entertainment and politics, these civic performances are not limited to people with low levels of education or political interest who have no "better" resources available. Nor do audiences fall prey to trivializing "effects" of politics in entertaining forms. On the contrary, the audience reactions show that effects arise from people's already existing ideological and normative standpoints through which they appreciate (or do not) these stories. They use the stories to express their understanding, reflection, judgment, and utopian visions of politics and politicians. In the last chapter, I will summarize my arguments about entertainment and citizenship and pick out three issues for discussion: the relation between entertaining citizenship and populism, its relevance to theories of political deliberation, and its politics of diversity.

NOTES

1. Using the combination of keywords "politics" *and* "entertainment," a search on June 11, 2004, among English articles in the Web of Science delivered sixty entries, of which twenty-one were on the topic of this book. Still, only three of them had a discernable historical angle (Berk, 1997; Haller, 1991; Thale, 2001). A guided search on June 13, 2004, for English books with the same keywords in the online catalog of the Library of Congress produced forty-six titles, among which appeared an address directory of celebrities in entertainment, politics, and business, but only four historical treatments (Baskaran, 1981; Oberdeck, 1999; O'Brien, 2004; Sacket, 1982). Other broader search terms did inevitably produce more results, but not a large body of work that systematically addresses historical articulations of entertainment with politics.

2. On the day that I was writing this, the Dutch national daily *Trouw* (November 18, 2003) published an excerpt from a prestigious yearly lecture about politics named after one of the founding fathers of Dutch democracy, the nineteenth-century liberal Thorbecke. The 2003 speaker, a professor of governance and leading Dutch social democrat, claimed, among other things, that we need "a journalism that does produce significant contributions to democracy. We could consider taxing trivial programs and genres and using the benefits to produce political programs that do discuss real backgrounds" (my translation).

3. Benjamin is a classic in this respect. Many authors, to support different arguments, however, refer to "The Work of Art in the Age of Mechanical Reproduction."

4. Hirsch (1980, 1981), for instance, has shown that the methodology of Gerbner has too many flaws to make his results reliable and valid. Freedman (2002) has criticized Gerbner's causal argumentation.

2

⊰⊱

Defamations: Politics as Soap Opera

In January 1999, the British Labour government issued a statement denouncing the obsession of national newspapers with "trivia, travel expenses, comment and soap opera," and condemned their reluctance to report on matters of political substance (Wintour, 1999). The government announced that it would seek other media outlets for its messages, such as the women's and ethnic press, regional media, and foreign news agencies. Tony Blair's official spokesman, Alastair Campbell, a former tabloid journalist himself, warned that "the papers' agenda of gossip, Concorde flights, soap opera and instant judgement" would inevitably produce "delusion [which] leads to disappointment which leads to cynicism about politics which finally results in the pessimistic sense that change is not possible" (White, 1999). Labour leader Tony Blair himself had already accused the national press of allegedly shallow political reporting.

Only some months later, in a perfect mirror of Labour's complaints, the leader of the opposition Conservative Party, William Hague, took on the Blair regime when he told the *Independent*: "I think the Government is actually in the business of promoting indifference to politics. It is systematically trying to diminish the substance of debate and conduct politics as soap opera and photo-calls" (Grice and Macintyre, 1999). He repeated his accusation at his address to the Conservative Party conference of 2000, saying that the Labour government had only been an act, with Tony Blair "the biggest actor in town" (J. Smith, 2000). He added: "We saw them last week, divided, arrogant and out of touch. What a bunch they are—this soap opera of a government. No ministers in recent times have lost touch so rapidly with the people who elected them" (Hague, 2000).

The media keep their end up in these quarrels and regularly charge both the government and its opposition with "soaping" politics: "Stop acting like a soap star, Mr. Blair, and start acting like a prime minister again," the *Independent* newspaper commented, on the occasion of a leaked government memo about ways to sell the government's achievements to the public ("Stop," 2000). The shadow chancellor of the Conservative Party, Michael Portillo, was warned by the press not to turn his own future into a soap opera, when publicly hesitating about his possible succession to the leadership, after the expected defeat of the Tories at the coming elections (Macintyre, 2000b).

Simultaneous with all these disparaging comments on the soaping of politics, Labour, the Conservatives, and the media alike have eagerly incorporated the soap format and its actors into their political campaigns and coverage. The Conservative Party produced soap opera–style election broadcasts featuring an ordinary couple discussing "issues" at their kitchen table (Ward, 1999a). The Labour government has turned its attention to existing soaps, trying—unsuccessfully—to convince their producers to insert story lines about government policies in the scripts (McSmith, 2000). The Labour election campaign was backed by a whole range of celebrities, among them soap actors from *EastEnders, Crossroad, Hollyoaks,* and *Emmerdale* (Dillon, 2001; Landale, 2001). The online edition of the *Guardian* newspaper made up "a new election soap running non-stop on all terrestrial and satellite channels until June 7." Tongue in cheek—admittedly—the newspaper revealed a story line in which main actor Tony B. worries about the body of Old Labour: "Tony and pals know it's securely buried under the patio at Number 10. But their enemies, headed by bungling Wee Willy Hague, are intent on rooting out the evidence" (Brooks, 2001).

What we see in these examples is the ubiquitous presence of the soap opera as a frame of reference both for presenting and understanding politics. This is by no means an exclusively British phenomenon. The stories of American president Bill Clinton's escapades with Monica Lewinsky and his other alleged affairs have repeatedly been told in terms of a soap opera, with the president appearing as the "entertainer in chief"—as one of his former aides said (Stephanopoulos, 2000). More generally, the use of film and television celebrities to endorse candidates and parties has always been part and parcel of American politics, with occasional actors becoming politicians and politicians becoming actors or talk show hosts (Brownstein, 1992). Likewise, politicians and parliamentary journalists from such diverse countries as Canada, Germany, the Netherlands, or Indonesia—and probably from a whole range of other countries as well—have applied the soap frame (respectively, Troost, 2001; Zipper zappt, 2001; Hoedeman and Nicolasen, 2000; Soetjipto, 2000).

Such use of the soap opera in constructing politics testifies to the fact that television culture has become a dominant, if not *the* dominant, means for interpreting social and political life. Whereas in previous times the theatre may have provided a more common figure of speech with which to mold political life, with, for instance, regular evocations of Shakespearean tragedy, nowadays, politics is more easily described in terms of television genres. The reality TV program *Big Brother* provides the latest variety: "I do at least know why Big Brother is so popular this summer. It's because the Labour Cabinet is on holiday and Big Brother is its natural replacement" (Kington, 2000). This, in fact, goes much further than simply saying that television has become the primary and unavoidable means of political communication and information. Television is indeed our prime source for learning about politics, and it provides the instruments for understanding, evaluating, and appreciating it. This generally shared acknowledgment—whether appreciated or criticized—is usually built on analyses of news, current affairs, and some infotainment programs (e.g., Iyengar and Kinder, 1987). The popularity of soap metaphors and symbols shows, however, that television culture has another, as yet unexplored relevance: through its entertainment genres in particular, possibly much more than through its informative programming, it provides narratives and perspectives to express and make sense of politics that may replace or transform the existing ones evoked through more traditional channels of political communication.

At present, as the examples given earlier show, the outlook of politicians and journalists on this prospect is highly schizophrenic: the soap simultaneously provides the metaphor with which to criticize the political behavior of opponents—be they politicians, parties, or media—and the symbols with which to create affirmative ties between candidates, constituencies, and possible voters. As I have argued elsewhere (van Zoonen, 1998a), this tension is typical for contemporary politics and has its roots in the contradictory social roots of politics on the one hand and popular culture on the other.

> The folkloric world of popular culture ruled by coincidence and marked by suspicion and sensation seems to be thoroughly at odds with the modern tradition of contemporary political institutions and culture, which is distinguished by a belief in rationality, progress and the capacity of people to take control over their own destinies. (van Zoonen, 1998a, p. 187)

This contradiction in itself does not explain why politicians or journalists who evoke the soap metaphor to frame political conflicts usually do so to express criticism and derision; nor does it account for the simultaneous, decided incorporation of soap narratives and soap actors in political campaigns. That paradox can only be understood by reading the gendered subtexts in the articulation of soap and politics.

GENDER, SOAP, AND POLITICS

Several authors have shown that the most common metaphors and symbols in politics are those associated with masculinity. Karen Wahl-Jorgensen (2000) uses the 1992 U.S. presidential campaign to show how metaphors and symbols perpetuate masculine hegemony in American politics. Candidates drew images and language from the domains of sports, the military, and the family to represent themselves and their issues, and these were readily taken over by journalists. Together with the central terminology of "the running mate," a discursive forum is produced, according to Wahl-Jorgensen (p. 63),

> in which male intimacy and power are closely linked. Engaging in publicly glorified male bonding, these men make decisions about the future of the country, and their decisions are guided by the very exclusivity and intimacy of their man-man relationships.

On the subject of the 1993 elections in Canada, Gidengil and Everitt (1999) contend that such "macho metaphors" conjure up an atmosphere of aggression, especially when it comes to the "struggle" between candidates for political leadership. Both candidates and journalists frequently used metaphors of warfare, sports, games, and general violence, whereas metaphors to do with the theatre and show business, nature, occupations, and movement were marginal. Only one metaphor linked a traditional female domain, cooking, to politics.

In the context of the dominance of masculine metaphors and symbols, the emerging symbolic and metaphoric articulation of soap with politics becomes all the more interesting. The soap is a genre usually considered appealing to women. In van Zoonen (1994, p. 121), the different factors that explain the popularity of soaps among women are summed up: the particular gendered pleasures of soaps are seen to originate from the centrality of themes and values associated with the private sphere. These themes are experienced and processed by the protagonists through extensive and never-ending conversations, showing different emotions and involvements at length; physical or immediate action is rare in soaps. The focus on women as protagonists, on their rational and calculated behavior, and on the destabilization of male power in the narrative forms some of the sources of pleasure for the female audience. Further pleasures stem from the ability of soaps to evoke a mode of reception that is simultaneously critical and involved. The particular scheduling of daytime soaps ensures that the audience tends to consist of housewives and others working outside the nine-to-five labor market. In addition, there is the cyclical narrative of soap: story lines never have a definitive ending, resolution of conflict is always only temporary, and even death is hardly ever the final word in soaps, for deceased characters regularly return from the grave. Some authors have made much-contested claims that such cyclical narratives accord particularly well with femininity. Modleski (1984), for instance, argues that they are in line with the "rhythms of women's work in the home," whereas Mattelart (1986, p. 15) contends that the repetitions and eternity in soap narratives are linked to women's experience of time.

This brief list shows that the generic features of soaps seem fundamentally at odds with the generic features of modern politics: soaps are about the private sphere, whereas politics is about the public sphere; soaps are about emotional involvement, while politics is about rational debate; the soap narrative centers around conversation, but politics contrarily is focused on planned action; soap solutions are always temporary, whereas political solutions are supposed to last. These oppositions are gender specific and, within the confines of dominant gender codes, the soap cannot take center stage in the masculine-encoded domain of modern politics. When political problems, debate, and conflicts are framed as resembling a soap opera, modern politics implicitly receives an accusation of feminization, of being effeminate and unmanly. As feminist political philosophers have repeatedly shown, the incorporation of "the feminine" in the political domain has been constructed by otherwise sharply opposed authors as undermining its rational and universal basis (e.g., Elshtain, 1981; Kennedy and Mendus, 1987). In the form of explicit treatment of the nature of politics, such views have disappeared from the public arena. However, when reviewing the experience of women in politics, their struggle with the dominant codes of conduct (Norris, 1996), and their representation in various media (Sreberny and van Zoonen, 2000), it is clear that as a practice, politics is still very much constructed as male territory. The only self-evident, unproblematic position for women that this territory allows for is one of support; support of the female colleague for the male leader or support of the wife for the husband in politics (van Zoonen, 1998b). Those are the gender arrangements that make it possible for the soap to be simultaneously mobilized as an inspiration to political campaigns and exploited as an instrument with which to condemn political acts and behavior. The position of the soap in modern politics is thus very much like the one of the first lady: accepted when being supportive to her husband, expelled when entering the field herself (Brown and Gardetto, 2000).

The naturalness of the discourse in which soap and politics are articulated is rooted in the modernist conception of politics as ideologically

informed conflicts and negotiations between rational actors who have
no personal stakes in political issues about the best organization of society. An informed citizenry, which relies on information, facts, and rational argumentation for its political sense making, is considered a prerequisite for modern politics and society (Habermas, 1989). In the
modernist understanding of politics that I discussed in chapter 1,
the only legitimate place for popular culture and for qualities traditionally associated with women (private life, emotional commitment, intuition, or care) is located outside the political domain as sources of
support rather than as part of the process itself. Whereas the soap
metaphor is obviously one means of accomplishing that exclusion, its
sheer existence and regularity are simultaneously a sign of the perceived
crisis in modernist politics. As the usual critical comment claims, information has been replaced by entertainment, political stature by personal
appeal, ideology by technicalities, political constituencies by taste communities, substantial campaigning by elegant marketing, political preference by consumer choice, and reproducible political deliberations by
melodramatic personal combat (for example, Hart, 1994; Postman,
1985). Such criticism expresses an archaic nostalgia for an ideal form of
politics and citizenship that has never existed (for example, Calhoun,
1992; Schudson, 1998) rather than a means to understand and improve
contemporary politics, in which the antagonistic requirements of popular culture and representative democracy need to be reconciled (van
Zoonen, 1998a). The soap metaphor, apart from reconstructing modernist political discourse and ringing its predicaments, may also provide
a way of exploring such reconciliation. I have looked, therefore, in more
detail at how soap metaphors have been applied to politics in a variety
of newspapers from the United Kingdom, the United States, Germany,
and the Netherlands.[1]

A consistent result of research on soap texts and audiences is that the
genre simultaneously evokes critical and referential modes of reception.
The critical mode constitutes a more or less detached way of viewing in
which the audience recognizes and criticizes the construction of the
story line and the quality of acting. Audiences bring all kinds of inter-
textual knowledge to their speculations on future developments. When
watching referentially, audiences tend to identify with story lines and
characters, and use them to make sense of their own experience (Geraghty, 1990; Hobson, 1989; Katz and Liebes, 1990; Seiter et al., 1989). I
will examine whether a similar double-edged reaction is prompted by
the soap metaphor in politics, assuming that in modernist discourse the
soap metaphor will mainly invite readers to review the acts and behavior of politicians in a critical and detached way, whereas in a more hybrid understanding of contemporary politics the soap metaphor would

enable readers to identify and connect with politics in ways that, like the soap opera, "often act as a catalyst for wide-ranging and open discussions" (Hobson, 1989, 66).

MODERNIST DISCOURSE

Scandal, conflict, and incompetence, both personal and political, provide one set of core ingredients for the soap metaphor in modernist discourse. With an occasional exception, all these stories contain distancing mechanisms, estranging readers from politics and politicians, rather than involving them.

Scandal

Bill Clinton's affair with Monica Lewinsky, which brought him close to impeachment, has become the quintessential political soap story, constituting a predictable frame of reference for other similar stories about the sexual misdemeanors of politicians. New York City's mayor Rudy Giuliani went publicly through adultery and divorce in May 2000, with the newspapers referring to the "Rudy-Judi-Donna-Cristyne soap opera" (Rich, 2000) as a "weeper [that] has everything: politics, stymied ambition, a marriage on the rocks, a bitter wife, whispers of an old love affair, a new girlfriend and a cancer menace" (Haberman, 2000, sec. B, p. 1). A Mississippi governor who seriously criticized Clinton's conduct in the Lewinsky affair found himself the subject of "soap" when journalists found him vacationing in France with a woman who was not his wife (Ayres, 1999). Californian congressman Gary Condit topped his colleagues when it was alleged that he was responsible for the disappearance of intern Chandra Levy; he became "embroiled in a tragicomic soap opera involving multiple secret girlfriends, allegations that he made unsavoury efforts to keep them quiet, lie-detector tests, DNA blood traces, and more" (Gumbel, 2001). This list could easily be expanded with other politicians presented as actors in their self-invoked personal melodramas. When the soap metaphor is used, it routinely contains an inventory of the story's ingredients, as the examples above show, pointing at the construction of the story and creating distance among the readers rather than inviting involvement or empathy with the characters. In the numerous marital scandals that journalists framed as soaps, only once was the common pragmatics turned around:

> This whole soap opera is in some ways a public service, since Mr. Giuliani, intentionally or not, helped unclose one of the most common traumas of

modern America—divorce. . . . For those of us who've been through divorce, there is cathartic value in seeing that the high, mighty and normally self-possessed can behave as childishly and be hurt as badly as the rest of us at that tragic moment when a marriage dies. (Rich, 2000, sec. A, p. 15)

The soap metaphor regularly encapsulates a wider range of scandals than just the sexual or marital:

The drama that has been unfolding here has all the ingredients of the convoluted soap operas that Brazilians love to watch: a power struggle, betrayal, sexual intrigue, jealousy, revenge. But most of all it's money, lots and lots of money, that has brought the downfall of Celso Pitta, mayor of Sao Paulo. (Rother, 2000, sec. A, p. 4)

Similarly, Peruvian presidential candidate Alejandro Toledo was said to have got caught up in affairs of soap quality:

It has also been heavy soap opera, rich in personal scandal that has obscured Mr. Toledo's campaign message and damaged his credibility. . . . A story of sex with prostitutes, cocaine use, abandonment of an illegitimate daughter, domestic violence and laundering campaign money. (Krauss, 2001)

It is no coincidence that in these cases, the soap metaphor was applied particularly to politics in new or deficient democracies in Latin American countries (Krauss, 2000), Russia (Gordon, 1999), or Asia (Hagedorn, 2001). These exotic locations help to address the reader as a distant, superior observer who frowns in benign surprise. Nevertheless, corruption occurs in Western democracies as well. Political corruption in the United States (Chen, 2000), France (Lichfield, 2001), and England (Blackhurst, 2001) has also been framed in soap terms. Again, the Clinton presidency provides an easy target for journalists: "An opulent mansion drenched in sex and money, where business and bedroom adventures abound, the over-the-top saga of a twisted dysfunctional family. It's not Titans . . . it's 'Clintons' in DC" (Dowd, 2000, sec. 4, p. 15). Journalists, even from the serious newspapers, seem to revel in the sheer deviance of it all, reporting sensational details: "A former ally videotapes two women engaged in lesbian trysts at a water-pumping station, later asks one to murder the other, according to the other, then tries to commit suicide himself" (Chen, 2000, sec. B, p. 1). Here, constructing the politician's behavior as completely beyond any kind of ordinary reality or moral standards creates the distance. Whereas the involved mode of watching the soap depends on the quality of its emotional realism (Ang, 1985), the soap metaphor for sex and corruption scandals in politics creates bewilderment and distance.

Conflict

While the soaps that went on in the U.S. government in the last decades centered on sexual escapades and loose financial mores, Tony Blair's soaps, according to the press's metaphors, are about strife in his cabinet. The *Independent* compared the Labour cabinet with reality soap: "The greater part of the fascination of the Labour cabinet . . . comes from wondering who is for the chop next at the hands of Tony 'Big Brother' Blair" (Kington, 2000). Rivalry and conflict within the cabinet opened the way for the Conservative opposition to apply the soap opera metaphor for "a government whose leading lights fight each other like rats in a sack" (*Guardian*, 2000). Another comment says, "The feuding has grabbed the headlines although the schemers knife each other in a virtually policy-free vacuum" (Richards, 2000). Apparently, the soap framing of personal conflicts was convincing enough to seduce German newspapers to repeat it in an analysis of tensions in the Labour cabinet (Kielinger, 2000). The occasions for the metaphor may differ, but the soap frame itself seems to have become inescapable for every conflict among Tony Blair's ministers and advisors:

> This is politics as soap opera: a Downing Street tale of broken friendship, betrayal and revenge that would not be out of place on BBC1 or ITV. Peter Mandelson and Alastair Campbell are now bitter enemies after one of the most spectacular Westminster falling-outs in living memory. (Maguire, 2001)

Evidently, the Labour government is not the only one to suffer from (seemingly) personal conflicts of soap quality. Different American primaries have witnessed "soap opera like drama" (Hicks, 2000a) and "scripts for a soap opera" (Hicks, 2000b); Gerhard Schröder's German cabinet has been typified as "Die Leute vom Reichstag—Die politische Daily Soap" (Zipper zappt, 2001); the Dutch Labour party saw its chairwoman withdraw because of internal feuds in soap opera style (Hoedeman and Nicolasen, 2000); and so on.

Wherever they come from, all these stories make great reading and must be fun to write.[2] However, the authors all apply the soap metaphor rather minimally, by forgetting that in real soaps, personal conflicts always have a substantial base. Sometimes the sources of conflict are so far in the past that only the most devoted viewers remember them; nevertheless, conflicts in soaps are never simply irrational feuds that are only based on likes and dislikes. They have good reasons, just as the political conflicts must have a substantial logic, but they tend to get buried in the metaphor. Only once, I found a soap metaphor applied substantially: when the Dutch *Volkskrant* paraphrased a rather complicated tax discussion between the minister of finance and the president of the national bank as "a lovely soap" and presented the different arguments in terms of daily episodes (Kalshoven, 1999). This exception notwithstanding, when the soap metaphor is used to frame conflict between politicians, it constructs them as exclusively personal and ignores the political. As journalists themselves acknowledge, this creates at best a distance and at worst evokes cynicism among the electorate (Macintyre, 2001). Journalists tend to blame politicians, however ("Do you think it is demeaning to treat the Labour cabinet as if it were a TV show, but that is how we have been taught to treat it"; Kington, 2000), rather than their own incomplete use of the metaphor.

Incompetence

Although it is not my intention to make cross-cultural comparisons, it is striking that in the Dutch applications of the soap metaphor, the incompetence of local, regional, and national governments was mostly the occasion: "One could write a soap opera about Council politics, which would make Peyton Place fade away" (*Algemeen Dagblad*, 2001, p. 7). The soap metaphor is used to point at unexpected and incomprehensible changes of conviction and policy. "In the soap about the Study House, it seems that Secretary of Education, Karin Adelmund, plays the part of fidgetter" (Hageman, 2000, p. 17).[3] Another observer criticizes regional policies as "episodes of the soap 'A shameless spectacle'" (Godschalk, 1999). An enduring debate about an unfinished flyover is typified as a regional soap (Broek, 2000). In the Dutch cases, these typifications are applied rather superficially and sometimes a little incoherently, for instance when a commentator wrote of the political aftermath of the Srebrenica drama as being "an unmitigated soap" as well as "a fascinating farce" (Faber, 2000). Such undeveloped notions of soap are likely to be caused by the short history of soaps in the Netherlands and Dutch consciousness, unlike the long history of British and American soaps.[4]

The Americas, both North and South, had their soap of political incompetence in the story of the Cuban boy Elian Gonzales (Lanting, 2000). In England, it was the inability of the Tories to come up with a new leader after William Hague's election defeat. Some journalists used the soap metaphor to claim that no one would be interested in the battle for the Tory leadership. It is hardly the most complex exercise in history, McElvoy (2001) claims, nor the most interesting one: "As brutal a shock as it must be to the main characters involved, there is precious little enthusiasm for an omnibus-length leadership soap opera." Other journalists equally put down the Tory party—"Before our very eyes, the Conservatives have become the party to hate itself"—but saw much more excitement in it: "Tory Story has had it all: betrayal, hatred, even that time-honoured staple of soap—the queeny matriarch loved by a few and condemned as a dragon by everyone else" (Freedland, 2001).

Spin Control

The soap metaphor is applied in a rather different way in stories that try to analyze the current state of the art in politics, calling it postmodern, personalized, Clintonized, popularized, artificial, spin controlled, celebrity politics, or whatever. At the heart of these analyses is the supposed lack of authentic political drive among politicians: "Politicians speak like performers in a Karaoke bar, mouthing the words of other people, and taking no responsibility for those words, once their performance has ended" (McLaren, 2000). Politicians are presented as the characters in a script sometimes written by themselves, but more often by their advisors, the infamous spin doctors. The champions of spin control, as many journalists remind us, were of course part of Bill Clinton's administration (Joseph, 2000; Wintour, 1999). However, in the most recent period, it is the Blair government that especially faces this kind of charge: "So was this the beginning of the end of the Blair soap opera? Will the events of the past week finally force the real Blair to stand up, free of spin doctors and advisers who have created such cynicism among traditional voters" (Ahmed, 2000; see also *Independent*, 2000; Rawnsley, 2000). As noted in the very beginning of this chapter, journalists blame Blair and his advisors for the current obsession with image, style, and polls, but Blair's advisors accuse the press: "He believes that he is more spinned against than spinning" (Hoge, 1999, sec. A, p. 4). A third party in this unhappy marriage between politicians and journalists is the public, who receives its blows from journalists and politicians alike, claiming, for instance, that it expects its "daily fix of soap opera" from politicians (Dowd, 2000, sec. 4, p. 15), that it sees politics as "just another open-ended, pointless soap opera, complete with artificial crisis, all of which are meaningless within a week" (Joseph, 2000), or that it is "riveted by the soap operas of public lives" (Dowd, 2000). Slightly more sophisticated analyses move away from the persons and the public, and point at the lack of real political disagreements and the loss of ideologies as the main source behind soap opera politics: "When real politics lacks life and death drama, the punters search for alternative entertainment" (Rawnsley, 2000). When politics lacks an ideological basis, says a Dutch observer, it descends to the level of personal relations and becomes a soap (Kleinrensink, 2001, p. 7). The German newspaper *Die Welt* particularly ascribes the lack of ideological conflict to the "Third Way politics" introduced by, among others, Clinton, Blair, and Schröder, resulting in supermarket logic in which every social democratic opportunist can select his own mix of products: "Eclectics and actors are the prototypes of the postmodern Democracy" (Weimer, 1999, translation by the author).

The stories of scandal, conflict, incompetence, and spin control that journalists have framed as soap opera do indeed contain many classic elements of the genre. A crucial part of many of the stories reviewed here is an inventory of these elements to prove that one is witnessing something like a soap. In addition, the unfolding of the narratives in these stories parallels the conventions of soaps, with stories and characters returning to haunt each other, and with political failure (or death) proving only temporary. The many resurrections of, for instance, Bill Clinton, "the comeback kid," attest to this. Nevertheless, the metaphor is also used in an extremely limited and biased way. Characters in these political soaps are invariably portrayed as immoral and spoiled (scandals), petty and vindictive (conflicts), or silly and incoherent (incompetence). All of them are continually scheming to cover up their wrongdoings and polish their own image (spin control). It is unclear whether, apart from a hunger for sex, money, and power, something more elevating motivates them. The political soaps thus feature wicked, self-centered people, mainly men, with despicable or incomprehensible motives. No channel manager in his right mind would accept such a scenario for prime-time soap, for audiences would be appalled by it, as appalled as they are often said to be by politics. In these modernist applications of the soap metaphor, there are no sympathetic characters one can identify with, like there are in real soaps; they are not driven by experiences one can understand on the basis of one's own life, like one can in real soaps; there are no story lines that people can recognize or sympathize with because they have been through it themselves. In short, the soap metaphor in these contexts positions the reader at a critical, superior distance, looking down on politicians and the political process as an extraterrestrial species primarily busy with itself. The resulting alienation is as much a product of occurring political abuse as it is a result of the limited way in which journalists apply the soap metaphor, only evoking its critical and detached mode of reception and failing to exploit its capacity to involve and connect people to characters and stories and thus—maybe—to politics.

Are there particular ways in which the engaging qualities of soap could bring politics to a more sympathetic and honorable level that is relevant to contemporary challenges put up by personalization, television, popular culture, and the supposed lack of ideology?

THE SOAP AS SAVIOR

Governments and politicians alike have embraced soaps and their actors as useful vehicles for their campaigns. The Dutch government, for instance, ponders how to convince soap producers to include health messages about the dangers of smoking (Deen, 2001). The Labour government also considered trying to get their messages across in TV scripts, a move that journalists describe as a "sinister scheme to woo the masses" (McSmith, 2000). The Tories would have liked the British soaps to include story lines that encourage marriage (Ward, 1999b). Both New Labour and the Tories have constructed their election broadcasts as small soap narratives (*Guardian*, 2000; Ward, 1999a). Soap celebrities have come to back the Labour campaign in particular, just like Bill Clinton had a strong constituency in Hollywood. The paradox of the soap functioning simultaneously as a means of denunciation and as an instrument of support has been explained earlier; it is the gendered subtext that enables politicians and government to hail the soap as a means of support as long as it does not take over their core business. Journalists, however, by and large ridicule the incorporation of soap narratives and soap actors in policy and campaigning, in another expression of modernist discourse that considers entertainment separate from politics: "[Celebrity endorsements] provide the two crucial ingredients that spin doctors and journalists crave during election campaigns: a new storyline, and with a bit of luck, an attractive female twenty-something" (*Guardian*, 2000). Of all the stories reviewed for this chapter, only a few considered the soap to provide an appropriate and stimulating narrative to cover politics and politicians. Mayor Giuliani's divorce and the Dutch tax debate have already been mentioned. Timothy Garton Ash, a fellow at Oxford and Stanford Universities, also presents a diametrically opposed employment of the soap metaphor—elaborate, elegant, and enthusiastic—in a comment on the American elections published in both the *Independent* and the *New York Times* (Ash, 2000):

> Now, in living rooms from Caithness to Kosovo, Europeans are watching a new American soap opera. After *"Dallas"* and *"Dynasty,"* we have . . . *"Democracy."* The cast is familiar. Here again are the powerful women, with strong, partisan hearts and the shoulder pads of righteousness. . . . Here are the silver-haired dynasts, advancing the interests of their houses with senatorial mien. . . . For ordinary viewers to identify with, there is the walk-on ordinary person, here played by Theresa LePore, hapless inventor of the butterfly ballot. . . . Does this mean the United States is making itself a laughing stock? Absolutely not. . . . The basic message is a positive one: Every vote really does matter. And, like it or not, a soap opera is probably the best way to get this message across to the largest possible audience. (sec. A, p. 29)

Here seems to write a true believer in the genre, applying the soap metaphor not only in a well-informed way (thus including female and sympathetic characters) but also recognizing the potential of soap to involve people in personal and public issues and make them discuss them among themselves. In a later piece about the Milosevic trial, Ash (2002) contends that the Serbian people are in a state of denial of the war crimes, a denial that is reinforced by the trial. He claims that the Serbian truth commission does not evoke the emotional response necessary for the nation to come to terms with its past. Serbian leader Kostunica says, "We don't want a soap opera," but Ash argues that soap opera might be one of the means to break through "the immensely strong psychological barriers of denial":

> It was only the 1970s American soap opera Holocaust which finally brought home to ordinary Germans, through personalising and dramatising, the true horror of the Holocaust. Today, Serbs have one historical soap opera on their television screens: the Slobo and Carla show from The Hague. They urgently need another: a domestically produced reality show. Only when they get it will people like Dule [a Serbian acquaintance of Ash] begin to face the facts and remember.

Ash's use and promotion of the soap metaphor are highly exceptional in the plethora of cynical applications that characterize the work of ordinary journalists. His views reveal the bias in journalists' articulations of soap and politics more sharply. It is not simply a matter of different personal viewpoints on the relevance of soap. The difference has also to do with Ash's position as an outside expert. Structural and ideological factors explain why journalists utilize the soap metaphor in their particular hostile manner. News values and organizational routines make the day-to-day news story primarily a negative one. The critical distance enabled by the soap metaphor fits easily into the professional routines that favor bad news and ignore good news. Time pressure and framing routines are as important as their personal dislikes to understand journalists' views on politics as soap (after having gone through all these stories, one wonders whether there are fans of soaps among journalists). In addition, professional ideology has developed in ways that make journalism one of the last bastions of "high modernism" as Hallin (1996) has called it, believing in progress, rationality, and universal truth or standards, making it run parallel with modern conceptions of politics. Despite all the different changes that journalism has gone through, including an increased attention for "soaplike" things such as human interest, private confessions, and the like, the use of the soap metaphor in the prestigious newspapers examined for this chapter shows that modernism still reigns supreme in the newsrooms. It is therefore unlikely that the articulations of soaps and politics as journalists construct them will enable the engaged investments that soaps are famous for and that politics needs desperately. Only the occasional story, such as the ones of Timothy Garton Ash, may realize such a reaction of the audience. That does not mean that the soap format is without potential for contemporary politics; it only means that it is unlikely to be accomplished in this kind of journalism. Soaps themselves may actually do a better job, as the immense critical and ratings success of the American series *The West Wing* suggests. I will briefly discuss this series here, and will come back to it in much more detail in chapters 7 and 8.

The West Wing is a weekly series that started on NBC in September 1999. It features the Democratic president Josiah Bartlet (played by Martin Sheen) and his staff, showing how they operate in the face of major and minor political crises and events, and how their political work is continuously informed and transgressed by personal convictions and private matters. Like other series in this genre (e.g., *ER* and *The Practice*), it has a weekly plot and narratives that cover several episodes. The show has been exported to numerous countries and has received more awards than any other series before. Audience comments on the Internet suggest that the series invites an engagement and discussion with politics that is very often simply affirmative and admiring, but also—as soaps tend to do—at times resolute and profound. Martin Sheen's presidential character is often put up as an example for the real president: "Can we have a President Bartlet instead of this Bush guy," "On countless occasions I've wished Josiah 'Jed' Bartlet were real and sitting in the real Oval Office," or "His character is not a saint, but one gets the feel that there is a decent man with a passion for a job he loves but doesn't necessarily like doing." Although people recognize *West Wing* stories as contrived for the purpose of good drama, nevertheless they seem to get a sense of the everyday political process.

Soap conventions thus may enable a hybrid understanding of politics, in which the different logics of rational policy development, ideological struggle, personal convictions and preferences, public relations requirements, occurring incompetence, and bureaucracy unite into a coherent and persuasive picture of "best possible" political practice. The incorporation of private matters and personal weaknesses, in particular, simultaneously redefines prevailing notions of masculinity in politics, upholding it as a balanced mixture of public and private experience. That does not make for a practice that ensures equal access and participation for women, however— almost on the contrary. Apart from press secretary C. J. Gregg (played by Allison Janney), the show features no women in power (and, for that matter, her power is derived from her position as the president's mouthpiece), nor does it make room for any key black characters. The common defense line that the reality of politics is no different does not hold here, for past and present American administrations have employed more women and blacks in high positions than *The West Wing* does. Film and TV critic Lesley Smith has argued that *The West Wing* is actually about male bonding, with "the ongoing delineation of male virtue the show's main concern" (1999). Masculine virtue in politics has clearly been redefined and is no longer dependent on stoic, rational, and unaffected behavior. Virtues traditionally considered feminine, such as sensitivity, intuition, and care, have obviously passed into pop culture's notions of the ideal politician. Popular magazines, too, have been seen to propagate such qualities in male politicians, but, as in *The West Wing*, it does not result in an equal place and appreciation of female politicians (cf. van Zoonen, 2000b). The case of *The West Wing* even suggests that for politics to transform itself with the help of "femininity," to be able to be the central theme of a soap, it needs to exclude women even more rigidly than before. One would not want to have one's masculinity questioned in the process, would one?

SUMMARY

I have reviewed various articulations of soaps and politics for the reason that they seem to become ever more frequent, and in the hope that some of the soaps' miraculous qualities of moving, engaging, and mobilizing people would transfer to politics. It showed, however, that the dominant use of soap metaphors in politics, firmly anchored in modernist discourse, both brought down politics and depreciated the soap by only exploiting its capacity to position the public as a detached and critical spectator. Within the confines of modernist discourse, a more beneficial contribution for the soap was only made possible in a supportive role as an endorser of parties or a narrative instrument for policy. This is very much in line with the traditional gender relations evoked by the subtexts of politics and soaps as respectively masculine and feminine genres. To introduce a metaphor for the role of soap in modernist politics: she is allowed the position of the first lady, supportive but powerless. One needs to look outside of the public realm of politics and journalism in the area of popular culture to find an articulation of soap and politics that enables the public to engage and invest in politics. The American series *The West Wing* does invite empathy with the public and private predicaments of politicians, and suggests a hybrid understanding of politics. I will pick up that discussion in chapters 7 and 8. First, it is necessary to examine another tension in modernist political discourse about entertainment, namely the abuse, exploitation, and neglect of popular music.

NOTES

This chapter appeared originally as my "'After Dallas and Dynasty We Have . . . Democracy': Articulating Soap, Gender and Politics," in *Media and the Restyling of*

Politics, edited by John Corner and Dick Pels (London: Sage, 2003). Reprinted by permission of Sage Publications Ltd.

1. My research assistant, Femke Bilderbeek, searched the online archives of British (*Independent, Guardian, Times*), American (*New York Times*), German (*Frankfurter Rundschau, Die Welt*), and Dutch (*Volkskrant, Trouw, Algemeen Dagblad*) newspapers for the combination of the terms "politics" and "soap" over two years (January 1999–September 2001). The selection of newspapers was dependent on the existence of an easily accessible online archive. Only those articles were selected in which "soap" was used as a metaphor or symbol: articles about soap preferences of politicians, for instance, were not used. The analysis was meant to provide a more detailed understanding of the range of interpretations of politics that the soap metaphor opens up and was not meant as a classic content analysis showing the number and distribution of metaphors along different countries and newspapers. The results therefore should be representative for the variety in discourse rather than for countries and newspapers (cf. Miles and Huberman, 1984).

2. Just as it was a joy to read them for the purpose of this chapter.

3. The Study House is a particular Dutch policy enabling high school students to learn on their own, under supervision of a teacher.

4. Think, for instance, of the national excitement around the questions "Who shot JR?" and "Who shot Phil?"

3

Confrontations: Popular Music and Politics

Like the soap opera, popular music is a genre of entertainment that has frequently met politics: politicians have similarly criticized popular music for its debased morals, and that criticism has also provided them with a means to occupy an ethical high ground. Unlike the soap, however, popular music has been in the middle of concrete political and legislative conflict, especially about self-regulation and censorship of sexual and violent lyrics and performances (Jones, 1991; McDonald, 1988). Moreover, bands and artists have used their music to express their social and political allegiances, and they have exploited their fame to endorse political positions and candidates. In other words, the encounters between popular music and politics have been far more politicized than the articulations of soap with politics. Many an observer has claimed that popular music constitutes a liberal, left-wing battleground in particular. John Street, who has done much work in this area, writes, for instance:

> From the birth of rock'n'roll in the 1950s, through flower power in the 1960s and punk in the 1970s, on into rap and dance culture in the 1980s and 1990s, pop music has been both a vehicle for radical sentiments and the object of conservative anger. (2001, p. 61)

Other authors have also made the observation that popular music has mainly supported a progressive political agenda. Garofalo (1992b) describes how folkloric musical forms were connected to the labor and civil rights movements, and claims that current popular music is above all associated with progressive causes. Yet there are popular music genres that seem to be especially well liked by people with conservative standpoints, such as middle-of-the-road hit music (Fox and Williams, 1974; Peterson and Christenson, 1987). What's more, genres differ within themselves when it comes to their conservative or progressive disposition, as one can see most vividly in the different appreciations of rap music: it has been simultaneously hailed as the voice of black inner-city protest (Rose, 1994), exposed as a misogynist carrier of violent sexuality (Bayles, 1994), and upheld as an arena for exploring alternative feminine identities (Skeggs, 1993, quoted in Stapleton, 1998). An assessment of the political position of individual songs is just as complicated. With his 1984 song "Born in the USA," Bruce Springsteen meant to lament the fate of Vietnam veterans in the United States. Instead, Ronald Reagan wanted to use it as his campaign anthem, and conservative forces picked it up as a song of American superiority over the Russians (Jaffee, 1987). Another example of such ambiguity can be seen around George Michael, who protested British allegiance with the United States' antiterrorist campaigns through his 2001 single and animated video "Shoot the Dog." His position was rather uncommon in the aftermath of the 9/11 attacks on the World Trade Center in New York. In the fund-raising "Concert for New York" that followed, music was a means to salute victims and rescue workers, and it offered a space for shared mourning. However, participating musicians also gave a voice to the retaliatory mood in the country, with lyrics like "I'll put a boot in your ass" and "I want an eye for an eye" (McNair, 2003). George Michael's "Shoot the Dog" was an obvious political exception, but while the animation of Tony Blair as George Bush's poodle attracted some favorable attention, other commentators contested the singer's political sincerity, because they suspected he tried to raise controversy for commercial purposes. If that was Michael's desire, his strategy was not very successful; the song flopped.

There are many other examples that tell of the contradictory interpretations of songs that have a political intent (e.g., Street, 1986). Such ambiguities are not limited to the articulations of politics and popular music, but are a specific case of a general phenomenon in media reception: as a result of the inherent polysemic nature of media texts, their reception is a multifaceted and relatively unpredictable phenomenon (Hall, [1973] 1980). It is therefore impossible to assess the particular political leanings of popular music genres and songs apart from their situated reception in the everyday lives of ordinary citizens. As Negus (1996, p. 190) says: "Any political content of a song has to be understood in terms of processes of mediation during which it can undergo change and be connected to various political agendas." The relevance of the reception context is further underlined by the fact that distinctly nonpolitical songs have acquired political meaning because of their use in a specific politicized context. The Portuguese Revolution of 1974 started when the Portuguese radio played

"Grandola Vila Morena," a run-of-the-mill love song that was an agreed sign for the young army officers to begin their rebellion against dictator Caetona. The song has ever since been considered revolutionary.[1] The multiple political interpretations of popular music make an assessment of its ideological leanings a futile exercise.

What is more interesting in the context of this book is whether and how articulations of popular music and politics enable or disable citizenship. There are already many good treatments of the connections between politics, popular music, and citizenship (e.g. Street, 1986; Negus, 1996). These authors, however, use a rather broad understanding of politics and citizenship. Pratt (1990, p. 4), for instance, understands politics to be about the ways in which "individuals and wider publics identify, name and may begin to work to satisfy" their basic and higher-order human needs. A partial focus on the specific relationships of popular music to the political field seems too limited from that perspective. Nevertheless, it is precisely this specific and limited relation that we intend to explore in this chapter. As we will show, it is from the articulations of popular music with the modern political field that the most interesting context to understand how popular culture can mingle with political citizenship emerges. We will discuss three particular articulations of popular music with politics. First, popular music regularly occurs as an issue of political conflict, for instance when it comes to industrial policy, content regulation, copyrights, and downloading. The question is how these focused encounters between popular culture and politics frame citizenship for actors who are otherwise absent from the political field. Secondly, political actors in the field have reached for popular music to position themselves within the multitude of consumer lifestyles that are current among their electorates. They also use popular music to communicate with supposedly hard-to-reach constituencies, such as youth and ethnic minorities. Modern politics thus seems to have broadened its range of communicative styles, and the question is whether that has implied a change in the appeal of citizenship. Finally, the question is what the broader political battleground that is constituted by popular music can offer to politics in terms of agendas, issues, arguments, conflicting claims, and public concerns. We will discuss these three articulations of popular music with the political field in more detail first, and then make the broader connection to the theme of entertaining citizenship.

POPULAR MUSIC AS A POLITICAL ISSUE

Various aspects of popular music have been subjected to political debate, policy formation, and legislation. Jones (1991) describes, for instance, how

U.S. immigration laws make it difficult for relatively unknown foreign musicians to perform their music in America. Wallis and Malm (1992) report on the cultural policies of small countries to protect their national music industries against the overwhelming presence of Anglo-American popular music. Trade restrictions, tariff barriers, and airplay quotas are the most usual measures taken (Negus, 1996). Copyright issues constitute other regular political conflicts around popular music. The Napster trials about the legality or illegality of downloading popular music from the Internet build on a longer history of legislation against illegal distribution and the implied loss of income for artists and the industry, as is apparent, for instance, in the taxation on empty audio carriers (Creech, 2001). However, protection, whether against foreign music and musicians or against income loss, is not what comes to mind first when thinking of politics attending to popular music. By far, the most visible and controversial intrusions have to do with content regulation and censorship. Evidently, in totalitarian regimes, censoring popular music and persecuting popular musicians are part and parcel of overall restrictions on freedom of speech and of the denial of citizenship in general (e.g., Street, 1986). Yet liberal democracies are not by definition tolerant toward popular music. Although in Britain, France, and other countries in western Europe, political elites have been relatively indifferent toward their popular music (Street, 1986; Chastanger, 1999), in the United States, the epitome of free speech and democracy, popular music has met with repression from its very beginning. In fact, Lynxwiler and Gay (2000) argue that the history of popular music in the United States can easily be written as a history of censorship (see also Cloonan and Garofalo, 2003). The adversaries of popular music have disapproved of specific beats, specific performances, and the private behavior of musicians. Jazz, early rock, and specific genres of house music (e.g., techno and trance) have all been accused of having a sexual or harmful beat (Jones, 1991; Ter Bogt et al., 2002). Elvis's hip movements shocked unreceptive audiences, as did later sexually explicit performances of, for instance, Prince and Madonna (e.g., Schwichtenberg, 1993). The satanic style and onstage destruction that have been essential to the performances of musicians like Alice Cooper, Kiss, or Marilyn Manson have infuriated many groups in society, who have seen their repulsion confirmed by the private misbehavior of musicians abusing drugs, women, and life itself (King, 1990). Singer Kurt Cobain of the Seattle grunge band Nirvana was accused postmortem of leading his fans into death by upholding suicide (Jobes et al., 1996), and rap music in general has taken the blame for the isolated violent and homicidal acts of some performers (Binder, 1993). Still, of all the targets that popular music offers to its opponents, song lyrics have attracted the most concrete and successful attempts at censorship. Dougherty (1985, in McDonald, 1988) reports that as early as 1940 more than 100 songs were banned by NBC radio. Traditional blues artists were prevalent among the first targets, officially because of their sexually explicit language, but many an author has pointed out the racist subtexts of restricting the blues (e.g., Oliver, 1970). Intolerance intensified when black musicians conquered the mass market in the 1950s and when white performers took up black musical styles:

> Much of the outcry against rock and roll in the 1950s was, of course, racially motivated. The fact that Chuck Berry and Little Richard became household heroes for millions of white middle-class youths was bound to draw attention from many people. (McDonald, 1988, p. 297)

According to Lynxwiler and Gay (2000), censorship issues built up as a result of the racial blending of musical styles and performers, but musical and political developments in the 1960s exacerbated them. To the mythical stories of the decade belong the imperative for the Rolling Stones to change the lyrics of their song "Let's Spend the Night Together" into "Let's spend some time together" before they were allowed to sing it live on the *Ed Sullivan Show*; the BBC ban on "With a Little Help from My Friends," a Beatles song supposedly referring to drugs; and the fining of the Jefferson Airplane and other artists for verbal abuse onstage (cf. Jones, 1991). While such interferences were primarily defended by an appeal to moral concerns, during the Vietnam War, the Nixon administration had a clear political purpose when it accused performers who were siding with the antiwar movement of undermining national strength and when it investigated and harassed artists for their views on U.S. policies. Those interventions were reminiscent of the McCarthy hearings in the 1950s that produced political victims among popular musicians who were blacklisted for their supposedly "un-American" messages.

As Jones (1991) and McDonald (1988) argue, censorship of popular music became most successful and institutionalized with the emergence of the Parents Music Resource Center in 1985. Chastanger (1999, p. 181) has even called the PMRC the "most formidable censorship machine in American popular music." The PMRC has adamantly positioned itself as a center that wants to inform and educate, and provide parents with resources to know what their children are listening to. It has fiercely denied any accusation of infraction on the First Amendment. Nevertheless, Chastanger suggests that its agenda eventually led to censorship: PMRC activities made it easier for authorities to charge individual artists on the basis of existing legislation on obscenity, and some local authorities used the PMRC warning labels to notify retailers that selling certain records could be illegal under existing obscenity laws. As a result, Chastanger says, both retailers and music companies became wary of producing and selling records of musicians using explicit lyrics. The heyday of the PMRC is gone, but a lasting reminder of its influence is the warning label that record companies agreed to sticker on albums when necessary: *Parental Advisory: Explicit Lyrics.*

Although the objections against popular music have at times been explicitly political—as in the McCarthy era and during the Nixon administration—the basic hostility has to do with the alleged violation of established social and ethical conduct. Lynxwiler and Gay (2000) therefore speak of "moral entrepreneurs" to identify the actors who believe all social ills are connected to popular music. The list of moral defects that are mentioned in the literature as supposedly caused by popular music is impressive: sexual excess, delinquent values, drug abuse, sexism, homophobia, addiction to pornography, occult activities, lawless behavior, indecent exposure, obscenity, rape, homicide, suicide, and so on. In fact, as Grossberg (1992) has suggested, one of the strategies of moral entrepreneurs like the PMRC is to first make a general claim about the relation between social ills and popular music, and then single out the lyrics and performance of specific genres or artists as unmistakable examples. In the opposite approach, specific and sad cases of teenagers following their music heroes into drug abuse or suicide have been used as general evidence of the overall appalling impact of popular music (Jones, 1991). Such incidents usually receive ample media coverage in which calls for further regulation and restriction predictably come up (Binder, 1993).

Although the main forces behind such proposals often belong to conservative groups and the religious right, the PMRC was founded by the wife of Democrat Al Gore and attracted supporters from across the ideological divide, including the National Organization of Women (Martin and Segrave, 1993). Likewise, while disapproval of lyrics belonging to black musical genres has been attributed to white anxiety, that is not the whole story. Black leaders have also strongly condemned violent and misogynist lyrics of black rappers (Lynxwiler and Gay, 2000). Other divisions may therefore also contribute to the confrontations over popular music, which becomes clear when we consider which actors are generally absent from the debates. Representatives from record industries, artists themselves, and independent academics are usually called in to defend the targeted genres.[2] Fans, however, hardly ever occur in the discussions, hearings, and relevant councils. Partly, this may have to do with the lack of formal organization among fans, but more relevant is that the discourse of moral decay eliminates them as legitimate participants. The fan, already irrational and susceptible by definition (for the fan is a fanatic), can only be considered the embodiment of the moral corrosion induced by popular music. Someone who actually likes satanic or porn rock, or who enjoys violent and sexist rap, is the problem in the discourse of moral decay and can therefore enter the debate merely as a possible target for redemption. This invalidation has a particular variety in the way that the discourse of moral decay positions youths. The PMRC typified children as having "virgin minds" that need protection against the sleazy world of adult music (quoted in Censorship Alert, 1986). That overthrows the uses, interpretations, and beliefs that youths themselves have about popular music. While they are at the center of the dispute, the right to participate in the deliberations, a basic right in terms of political citizenship, is denied to them. Like the fans, they are not considered legitimate and serious agents in these deliberations. This discursive exclusion holds for all fans and youths, but there is a conspicuous overlap with existing social formations: heavy metal and rap, at the center of attacks, are the genres most appreciated by working-class white and black youth respectively. On the surface, then, censorship issues in the confrontations between popular music and politics may seem to express a clash between conservative and progressive values, and a white anxiety against black culture. As important, however, are the dividing lines between conservative, progressive, black, and white elites on the one hand and "the people," as John Fiske (1992) would say, on the other. The "people"—in this case, the grown-up and young consumers of the wrong genres—are constructed as morally immature and therefore not entitled to the basic citizenship rights to deliberate and participate. The option that the elite may be wrong in their assessment of the impact of popular music is foreclosed, as is the possibility that fans and youths may be morally sound citizens despite their musical preferences.

POPULAR MUSIC AS A CAMPAIGN INSTRUMENT

Amidst the moral and political controversies surrounding popular music, for politicians to embrace songs and performers to endorse their campaigns is a risky strategy. When Ronald Reagan invited the Beach Boys to the White House to celebrate the Fourth of July, his fellow Republicans raised at least one eyebrow: "Did the Beach Boys represent the family and fun, or drugs and decadence?" (Street, 1986, p. 48). During the Dutch 1994 election campaign, the Greens organized a house party to entertain young voters. Green members of parliament danced along with the crowd and issued condoms with the logo *Vote Safe Vote Green*. But other attendants distributed drugs, and the ensuing public scandal has often turned up as an explanation of the Green electoral defeat of that year (Van Zwol, 1994). Still, popular music and artists have been routinely integrated into election campaigns. Street (1986) traces this habit as far back as the New Deal era of the 1930s, when politicians experimented with the idea that popular music provided a new vehicle with which to reach their electorates.

The expectation that popular music may deliver new electorates to politicians and parties remains dominant today, especially when it comes to groups outside the reach of more traditional means of political communication. Young voters are the main targets for these efforts that come from nonpartisan institutions and political parties alike. Rock the Vote is one of some long-standing initiatives to attract young voters to politics. Founded in 1990 by the American record industry canvassing against censorship, it is now primarily aimed at registering young voters and encouraging their political awareness (Rock the Vote, 2002). In 1996 a British version of Rock the Vote was launched (Cloonan and Street, 1997). The American campaign includes the placement of voter registration tables at rock concerts, public service announcements on the music channel MTV, information about voter registration on toll-free telephone lines, popular musicians endorsing voting, awards for politically active musicians, press releases, and other strategies. Rock the Vote claims to have increased voter registration among the young with some 400,000 to 500,000 for consecutive elections. Its additional campaigns to encourage actual voting are said to have caused a 20 percent increase in youth turnout in the American presidential elections of 1992 (Rock the Vote, 2002). MTV set off a similar but more focused campaign in 1992: they transformed their incidental coverage of presidential elections into an intensive and habitual campaign, Choose or Lose. MTV wanted to educate its viewers and advance their registration as voters. The initiative met with considerable public support, and politicians regularly visit MTV to secure exposure among young audiences and to make politics "hip" (Smillie, 1992).

George Bush Sr. initially refused to appear on MTV:

> I think in a campaign year, you've got to draw the line someplace. . . . I don't want to turn this thing into a call-in show. I'm not going to be out there being a teenybopper. At 68 I just cannot do that anymore. (Quoted in Bare, 1993)[3]

On the eve of the election he had to give in, fearing too big a loss among young voters. Nevertheless, the actual effectiveness of both Rock the Vote and Choose or Lose is difficult to evaluate. While Rock the Vote claims success in getting youths to register as voters, its impact on the young actually voting is unclear. Knack (1997), for instance, claims that the rise in youth turnout in 1992 cannot be attributed to Rock the Vote alone and suggests that whereas Rock the Vote might have made it less acceptable for youth to admit nonvoting, it did not actually bring them to the voting booths. Research on MTV's Choose or Lose campaigns corroborates both the idea that such efforts are not successful and the hope that they do connect youth to politics (Hollander, 1995; Johnson, Braima, and Sothirajah, 1999; Roberts and Lundin, 2001).

Next to such general endeavors, particular political parties and politicians have associated with bands and artists. In the 1980s the British Labour Party became involved in Red Wedge, a touring mixture of a political rally and a pop concert at which Labour politicians, musicians, and youth campaigned against Thatcherism. Although most young voters chose Labour in the following election, Frith and Street (1992) show that other factors were at least as important. Direct effectiveness on voting behavior, however, may not be the best criterion to judge the significance of politicians blending with popular music. The resulting branding is more relevant. Musical taste and alliances are presumed to communicate lifestyle, social milieu, personality, and a general capacity to understand the everyday tastes of ordinary people. Consecutive American presidents have therefore invited popular musicians and other artists to the White House: Frank Sinatra sang for Kennedy, Nixon liked the Carpenters, Carter listened to Dylan and the Allman Brothers, and Reagan called the Beach Boys. Megabands and stars have found themselves courted by politicians from both sides of the political spectrum. Thus Frank Sinatra later switched to the Republicans, both the British Conservatives and Labour hurried to express their admiration for the Beatles, and Republicans and Democrats alike have exploited Bruce Springsteen's music.[4] Street (1986) observes that while the use of popular music may have been prevalent in progressive parties, the increasing use of marketing techniques in politics has intensified the use of popular music across the ideological gamut. It has, for instance, become common practice to adopt a specific song as a campaign anthem, in the vein of Clinton's use of Fleetwood Mac's "Don't Stop (Thinking about Tomorrow)" or New Labour's handling of "Things Can Only Get Better" by D:Ream. Musical preferences have now become part of the branding of politicians as people close to their constituencies. This is facilitated because unlike their predecessors, the latest generations of politicians grew up with popular music. The young Tony Blair, for instance, played in a band himself (Harris, 2003). While the 1997 elections in Britain witnessed a campaign battle of the pop stars with the Spice Girls supporting the Conservatives, it still seems that progressive politics offers the more natural allies to popular music. Harris (2003) describes how in Britain in the 1990s a more or less predestined alliance emerged between Britpop and New Labour. After more than a decade of Conservative rule, a new era, Harris claims, began both in pop and high culture. Movements like the Young British Artists, lad culture, and Britpop made London the city to be in during the 1990s. The inevitable mission for New Labour was to realize an association with

Britpop that would make Tony Blair and his people look cool. Oasis, Blur, and Suede were only a few of the bands and performers that were heavily courted. The endorsements and manifestations of Old Labour's Red Wedge, however, were passé. Nothing so concrete was looked for: what mattered primarily was the impression of a shared political and cultural movement toward renewal. The New Labour victory of 1997 seemed the ultimate evidence: Cool Britannia had arrived in a composite effort of politics and pop culture.

It is precisely the element of branding that has made popular musicians and their fans wary of politics using popular music. John Street (1986, p. 46) quotes James Brown, the American soul artist who said that politicians are little more than parasites upon the skills of musicians: "My stage act is so organized the whole establishment want to steal it from me, they want to know how I can command the love of people." The Britpop musicians found out to their dismay that New Labour was more interested in how they made Tony Blair and the party look up-to-date than in their issues or opinions. A member of Blur, for instance, thought New Labour's courting was very much like Camel sending the band free cigarettes and Prada giving them free clothes (Harris, 2003). Young voters' perceptions of the late and reluctant appearance of George Bush Sr. on MTV were devastating: they recognized it as an opportunistic attempt to woo their vote without listening to them (Bare, 1993). Reactions like these suggest that while popular music has been regularly called the *voice* of this or that generation, that should not be taken too literally, for it is rare to see popular music occur in political campaigns other than as branding instruments. The sole exception may be the world leaders receiving Bono, the lead singer of the Irish megaband U2, on his 2002 international political tour. He used his fame to plead for a complete discharge of Third World debts with George Bush Jr., Nelson Mandela, and Tony Blair—among others— who gave him a serious hearing and welcomed the photo opportunity. The more regular incorporation of popular music in politics suggests that what is at stake is the image of politics and politicians, rather than the possible political relevance of popular music. The use of popular music thus primarily restyles the appearance of politics and makes the position of particular parties and politicians in terms of lifestyles and taste more clear. Such branding has become an integral part of contemporary politics (e.g., Scammell, 2003) and is imperative given the necessity for contemporary politics to *entertain* citizenship in the triple sense of the word laid out in chapter 1. The conditions, of course, are that a particular connection between politics and popular music makes sense and that the politicians and performers involved are comfortable with it. Whereas the connection between New Labour and Britpop was highly plausible in the context of the shared cultural and political fatigue with Thatcherism (Margaret

Thatcher's favorite song was "How Much Is That Doggy in the Window?" for that matter), the ensuing disappointment of musicians shows that jointly these two conditions are not easily met. The access to new and alienated electorates that is at stake in the search for entertaining citizenship will therefore not simply be realized by using popular music to embellish politics. One might contend that most popular musicians, even the ones who endorse particular candidates, do not aspire to be heard politically. One might add that audiences appreciate their favorite music for other reasons than political ones, and vote for other reasons than musical ones. Nevertheless, there is a significant political tradition in popular music that makes it an alternative forum and source of knowledge about political concerns and debate.

POPULAR MUSIC AS POLITICAL FORUM

To be sure, just a minor part of the whole realm of popular music functions as a political medium. Brown and Campbell (1986) claim that 20 percent of all video clips can be considered "political"; Baxter et al. (1986) reach an amount of 14 percent, whereas other authors (Christenson and Roberts, 1998) argue that "political" songs never make up more than 10 percent of the total output. The dilemma here, of course, is the particular understanding of "politics." It is rare to encounter a song that addresses the issues and actors of the political field directly: Pulp, one of the Britpop bands, produced "The Day after the Revolution" about the victory of New Labour; George Michael's "Shoot the Dog" confronted the British acquiescence with U.S. plans to counter terrorism; and Dutch rapper Raymtzer made "Kutmarokkanen"[5] as a judgment on an Amsterdam alderman who was caught whispering this racist insult while ostensibly off camera. "Kutmarokkanen" made headline news and forced a public comment from the alderman, who had to invite the rapper to discuss the matter. Depending on one's own particular location in space and time, other examples of such concrete exchanges between the political field and popular music will come to mind, but they are incidental rather than systematic. The more common and sustained political expressions of popular music occur in relation to the social movements that have consciously operated outside of the political field (Garofalo, 1992a). According to Street (1986, p. 51), the reason for the manifold connections between new social movements and popular music is that "popular musicians share with political movements the preference for a politics around a cause, rather than an ideology or an electoral campaign." In addition, because most social

movements have a political and a cultural dimension, popular music
functions as a means to express and reinforce the identity and lifestyle dimensions involved. In women's bars and discos, for instance, the main
sound comes from not only female performers (see Lont, 1992) but also
mainstream disco hits such as Gloria Gaynor's "I Will Survive," which
have been turned into feminist dance classics. Thus, in social movements
from the right to the left, popular music has turned up both to convey the
issue at stake and to build a sense of community among the movement's
supporters. If popular music constitutes a political forum, then, it is usually around a movement issue, such as peace, the environment, equal
rights, urban decay, or freedom when it comes to popular music enhancing the struggle against totalitarian regimes (Garofalo, 1992a). One can
even recognize a certain degree of "issue ownership" across particular
genres. Rap music, for instance, holds the crisis of the American inner
cities (Rose, 1994; Stapleton, 1998) whereas world peace was particular to
folk music of the early 1960s and 1970s (Pratt, 1990; Sprague and Turner,
1990). Street (1986) lists how extreme right youth in the 1980s in Britain
colonized certain aspects of punk and Oi music, and qualified new wave
dance bands such as the Human League and Spandau Ballet as making
"traditional Aryan music." That happened despite punk's history as an
expression of broad youth disenfranchisement focused against images of
established authorities and the monarchy. Interesting, for that matter, is
that older advocates of the extreme right thought popular music an overall source of moral decline, with the exception of country and western. In
the United States, too, country music has been associated with the extreme right through the activities of the Ku Klux Klan and has given a
voice to mainstream conservative nationalism.[6] It has also been a favorite
genre among white South Africans. Such examples of issue ownership
suggest strongly that lyrics are not the only dimension of popular music
that transforms it into a "political" voice. Rap lyrics may concretely express inner-city protest, but in addition its performers are mainly black,
and the form builds on a long-standing African oral tradition to which
their sartorial style also refers (Stapleton, 1998). Country artists express—
indeed—a love for the country and a nostalgic view of a simple life
through their lyrics, their dialect, their dress code, and their choice of instruments. Punk bands, while themselves mostly not explicitly political
let alone extreme right wing, were nevertheless easy prey for the extreme
right because of their use of Nazi symbols and their general anti-
establishment attitude that was expressed in musical nihilism as well.

The "politics" of popular music is therefore not simply in the lyrics.
Lyrics on their own, in fact, may be a rather poor political indicator, since
most young audiences only have a cursory relation to lyrics; they miss
symbols and metaphors, and assess the content of a song basically from

song titles and band names (Prinsky and Rosenbaum, 1987). Rather than from the lyrics themselves, then, "politics" arises—often intended, sometimes unintended—from a specific articulation of lyrics, genre, artists, and audience appropriations. Whenever these articulations have been exploited and organized in concert, so to speak, popular music has become an alternative forum to the political field. The most explicit and political of these endeavors have come in the form of "Rock against . . . " concerts. British punk artists took the first initiative in 1976 for a chain of events that was called Rock against Racism. They wanted to express their outrage about guitarist Eric Clapton, who stated support for conservative politician Enoch Powell, notorious for his strong anti-immigration views. In 1979 representatives of the alternative press, music studios, rock clubs, and bands organized the first U.S. follow-up. Ever since, concerts, tours, festivals, and manifestations have been organized taking on various other causes too (e.g., Widgery, 1987). As a brand name, "Rock against . . . " is no longer limited to the popular music scene. Other actors have used the label to rally support for their issues. When the United States got the Olympics in Atlanta, for instance, opponents organized "Rock against Racism/Rap against the State" to

> expose the commercial nature of the Olympics, the warlike nation-state basis of the "competition," the police state activities of Atlanta and the United States government to prepare for the Olympics, the farce of the 1996 elections and the deteriorating economic/political conditions of the U.S.A. and the world in general, which the Olympics is designed to cover up.[7]

Live Aid stands out among the variety of manifestations. The fourteen-hour-long concert featuring over forty different bands was held simultaneously in Philadelphia and London in 1985 and was broadcast live by the BBC, MTV, and ABC. It was meant to raise money for the victims of the famine in Ethiopia and built on the success of Band Aid, a collective of popular British musicians that Boomtown Rats singer Bob Geldof brought together to record a Christmas song for Ethiopia ("Do They Know It's Christmas?"). Through Live Aid and Band Aid, about $120 million was raised. As a result, popular music became more respectable as a realm with social and political relevance (Garofalo, 1992a).

We can conclude that when popular music claims an explicit political role for itself, it is usually in association with social movement politics, constructing and confirming the sense of togetherness around a particular shared concern. Through social movements, then, popular music has been firmly tied to liberation movements in the former communist bloc, and in the Latin American, African, and Asian dictatorships (Garofalo, 1992a). It has also been said that specific popular music genres and events have constituted social movements in themselves. Thus, rap music has been considered as the 1990s version of the civil rights movement (Martinez, 1997), while Live Aid has been put up as a movement against famine in the Third World (Garofalo, 1992b). In terms of raising public consciousness and money for otherwise distant issues such as world famine or the problems of the inner cities, such assertions may be valid. It is also true that popular music offers a vehicle for musicians who want to express and share their political opinions. Popular music, at times, does put across a sense of injustice, a need for action, or a call for better societies that appeals to different audiences with varying intensity. For it to be *political* in the sense that we use in this book, it also needs to be listened to by political actors in the field, voluntarily or as the result of lobbying, pressure, or force. Live Aid is one good example of where the "politics" of popular music stops. While it did raise awareness and involvement with Third World famine, and while its organizer Bob Geldof was knighted for his efforts, Live Aid did not manage to reach to the field of politics in the sense that it opened up a discussion about U.S. and UK foreign policies in the respective parties and governments. In the end, the success of the event was along lines of charity rather than of politics.

CITIZENSHIP?

How do these associations between popular music and politics entertain the citizen? In other words, how do they enable the consideration of what citizenship means, how do they provide a hospitable surrounding for citizenship, and how do they work to make citizenship a pleasurable experience? By and large, the answer to those questions comes out negative. The existing relations between politics and popular music can be characterized in terms of domination, exploitation, and neglect. In the attempts to morally and politically discipline popular music and its performers, it is clear how politics regularly exerts direct power over popular music, submitting both artists and their fans to the unilateral regime of the cultural elites on all sides of the political spectrum. The simultaneous exploitation of popular music in campaign times can just as much be considered a one-sided exercise of power, especially because a more lasting input from popular musicians and their fans is not looked for, even if some artists and genres seek and have definitive political relevance. While the use of popular music as a campaigning instrument suggests awareness that different publics may require different communicative repertoires, in practice politics and popular music remain two separate fields with separate understandings of politics. The politics of popular music is the product of often-inchoate lyrics, beats, performance, and personal beliefs of musicians and is carried by a public that does not identify itself as political. Popular music thus has an easier connection to social movements, which also harbor a relatively disorganized mixture of interests, lifestyles, and sentiments that are political in the wider sense of the word and that for a larger part take place outside of the specialized field of politics. These features do not easily correspond to the requirements of the political field in which popular music, therefore, has hardly been considered a legitimate source of information, experience, and views of particular social groups. What the modern political field assumes is that individuals define and contend with their social needs among themselves and through political mediators such as candidates, parties, or news media in a well-informed and rational way. It is based on the ideal of an informed citizenry that weighs various political and policy alternatives and leaves little room for the affective, intuitive, and sensuous beliefs that arise from popular music as politics.

The confrontations between popular music and politics actually have a counterproductive tendency in terms of enhancing political citizenship, for instance when it comes to young voters. As was clear in the discussions about censoring popular music, fans of the targeted genres—often working-class white and black youth—are positioned as objects of policy rather than as legitimate political actors who have a right to participate in discussions about their tastes and pastimes. The young only seem to become interesting in election times, when performers and bands are exploited to suggest an intimate connection between politics and these possible constituencies. On top of that, the political experiences and beliefs that do emerge from popular music hardly ever reach politics as relevant expressions of problems or interests that need attention. In this context, the often-observed absence of political interest and involvement among the young can hardly be seen as a sign of their immaturity and deviance. Instead, it may be read as a perfectly legitimate and comprehensible response to a process of exclusions and submission (see Buckingham, 2000).

What we see, then, is that the concrete confrontations between popular music and politics, in spite of all the lip service paid, assume and reinforce the distinction between modern politics and entertainment as inequitable fields. Both the popular music and the soap opera cases that were discussed in the previous chapter thus show the exclusionary pragmatics of politics: while it will absorb all expressions of popular culture to its own benefit, politics will hear and allow only one mode of expressing public concerns and conflict: the discourse rooted in the ideals of the Enlightenment and the modernist traditions of the public sphere (see chapter 1). What would happen, however, if we took the soap and popular music as exemplary for politics, as instances of popular culture from which one could learn how citizens can be informed, engaged, and

mobilized in our contemporary entertainment societies? That is the subject of the following chapter.

NOTES

This chapter was written with Chris Aalberts, Ph.D. student at the University of
Amsterdam.

1. For this example, I am indebted to my colleague Ido de Haan, professor of modern history at the University Utrecht, Netherlands.
2. The moral entrepreneurs targeting popular music call in other independent
academics.
3. Bare takes his quotes from research in progress by Anne White, School of
Journalism and Mass Communication, University of North Carolina at Chapel
Hill.
4. Examples taken from Cloonan and Street (1997) and Street (1986, 1987).
5. Translation: "fucking Moroccans."
6. The Dixie Chicks, an all-female country and western band claimed to be the
best-selling women's band ever, is a striking exception. One of their singers said
in a television interview that she was ashamed that George Bush Jr. came from
their home state of Texas, and criticized the planned intervention in Iraq. While
other artists made similar comments, "The Dixie Chicks found out the hard way
that such sentiments didn't fly as well with the flag-waving country set" (Skanse,
2003). A conservative backlash followed including death threats, boycotts, and
talk radio attacks.
7. Atlanta Olympics Protest Committee, www.webcom.com/~peace/PEAC
TREE/stuff/stuff/html/0255.html (accessed June 13, 2004). Many other examples
of "Rock against . . . " can be found with any Internet search engine.

4

⊰⊱

Connections:
The Fan Democracy

The previous three chapters showed how modernist political discourse constructs a vast distance between popular culture and politics. Academics have identified popular culture and politics as distinct fields with different logics that should be kept apart. Journalists have used a particular genre of popular culture, the soap opera, to disqualify particular events and actions. Politicians have come down on popular music as a genre of moral ignominy, and have suppressed the politics of popular music.

In this chapter, I will take the first step to an alternative view that brings out relevant connections between popular culture and politics rather than presumes insurmountable differences. I will first look at whether and how the intense investments that audiences make in their favorite popular genres and stars have any bearing on the possible activity and involvement of people in the political field. I will then propose three analogies between fandom and citizenship: first, both fan communities and political constituencies come into being as a result of performance; second, fan groups and political constituencies resemble each other when it comes to the endeavors that make one part of the community; and—finally—both rest on emotional investments that are intrinsically linked to rationality and lead to "affective intelligence." These analogies make it possible to develop the contours of entertaining citizenship in the subsequent chapters.

AUDIENCE ACTIVITY AND INVOLVEMENT IN POLITICS

Popular culture harbors an array of media and genres that are all able to draw intense involvement from their audiences and become infinitely salient in their everyday lives. The soap opera, for instance, has been shown to structure household routines by defining moments in the day for family gatherings or for individual breaks from everyday chores (Seiter et al., 1989). It also presents a recurring opportunity for conversation, moral judgment, and shared pleasure about the predicaments of the main characters (Hobson, 1989). Such exchanges take place between family members, neighbors, colleagues, friends, and—after the arrival of the Internet—otherwise anonymous fans from across the country (Baym, 2000). Popular music is similarly integrated in everyday lives. It is both a strong individual mood manager and a means to experience and express a collective humor (Christenson and Roberts, 1998). Particular songs are enduring markers of the first dance, the first kiss, and other significant moments in life. Fans may decorate their bedroom walls with posters of their favorite performers and go out of their way—financially and geographically—to see "their" band or artist play live. One could compare these examples with the passionate attachments that people have for their favorite sports teams, or for a specific movie or television program; the list of fandom and fan communities is endless and well researched (e.g., Hills, 2002). In all cases, one would see that popular culture has been able to activate audiences into discussion, participation, creativity, intervention, and evaluation.

Currently, popular reality television genres have intensified such audience activities by offering the opportunity to intervene in the course of a program by voting for one's favorite candidate. While *Big Brother* was not the first program to incite such audience involvement, it did take it to unprecedented heights. Aired for the first time in the fall of 1999 in the Netherlands, it took the rest of Europe by storm and has now become a popular format in twenty-seven countries and regions.[1] At the heart of the program is a contest between twelve ordinary people who submit to voluntary confinement in a specially constructed house for a period of some three months. Video cameras follow their everyday interactions and negotiations; audiences can watch these camera streams live on the Internet, or edited into daily segments on television. At regular intervals, the house residents nominate two or three of their fellows to be voted out by the audience. Through the Internet, SMS (short text messages sent from mobile phones), and telephone connections, audiences then cast a vote for their least favorite person. Three candidates remain in the end, the winner again selected by audience call-ins.[2] Throughout Europe, the popularity of *Big Brother* was astonishing: huge audience shares running up to 70 percent, intense public debate, passionate Internet discussions, and colossal voting turnouts. Even in the United States, where *Big Brother* pulled only a moderately sized television audience, involvement and commotion among them was high, as, for instance, the record number of site visits testifies (see van Zoonen, 2001). Many similar formats have followed since then, each of them inviting audiences to take part, discuss, vote, or even become candidates themselves. The latest peak in these genres came in 2002 in the form of 19/FremantleMedia's *Pop Idol*, a British format that has a national talent contest as its main feature (titled *American Idol* in the United States and *Idols* in European countries). Thousands of young boys and girls audition in front of a four-person professional jury that has no mercy in its verdicts. In the initial weeks of the program, audiences can only watch the moving, funny, embarrassing, ironic, or absurd attempts to survive the first selection, with some highs and many lows of talent alternating. In several, again ruthlessly televised cycles, the jury limits the final number of contestants to ten: then the audience comes in and votes every week to keep their favorite in the race. The sequence culminates in a final between the two last remaining rivals, of whom only one will end up with the title *Idol*, again decided by the audience. Like *Big Brother*, *Pop Idol* does have its predecessors and lookalikes, but it has outweighed all of them in terms of ratings, discussion, activity, involvement, and voting numbers.

Audience-participation programs such as *Big Brother* and *Pop Idol* make visible what audience research has claimed extensively: that audiences are not the passive couch potatoes, the mindless dupes, or the vulnerable victims that they are often made out to be by television's critics.[3] Digital interactive technologies have now given audiences a possibility to *act* on their involvement with a program and to *intervene* in its course. The interpersonal communication that always takes place around television programs (e.g., Katz and Lazarsfeld, 1964) has now acquired an additional, more public outlet in the various communicative possibilities of the Internet and mobile telephony. The ever-present sympathies and antipathies of audiences for television characters can at this time be translated into a definitive act to foster or obstruct their fate, through SMS decrees, phone-ins, or Internet ballots. The interpretative communities that have existed around all television and other popular genres have acquired new vigor in Internet forums, which contain comment, reflection, advice, and creative input on particular programs. This occurs, for that matter, not only with the genres that particularly invite such interaction, like *Big Brother* or *Pop Idol*, but also with more classic "one-way" genres such as sports, science fiction, and soaps.

The classic work on such pre-Internet audience activity is Janice Radway's (1984) study of reading communities around romance novels who discuss, evaluate, and criticize the huge offering of such books, and who occasionally transform their interest into the actual production of new novels: readers become writers. What Radway's and other similar reception research has shown to the academic world, and what *Big Brother*,

Pop Idol, and their counterparts have thrown into the public eye, is the enormous energy that people invest in popular culture, the creativity that they draw upon to make sense of it and adapt it to their needs, the intensive meanings it can acquire in everyday life, and—particularly—the participatory mechanisms it can set into motion.[4] These mechanisms make a parallel with the political process inevitable: the discussion, participation, creativity, interventions, judgments, and votes that take place around reality television are all activities that would qualify as civic competences if they were performed in the context of the political field.

Daniel Dayan (2001) confronts the parallel between such audience activities and civic performance and asks how fan groups compare with traditional political publics that have emerged around particular issues or affairs. Dayan defines these publics as social, stable, loyal, and reflexive; as engaged in internal debate and external debate; and as making demands about and toward their objects. Whereas Dayan acknowledges that fan communities expose precisely these features, he does not want to qualify them as publics because they function outside of society

> in a sort of parallel universe. The activities of the fan reflect a world of play and mimicry, a social reality that could be described as closed off, marginal, a game. Something essential seems to be lacking. Here is a public without a commissive dimension, without a sense of seriousness. (p. 752)

Dayan's distance between fan activities and civic performance builds on the normative desire to separate entertainment from politics that I discussed in chapter 1. Supposedly, entertainment brings audiences consisting of fans into being, whereas politics produces publics composed of citizens. Audiences and publics, fans and citizens, are thus constructed as involving radically different social formations and identities. As I discussed in chapter 1, that is not a tenable position, for it separates the political field from mainstream culture, which is ridden with entertainment, and it denies the increasing presence of entertaining means of communication in political practice, as one can see through the inclusion—however opportunistic—of soap narratives (chapter 2) and popular music in election campaigns (chapter 3).

There is also an urgent practical need to explore and imagine how fandom and citizenship can be connected. The success of reality entertainment like *Big Brother* and *Pop Idol*, in which audiences can vote for or against their favorite candidates, has inspired many initiatives to transport the appeal of these genres to the political field. In the UK, *Big Brother* inspired the Hansard Society, an independent nonparty organization, to explore possible lessons that the *Big Brother* house could teach the House of Commons (Coleman, 2003). The report suggests, on the basis of a survey among political "junkies" and *Big Brother* fans, that the *Big Brother* experience shows the desire of audiences for three indispensable but currently marginal dimensions of political culture: transparency and authenticity, interactivity and control, and respect for diverse epistemologies. In Argentina, an actual experiment with a political reality television program was produced: a Buenos Aires television channel programmed a reality show in the fall of 2002 that enabled people to choose their own candidate for the 2003 congressional elections. It had a similar format to *Pop Idol* with a jury deciding on who, of the many people who came forward, was allowed to campaign in the program ("Reality TV Search," 2002). The program did not fare too well; it was quickly rescheduled due to disappointing ratings. Finally, it was canceled altogether, and it ended on the year's list of biggest television failures ("El Fracaso," 2003). The reasons for this fiasco are unclear; however, the program looked like an average political talk show embellished with brief reports of the candidates' everyday lives. It seemed to lack the spectacle and excitement of its prototypes.[5] In the United States, FX network, a division of Fox, has seriously considered a similar idea, *The American Candidate*, a format proposed by R. J. Cutler, the documentary maker who created *The War Room*, about the 1992 presidential elections. It was meant to find a grassroots political candidate who would run as an independent candidate in the 2004 race for the White House. The program would start on the Internet, where the applicants could build their support base and debate their opponents. A selection from these people, elected by a professional jury, would end up in the television show competing for the audience vote ("All Hail," 2003). The extensive publicity and preparation notwithstanding, FX canceled the program because it was said to be too expensive and logistically demanding ("FX Won't," 2003). Predictably, these articulations of entertainment with politics have met with fierce disapproval. On account of *El candidate de la Gente*, Argentine philosopher Sergio Marelli claimed (2002, no page):

> The ties of representation of the town and the politicians do not reconstitute magically. The only way to return credibility to the politicians is through the indispensable social transformation that is associated with ethics, and not through spectacle. Such an objective is very far from the intentions and the possibilities of a television program. (Editor's translation)

The American Candidate received a similar comment: "Leave it to Fox to find a way to further diminish politics and public life in America," said Thomas Mann, a political analyst at the Washington-based Brookings Institution. "It's a sort of antiparty, anti system, celebrity based approach that reinforces the worst tendencies of our politics. It's sad—but not surprising"

(Cernetig, 2002, no page). Stephen Coleman, the author of the British
Hansard report (2003), writes that he encountered derisive laughter and
snobbery when discussing the research and its outcomes. Asking a group
of people profoundly interested in and conversant with politics how *Big
Brother* could inform politics, the more common reply was "staggeringly
hostile" (p. 23):

> The best thing an MP could do about this "voyeurism" telly is to push
> through a Private Members Bill putting a stop to the whole degrading, point-
> less, imbecilic trend. I really don't care if that makes me undemocratic or not.
> . . . It's for the good of the nation. (p. 24)

In these three comments, the familiar apocalyptic denunciations of the
articulation between entertainment and politics come up again. Obviously, the people proposing political *Big Brothers* or *Idols* do not share
these beliefs. They claim that there are useful parallels between the involvement of people in reality entertainment and the commitment one
would want people to have toward politics. That claim, however, has not
been theorized other than the observation that both require a commitment
to candidates and a willingness to vote in elections. That parallel is only
the superficial expression of more profound analogies between the fans of
entertainment genres and the citizens involved in politics. I will demonstrate first that fan groups are social formations that are structurally
equivalent to political constituencies.

POLITICAL CONSTITUENCIES AND FAN COMMUNITIES

The social and cultural fragmentation considered so typical of the postmodern condition is also evident in the instability and unpredictability of
political constituencies. In the decreases in political membership, the
diminishing of party identifications, and the increase in the number of undecided floating voters, Clarke and Stewart (1998, p. 363) see "the characteristic signatures of an era of partisan dealignment." These processes have
been attributed to a dissolution of the social, religious, and psychological
determinants of political preferences: the assumed one-to-one relations between, for instance, the working class and Labour, or Catholicism and
Christian Democrats, have by and large disappeared. The enormous electoral defeats that—in particular—many social and Christian democratic
parties in western Europe have witnessed in the past decades have been
taken as watertight proof of the loss of their self-evident social and psychological base. Mulgan (1994) argues that there is a crisis of *modern* politics that is characterized by, among other things, the erosion of "clearly

defined class interests by changing economic, occupational and social structures, and by a loss of much of the cultural homogeneity that bound class movements together in the past" (p. 12). There is a clear parallel here with the crisis that emerged in marketing when social positions and economic status no longer predicted consumer behavior and media use, and the allure of specific products in itself turned out to be the decisive factor in consumer behavior. Not surprisingly, therefore, political campaigns have incorporated modern marketing techniques in extenso, with focus group discussions, segmentation of the electorate, and branding of the party and its leaders as only some of the instruments employed (e.g., Newman, 1999). It is, however, not the congruence between political communication and marketing techniques, collapsing parties and products, that I want to point out here, although that is an inevitable part of the situation and discussion at present. Rather, I wish to focus on the different conceptualization of "constituency" necessitated by the present disappearance of traditional electorates. Political parties and candidates now have to *produce* their constituencies on the basis of their appeal rather than relying on already existing social commonalities. Adherents of political parties seem to share no more than their appreciation of the performance of that party and its candidates; they may have social factors in common, but that does not sufficiently explain their alliance with particular politics. An intermediate process of identification takes place, which is evoked and mobilized through the particular appeals of parties and their candidates.[6] The cognitive rational bias of political theory notwithstanding, these appeals also include emotional, affective, moral, and aesthetic components (e.g., Marcus, 2002). The politician, claims Mulgan (1994, p. 33), has a different role to play in these processes, not one of representation but one of mobilization: "What will make them representative and legitimate will not be election so much as their ability to define constituencies and common interests, representing them to others and to themselves."

The structural relationship of the political field to its constituencies as communities, which materialize as a result of performances and appeals, has an equivalent in the articulation of mass media with their audiences. Street (1997, p. 60) says, for instance, that

> politics, like popular culture, is about creating an "audience," a "people" who will laugh at their jokes, understand their fears and share their hopes. Both the popular media and politicians are engaged in creating works of popular fiction which portray credible worlds that resonate with people's experiences.

This analogy has not gone unnoticed, of course, and the concept of an "audience" and "spectator" democracy that resides primarily in the mass media, who show political leaders as the telegenic embodiments of particular ideals, has been used by, among others, Manin (1997). Whereas such a term may capture the reality of contemporary politics as a mass-mediated phenomenon, it assumes that audiences are relatively passive bystanders and does not at all address the dynamic and complex relations of individuals and collectives with mass media and among themselves. Abercrombie and Longhurst (1998) have developed a continuum of audience involvement that ranges from consumers on the one hand and petty producers on the other, with fans, cultists, and enthusiasts in the middle. Paraphrasing their understanding of the three middle categories in political terms, one can see how they capture the way constituencies are called into being by (mass-mediated) politics:

> "*Fans* are those people who become particularly attached to certain programmes or stars within the context of a relatively heavy media use" (p. 138). These could be considered, in other words, the voters of a party for a party or a candidate.
> "*Cultists* are more organized than fans. They meet each other and circulate specialized materials that constitute the nodes of a network" (p. 139). The political parallel here is with the volunteers of a political party.
> "*Enthusiasts* are, in our terms . . . based predominantly around activities rather than media or stars" (p. 139). Enthusiasts would be analogous to party representatives in various governing bodies.

Abercrombie and Longhurst (1998) add that their continuum may also be read as an audience career path, as it were (p. 141), in which—again— lies an analogy with politics: starting as a relatively indiscriminate consumer of politics, one may become a fan and then travel through the phases of cultism and enthusiasm to that of the political professional. Structurally, then, electorates are positioned in a similar relation to parties and politicians as fans are in relation to programs or stars. They also share internal distinctions based on different levels of interest, commitment, and activity. Nonetheless, even if electorates are structurally similar to fan communities, they may engage in totally different kinds of activities. If that were the case, the analogy between fans and electorates would not stand.

FAN ACTIVITIES AND POLITICAL ACTIVITIES

Given the common appreciation of fans as mindless followers of their heroes and citizens as responsible political participants, it is probably more necessary to dwell on the existence and nature of fan activities than on the reality of political activities. Fans suffer from stereotypical images, which put them down as mindless followers of their heroes, accepting whatever they offer them without criticism. Fandom is thought to be based on an affective appreciation of specific objects rather than on a critical cognitive assessment (see Jenkins, 1992). Political activities, on the other hand, are generally considered to be the quintessence of good citizenship: acquiring information about public affairs, developing informed opinions, discussing them with fellow citizens, taking action on these discussions (ranging from, for example, individually sending an e-mail to organizing collective protest), and taking responsibility for neighborhood, local, or national political affairs are only a few of the activities assumed to anchor democracy in everyday actions (e.g., Fisher and Kling, 1993). Juxtaposing fans and citizens in such commonsensical terms suggests that fandom cannot be a beneficial model for political citizenship; on the contrary, the passive fan and the active citizen are constructed as absolute opposites. Actual studies on fan communities present entirely different pictures, though. Hills (2002, p. 2) has observed the absence not only of a general theory but also of a comprehensive empirical outline of fandom: "Works have focused on single TV series, singular fan cultures, or singular media ('TV fans' versus 'cinephiles')." Yet these dispersed studies do show that many, if not most, fans actively, creatively, and communally engage with their favorite texts, be they stars, programs, genres, or media (Lewis, 1992). A detailed account of such fan activities can be found in Nancy Baym's (2000) case study of the Internet community that evolved around the American soap *All My Children*. Baym, a fan of daytime soaps herself, participated in the Usenet news group and observed the interaction between its participants between 1990 and 1993.[7] She returned to the group in 1998 to see whether the many changes and the greater availability of the Internet had changed the practices in the group. The conversations between the participants (mainly women) were primarily concerned with the interpretation of soap stories and characters. Fans process the soaps, for instance, by relating them to their own lives or by speculating about future events. As Baym shows through extensive quotes from the multitude of postings in the group, these interpretations emerged in dialogue and deliberation, which both have a playful and an emotional component. Part of the pleasure of the news group is in the common evaluation of the quality, realism, and underlying messages contained in soap texts. The participants prove to be a highly competent audience expressing critical assessments of the show that often surpass the knowledge of the producers. Some longtime fans feel they know the characters and their fictional community better than the writers and are struggling—as it were—with the writers about the ownership of the series. Baym shows how participants come up with new and better story lines, which they exchange among themselves in a humorous display of creativity and wit. The deliberation around these new stories is conducted in a general sphere of friendliness and consensus seeking. The fact that these participants are mostly women contributes to the group's atmosphere, according to Baym. However, it is not gender alone that is an explanatory factor here, but also its articulation with the specific textual features of the soap operas that call for diverging meanings and interpretations. The passionate involvement found by Baym is not limited to soap fans but is characteristic of all fan communities, and has been found among the fans of such dispersed programs, films, and stars as *Dr. Who, Star Trek, Casablanca,* Madonna, *Inspector Morse, Betty Blue,* and Elvis (see Hills, 2002; Jenkins, 1992; Rodman, 1996; Schwichtenberg, 1993; L. Thomas, 2002). Abercrombie and Longhurst (1998, p. 127) summarize the features of this involvement in the following way:

> Fans are *skilled* or *competent* in different modes of production and consumption; *active* in their interaction with texts and in their production of new texts; and *communal* in that they construct different communities based on their links to the programmes they like. (italics in original)

Such practices of community building are part of a social process that concerned observers have seen disappearing from social and political life in the past decades. Robert Putnam's *Bowling Alone* (2000) has become the almost proverbial reference in this context. On the basis of a vast array of miscellaneous social indicators, ranging from participation in voluntary organizations to going out for a picnic with the family, Putnam argues that such social capital has declined considerably. Since Putnam considers social capital to be the backbone of people's capacity and willingness to engage in public debate and participate in political activity, its demise represents not only a serious threat to social cohesion but to democracy as well.[8] "Voluntary associations, from churches to professional societies to Elks clubs and reading groups, allow individuals to express their interested demands on government and to protect themselves from abuses by their political leaders" (Putnam, 2000, p. 338). Weakening social capital can therefore be considered as the root of political degeneration in the United States, as expressed in declining political knowledge, dropping turnout rates, and other signs of decay (e.g., Galston, 2001). It is tempting to extrapolate Putnam's claims and propose fan activity as a contemporary locus of social capital: in fan communities, then, important capacities and conditions for democracy would be seen to arise and mature. It is, however, precisely the missing link between social and political capital that has been at the heart of the many critical assessments of Putnam's work: "At no point does Putnam establish any connection between the social and political realms that would permit such far-fetched claims about the impact of social capital" (Boggs, 2001, p. 285; see also Durlauf, 2002). Rather than construing fan activities as an embryonic step to acquire more relevant civic qualities and virtues, I would argue for the equivalence of fan practices and political practices, an equality that facilitates an exchange between the domains of entertainment and politics that is commonly thought to be impossible. Fans have an intense individual investment in the text, they participate in strong communal discussions and deliberations about the qualities of the text, and they propose and discuss alternatives that would be implemented as well if only the fans could have their way. These are, in abstract terms, the customs that have been laid out as essential for democratic politics: information, discussion, and activism (e.g., Fisher and Kling, 1993). Maybe, then, the only difference between fans and citizens is located in the different subjectivities on which they seem based; affective relations in the case of fans, cognitive processes in the case of citizens. Is this difference bona fide, though?

FAN INVESTMENTS AND CIVIC INVESTMENTS

As is clear from various accounts of fan engagement, the relation of a fan with his or her favorite object is primarily based on affective identifications. Baym's (2000) work on the fans of the soap *All My Children* shows that their dialogues are typified by playful and emotional interactions, the latter occurring in particular when participants in the news group relate the televised stories to events in their own lives and use the alternative story lines to make meaning of their personal experience. Other genres invite other kinds of emotional investment, sometimes with a much nastier face: soccer fans, obviously, are infamous for their hostility toward the fans of other teams or nations (e.g., Brown, 1998), and pop music has also been seen to produce rather passionate divisions between fans (e.g., Frith, 1978). A more detailed review of different kinds of fan engagement would inevitably reveal considerable differences resulting from, for instance, the interactions of gender and genre, and striking similarities arising out of the common practice of "affective play" (see Hills, 2002). Most important in this context, however, is that such an appraisal would also show how much research has constructed an imagined fan subjectivity seemingly fundamentally at odds with the traditional requirements of politics. Pleasure, fantasy, love, immersion, play, or impersonations are not concepts easily reconciled with civic virtues such as knowledge, rationality, detachment, learnedness, or leadership. It is not my aim to argue instead that fandom is based on cognitions and rational powers (although the historical and statistical knowledge of sports fans is at times bewildering), nor to pose affective fan engagement as the adequate alternative to failing contemporary political involvement. To do either would be to fall victim to an academic romanticism that has been adequately dismantled by Hills (2002). Fandom, however, is built on psychological mechanisms that are relevant to political involvement: these are concerned with the realm of fantasy and imagination on the one hand, and with emotional processes on the other.

Emotions have never been denied their proper place in politics. Although Max Weber (1918) typified the state of affairs existing at his time as already being a "dictatorship resting on the exploitation of mass emotionality," he also observed that if politics was to be a genuinely human action, rather than an intellectual game, "dedication to it can only be generated and sustained by passion" (1918). Marcus (2002) disentangles the emotional prerequisites—devotion, veneration, and well-confined passion—that the American Founding Fathers formulated in their blueprint for the country's government. In current political research, emotional political motivations have found their way into the widely used concept of *party identification*, which has been defined as an affective orientation toward a group or party that results from early life socialization processes taking place mainly in the family (Campbell et al., 1960). Also, Lodge and Mc-Graw (1995, p. 12) claim that affect or "hot cognitions" have ordinarily been taken up as relevant factors in research on the structures and processes of political judgment. In everyday political practice, emotions are ritualized in characteristic political ceremonies, which evoke fan behavior rather than civic behavior among their participants. Election nights, for instance, are invariably staged as a theatrical climax with ear-splitting music heightening expectation and exaltation. When the party leader arrives, the scenes of crowds yelling and cheering are not so different from the sight of fans shouting for their favorite sports or movie star. While the privileged party members who are allowed entrance to election nights can otherwise be considered classic citizens in *optima forma*, at such occurrences they seem only too eager to throw off the yoke of rational cognitive citizenship: they yell and cheer, admire and love, or cry and mourn with the leadership. They behave, in other words, like highly ecstatic or deeply bereft fans. The significance of such political rituals is evident: party leaders, active members, and—at a televised distance—passive members and voters are, however volatile, forged into harmony, briefly united in joy or sorrow. The indispensable affective ties contributing to the communality in political parties are forcefully addressed and temporarily tightened (see also Edelman, 1964).

Despite the commonplace occurrences of affect in political processes, the ritualized display of emotions, and the significant research tradition into psychological processes among politicians and voters, emotional investments have hardly been *theorized* as indispensable, desirable, and commendable components of political involvement, as relevant as information processing, cognitive evaluations, and rational assessment of alternatives. Rather, emotions have been theoretically understood as a secondary component of politics, accepted for strategic reasons at best, but worrisome and undermining when taking center stage, as observers as long back as Weber have feared. American political scientist George Marcus (2002, p. 5) summarizes these positions succinctly by saying that emotion is considered "a troublemaker, intruding where it does not belong and undermining the undisturbed use of our deliberative capacity." His alternative theory of affective intelligence counters the common case against emotion in politics by showing how it is—on the contrary—the key to good citizenship because emotional processes enable the use of reason (also Marcus, Neuman, and MacKuen, 2000). Building on current insights from the neurosciences (Damasio, 1995), Marcus and his co-researchers propose that two "affective subsystems" in the brain are crucial for the understanding of political judgment and behavior. The disposition system, Marcus's shortcut term for the more commonly used "habit learning and execution system," is concerned with the development and maintenance of routine behavior. Such routine behavior can only be useful and successful if the subsystem has feedback on how it is doing; for the disposition system, the sensation of "enthusiasm" provides the brain with the cue of whether it is doing well. "If all is not going well, then at [the] precise moment of mismatch a decrease in the sensation of enthusiasm provides an alert that an adjustment must be made" (Marcus, 2002, p. 81). The anxiety resulting from such systemic breakdown calls the surveillance system in the brain into action, which produces the need to stand still, analyze the situation, think about alternatives, and develop new routines. The disposition system, based on enthusiasm, and the surveillance system, based on anxiety, correspond to specific types of political judgment and behavior, according to Marcus's group. If the disposition system were the ruling one in people's engagement in politics, then their choices and behavior would be habitual, based on long-learned opinions and behaviors. The relative tranquility of the situation enables the free flow of associations, daydreaming, and fantasizing that is necessary for imagining modifications and alternatives. Election outcomes would be fairly predictable and campaign efforts would have to be aimed at maintaining a sufficient amount of enthusiasm among the party's own constituencies, and at producing apathy in the camp of the opponents. When the electorate is anxious for some reason, then the surveillance system will identify the need for information, learning, and making decisions that will enable a return to the disposition system.[9] Here, campaign strategies need to be aimed at persuading anxious groups of voters that specific partisan policy measures are better than others; in other words, they will relieve the anxiety. Marcus and his co-researchers (2000, p. 64) conclude therefore that the common presumption in politics that emotions lead to the failure of reason and a lack of sound judgment "is almost certainly false. Emotional, behavioral and judgmental consequences are not uniform across the emotional subsystems. Understanding the effects of emotion requires that one know which emotional system is engaged." Their alternative, which they label a theory of affective intelligence, shows "how emotion and reason interact to produce a thoughtful and attentive citizenry" (Marcus, Neuman, and MacKuen, 2000, p. 1). Without the affective investments resulting from enthusiasm and anxiety, political interest and commitment would falter, according to Marcus, just like fan communities would wane without the emotional input of their members.

CITIZENSHIP?

Having thus constructed a three-dimensional equivalence between fan communities and political constituencies, I will now return to the relevance of entertainment for political citizenship. That should not be sought in its informative qualities, its appeal to cognitive capacities, or its encouragement of rational deliberation. As has been shown ad nauseam, its capacities in these realms are highly limited. That does not automatically mean that entertainment should be separated from politics, as many authors keep claiming. Popular culture genres have shown that they are extremely capable of creating short- and long-lived fan communities. Such fandom has long been an intrinsic feature of audience behavior, even before participatory genres and interactive technologies intensified its manifestations. Since fan communities and political constituencies bear crucial similarities, it is clear where the relevance of popular culture for politics lies: in the emotional constitution of electorates that involves the development and maintenance of affective bonds between voters, candidates, and parties. This does not preclude political discussion and activity, as the research on the practices of fandom shows, nor does it forestall the use of cognitive capacities and consideration, as the discussed work of Marcus and his co-researchers points out. On the contrary, articulations between politics and entertainment should be seen as inviting the affective intelligence that is vital to keep political involvement and activity going.

The remaining question then becomes whether and how politics can borrow from the elements of popular culture that produce these intense audience investments, so that citizenship becomes entertaining. The simple transfer that is present in proposals like *The American Candidate* to produce "reality politics" will not do, because—as said—they only take the superficial resemblance of the voting process as the common basis. The more relevant connection, justified by the similar processes in fandom and citizenship, would have to come from the specific generic features of popular culture on which the immense audience investments are built. For this purpose, the common distinction used in semiotics between syntagmatic and paradigmatic structures is helpful (e.g., Hodge and Kress, 1988). "Syntagmatic structure" refers to the way in which particular signs in culture are combined into a relatively consistent unity, while "paradigmatic structure" refers to the particular choice and absence of signs. John Fiske (1987, 1989) has developed a semiotic approach that is specific to the features of television and popular culture, and argues that in these two areas the key features of syntagma and paradigma are, respectively, "narrative" and "character." "Narrative structure demonstrates that people and places are not anarchic and random, but *sensible*, and then combines the paradigmatic sense of places and people with the syntagmatic sense of events and time into a grand signifying pattern" (Fiske, 1987, p. 129). A semiotic approach to the political field would thus examine its paradigmatic and syntagmatic structure: who is present and absent as "politician" (paradigma), and what stories politicians tell and which ones are told about them (syntagma). I will therefore examine the personalization and the particular narratives of politics in the following chapters.

NOTES

This chapter builds on my "Imagining the Fan Democracy," *European Journal of Communication* 19, no. 1 (2004): 39–52. Sage Publication Ltd. holds the copyright for the original version.

1. Pan Africa, Australia, Argentina, Belgium, Brazil, Colombia, Denmark, Ecuador, France, Germany, Greece, Netherlands, Hungary, Italy, Mexico, the Middle East, Norway, Poland, Portugal, Romania, Russia, South Africa, Spain, Switzerland, Sweden, United Kingdom, and the United States, as of December 2003.

2. The format has been adapted to national television cultures, which produces variety in, for instance, the length of the series as a whole, the number of contestants, presentation formats around the show, staging of the final, and so on. See Hill and Palmer (2001).

3. Although there are, of course, critics who argue that they are exactly that, since the positioning of SMS voting and their options in programs including and subsequent to *Big Brother* can be seen as a purely cynical exploitation of an alternative revenue stream by producers and broadcasters.

4. Of course, much television goes by unnoticed and is as relevant to audiences as the proverbial wallpaper. Following Joke Hermes' (1995) observation

about reading women's magazines, much television has become so mundane, so routine, that it often fails to leave any impression at all.

5. My sincere thanks to Marcelo Cohen of Endemol Argentina for sending me a tape of the program.

6. This process of identifying should not be confused with the idea of party identification as commonly used in political science. This points toward a relatively stable individual's affective political orientations resulting from early life, primarily familial socialization, occupational and social networks, and exposure to politics (see Zuckerman, Kotler-Berkowitz, and Swaine, 1998). The concept is less dynamic than the process I want to identify here as the result of the way political parties "construct" their electorate.

7. The summary provided here is taken from van Zoonen, 2000c.

8. Putnam also argues that social capital is a prerequisite for health and happiness, an argument that I will not go into at this point.

9. This is, Marcus claims on the basis of neuroscience, the state that human beings desire.

5

⊰⊱

Personalization: The Celebrity Politician

The paradigmatic analysis of politics proposed in the previous chapter directs the attention to the position and performance of politicians. The individual politician is becoming ever more important due to three connected political and cultural developments. First, in the ever-increasing load of entertainment texts and images, the individual performance of politicians provides the much-needed shortcut to the information that people need to make political judgments. Different political psychologists have labeled citizens as cognitive misers who will seek to minimize the time and effort needed to learn about political issues by judging the individual traits of politicians instead (e.g., Iyengar and McGuire, 1993). In an entertainment culture, such a shortcut need not only be brief, but also pleasurable. Second, entertainment and its respective genres provide the dominant cultural framework within which to make sense of politics. The codes and conventions of these genres favor individuals over processes, psychological motives over power structures, and personal efficiency and decisiveness over abstract social developments (Sparks, 1992). "The politician" fits those cultural requirements much better than "politics" and must thus take center stage. As a result, thirdly, politicians have to commute constantly between the different requirements of politics and entertainment in order to maintain their position and status in the political field, as well as their relevance to the everyday culture of their constituents. As a result of these developments, contemporary politics has become thoroughly personalized, to the dismay of authors who favor a modernist understanding of politics. For them, "personalization" is almost a four-letter word suggesting that politicians and citizens have become obsessed with the behavior and individual capacities of politicians at the expense of the proper exchange of ideas, expressions of interests, and debates about issues proclaimed to be at the heart of politics proper (e.g., Carmines and Stimson, 1980).

In this chapter, I will first discuss the modernist disgust of personalization; I will then show that personalization is not by definition antipolitical but rather is the result of a complex but balanced articulation of politics and popular culture, which finds its expression on different stages. A concrete analysis of the appearance of the Democratic candidates in television talk shows for the U.S. presidential elections of 2004 demonstrates in detail how the requirements of politics and popular culture come together in the performance of politicians, and leads to the concluding typology of political performance in the fan democracy.

FEAR AND LOATHING

When Arnold Schwarzenegger, the Austrian-born bodybuilder and star of many violent action movies, won the gubernatorial elections for California in 2003, critics saw their worst fears confirmed: celebrity had become more important than political substance, and people voted on the basis of a superficial Hollywood appeal rather than on a reasonable assessment of policy alternatives. Exacerbating their aversion was the fact that the campaign itself was full of candidates who did not run for governor but for the publicity opportunities the campaign offered to them (a porn star) or to their companies (two brothers with a beer company).[1]

Neil Postman (1985, p. 135) already warned about the "celebrity politician":

> Television frees politicians from the limited field of their expertise. Political figures may show up anywhere, at any time, doing anything, without being thought out of place. Which is to say they have become assimilated into the general television culture as celebrities.

Schwarzenegger's victory seems to prove that the opposite takes place as easily, for celebrities have become politicians as well (see Meyer, 2002, pp. 77–80, for other examples). Evidently, for the critics, such mergers between celebrities and politicians are only the putrefied excess of the personalization of politics. In *The Fall of Public Man*, Richard Sennett's eloquent argument against personalization in public life, the problem is phrased as follows:

> We see society itself as "meaningful" only by converting it into a grand psychic system. We may understand that a politician's job is to draft or execute

legislation, but that work does not interest us until we perceive the play of personality in political struggle. A political leader running for office is spoken of as "credible" and "legitimate" in terms of what kind of man he is, rather than in terms of the actions or programs he espouses. (1974, p. 4)

Sennett, writing in 1974, locates personalization firmly with "us," failing citizens who are obsessed with "the play of personality" and can only understand public life as a realm of psychological relations. Edelman (1964) attributes "our" incapacities to the burdens of mass society in which bewilderment, uncertainty, and atomization reign and in which personalized leadership conveys the promise to make the world understandable and controllable. Although Edelman ascribes similar functions to people's psychological identifications with political parties, more recent authors have seen the weakening of party attachments as responsible for the intensified personalization in politics (Dalton, 2000). Television, predictably, is repeatedly pointed out as the driver of personalization. British political scientist Bob Franklin (1994, p. 10) says, for instance, "Persistent television portrayals of a select clique of 'telegenic' politicians, mouthing prerehearsed slogans and automaton sound bites, has supplanted the rational and sustained advocacy of policy." Roderick Hart (1994) argues that the visual language of television, with its close-up focus on faces, encourages a personalized, psychological attitude toward politicians. Thomas Meyer (2002) argues that the dramaturgical rules of television have removed the traditional politician from the field. For Meyer, the traditional politician is someone who studies administrative documents about which he then talks, negotiates, and decides. The celebrity politician of television, on the other hand, "does not have to depend on anything else or anyone else except his own talent as a performer. He owes nothing to any lobby, association, interest group or party, as long as the media aura of his public body lasts" (p. 79).

Authors who claim that politics has always been about performance by individual political actors have countered the modernist dismay at personalization.[2] They point to the classic art of political rhetoric, the modes and techniques of speech available to persuade a public. In ancient Greece, a distinct group of teachers, the Sophists, were responsible for exploring, developing, and refining the art of rhetoric (see Witteveen, 1992). They also gave rhetorical advice and wrote political speeches; they were the spin doctors of their time, in other words. Corner (2003, p. 68) quotes Machiavelli to indicate the historical continuities present in the performance of political personality:

It is unnecessary for a prince to have all the good qualities I have enumerated, but it is very necessary to *appear* to have them. And I shall dare to say

this also, that to have them and always to observe them is injurious, and that
to appear to have them is useful.

Machiavelli's writings, although often read as the ultimate cynical attitude toward politics, show that the union of personality and performance
into a convincing political persona is neither new nor immoral, as modernist critics suggest. On the contrary, for the classic authors, virtue in politics was a matter of a great performance. What may have changed under
the influence of entertainment culture are the conditions in which political performance takes place. While previously political performance may
have been framed as persuasion realized through rhetoric and acted on
stages similar to the theatre (e.g., Witteveen, 1992), the current appropriate observation might be that political performance is about evoking identification through the means of melodrama played out on television. Thus
John Street (2003, p. 86) says—without any of the commonplace denunciations discussed in chapter 2—that politics *is* soap opera. Whether
comparing politics to performance in the theatre or the melodrama of television, in both cases the politician is perceived as an actor performing a
relevant "persona," a self as revealed to others. In the contemporary entertainment-political complex, this persona should be the embodiment
not only of political histories, issues, interests, and communities, but also
of the ingredients of celebrity culture.

Political science research suggests that, indeed, people use both these
dimensions to evaluate politicians. A. Miller and his colleagues (1986) examined data from a succession of American election studies (1952–1984)
and identified five stable categories that people use in their perception of
political candidates: competence, reliability, integrity, charisma, and personal traits. The first three indicators are related to political performance,
according to Miller and his coauthors: has she or he been successful in
politics, can I expect him or her to achieve something, and can I trust him
or her? These dimensions of candidate assessments suggest that, in fact, a
political evaluation is hidden in personalization. In contrast, charisma
and personal traits, the last two dimensions, are entirely based on the perception of private features and thus cover the celebrity dimension of the
contemporary politician.[3]

What is at stake, then, is *persona*-lization understood as the performance
of political actors operating at the intersections of politics and entertainment, instead of personalization as a perverted superficial relation between
politicians and volatile fans. To be more precise, persona-lization requires
an analysis of the personal features of politicians (who are they) and their
performance on the stages particular to politics and entertainment culture.
I will provide such an analysis on the basis of talk show interviews with the
Democratic candidates for the 2004 U.S. presidential elections.

PERSONAL FEATURES

If one were to pick a politician randomly from any parliamentary body in the Western democratic world, the odds would be that a white man would come up, aged somewhere between forty-eight and seventy, highly educated, and with a professional history in the civil service, law, economics, or education. Over half of the sitting U.S. senators in 2003, for instance, were sixty years old or older. In the national parliaments of the world, women are a minority, although that implies anything ranging from total absence to an over 35 percent presence (the latter primarily in the Nordic countries; see Center for American Women and Politics, 2003a). The demographic profile of politicians as a group is thus decidedly partial in comparison with the demographic profile of the overall populations they are supposed to represent. Next to women and ethnic minorities, younger, working-class, and rural representatives are conspicuously absent from the various communities of politicians. Does that mean that those groups lack the capacities to perform "politician," or is politics a field that favors one type of actor over others?

Both arguments have been extensively examined in relation to the absence of women. It has been pointed out that the aggregate of women is less well educated, has less relevant professional and political experience, and is hindered by their family situation (see Leijenaar, 1992). The sheer demographic composition of the field has produced a cultural model of "politician" among women themselves, politicians, campaign strategists, and voters into which women do not easily fit (Iyengar et al., 1997). The political field has been exposed as dominated by rational, detached, competitive, aggressive, and individualistic behavior that is thought to be in contrast to the way women say they (want to) operate: emotionally involved, committed, modest, cooperative, and working for a common instead of an individual cause. Whereas such a disparity may sound highly stereotypical, both male and female politicians have expressed gender differences between politicians in these terms (e.g., Ross and Sreberny, 2000). Their experience seems supported by research into the personality traits of politicians. Popular and academic psychology has described politicians as having excessive masculine traits that in a pathological form would produce an authoritarian personality whose main motive for political activity would be a hunger for power (Adorno et al., 1950; Lasswell, 1948). However, most political positions do not yield unlimited power and can be stressful as well as unrewarding; the relentless criticism of colleagues, journalists, and voters adds to the pressures of long working days. Therefore, as other psychologists have pointed out, one needs a stable instead of a pathological personality to operate successfully in politics. Traits such as dominance, self-confidence, ambition, independence, and leadership have been found to be more salient among politicians than among the general public (Simonton, 1987). By and large these are traits considered masculine. Female politicians, as a result, often feel like outsiders in a political field in which there seems to be little room for compassion, intuition, warmth, and kindness, supposedly specifically female qualities. They are confronted with an unsolvable dilemma: when they stress their political merits (independence, strength, decisiveness), they will lose their femininity; when they stress their qualities as a woman, they may be considered failing politicians (e.g., Kahn and Gordon, 1997; van Zoonen, 1988).[4]

Without denying the validity of these experiences, and without denying that one needs specific personality traits to not only survive but also enjoy a life in politics, what observations like these ignore are the performance requirements that political personality traits pose. Political psychologists themselves have acknowledged that the behavior of politicians is as much the result of the particular situation in which they find themselves as of their personality traits (e.g. Etzersdorfer, 1997; Gaffney, 2001). Sidney Blumenthal, senior advisor to Bill Clinton, describes him as exploiting his "cloudbursts of anger" when necessary: "He understood his effect on people while he was having it, an unusual combination of instinct and self-awareness. . . . 'If an actor can become a president,' Bill Clinton said, 'a president can be an actor'" (Blumenthal, 2003, p. 272). Blumenthal's observation brings back the notion of the politician as projecting a persona instead of simply expressing his personality. Personality traits are not irrelevant altogether, because they set limits on the kinds of performance that a politician can give. Because politicians are not the great actors who can play every role that is necessary, their persona needs to be close to their sense of self; otherwise, their performance will be exposed as manufactured and artificial. "Be yourself" is therefore a common advice to political candidates, be it an increasingly unhelpful one, because which "self" would be appropriate for the many different stages on which politicians are playing nowadays?[5]

STAGES

John Corner (2003) has identified three stages (he calls them spheres of action) on which politicians must perform. There is the stage of political institutions and processes (in this book called the political field), where performance relates to the development of political programs and policies, negotiation, and the exercise of administrative power. Then there is the stage of private life, which is often considered "offstage" but is an obvious platform for politicians. Lifestyle, leisure preferences, cultural taste, family life, and friendship networks are all means to perform oneself in the context of private life, and they offer the connection with celebrity culture to which I will come back later. Thirdly, Corner distinguishes the stage of the public and the popular, where performance is most explicit. Here the qualities of the persona in the political field and the stage of private life are presented in concert to a wider audience. The performance requirements on the stage of the public and the popular are much more intense and wide-ranging than those on the two other relatively stable and homogeneous stages, because the genres of performance are so immensely heterogeneous. They include the classic political speech for a live audience; the town hall meeting with local citizens; the work visit to factories, schools, hospitals, or neighborhoods; door-to-door canvassing in election times; online discussion in Internet forums; personal web logging on the Internet; TV debate with citizens, political opponents, and journalists; sound-bite presentation for the many news programs; emoting in talk shows; "revealing" oneself in behind-the-scenes documentaries; and appearances in game and celebrity shows. Since the celebrity politician is built from a political and a celebrity dimension, in all these public and popular genres his or her persona must fit both the cultural model of "politician" that the diverse audiences have *and* their diverse ideas of what a celebrity, male or female, should be. As was noted, the cultural model of politician is much closer to ideas of masculinity than of femininity, which will make a successful performance more complicated for women (see chapter 6). In addition, performance must be consistent across the various stages and genres, because if anything will devastate a good performance it is its detection as a performance, as the ancient Greeks already knew about rhetoric. The best rhetoric is not recognized as such and thus, paradoxically, what must be performed on the different stages and across the variety of public and popular genres is authenticity. Blumenthal (2003, p. 272) argues likewise: "Being oneself is the hardest thing to achieve in politics, and it demands an undetectable self-control."

But what kind of persona—or, better, what kind of performance of the "authentic self"—fits both the cultural demands of the political field and those of celebrity culture? Current theory and research on the political persona have focused mainly on the political stage, using narrative analysis to elucidate stories of political struggle, and examining the metaphors through which politicians portray themselves. Myth is a common narrative form to map onto the political process. Rutherford Smit (1979, in Witteveen, 1992, p. 48) says, for instance, that the dominant narrative about politicians is mythical because they are presented as "an omnipotent elite, beyond both marketplace and law, struggling with each other to determine the rules under which the rest of us must live. The Greek gods on Mount Olympus were no less remote and only slightly less powerful."

The hero is, of course, the key to the mythical narrative and the ultimate quality for the politician. According to Schwartzenberg (1977), the hero can derive his authority from his great works and his charisma. Former military leaders therefore make good candidates and many metaphors from the military circulate in politics (Jamieson, 1996), but the wise father or the uncontested winner are other metaphors through which heroism is evoked. Other manifestations of heroism can come from the ordinary man who manages to change political seclusion, and he has been seen to draw on metaphors of the family man or the reliable mate (Wahl-Jorgensen, 2000). *Packaging the Presidency*, Kathleen Hall Jamieson's detailed history of American presidential campaign advertising, can be read as an analysis of the different evocations of heroism that candidates have tried to convey in their campaigns, with familiar figures like the soldier-statesman (Eisenhower), the crusader (Goldwater), the commoner (Carter), and the leader (Reagan) coming by. What hampers the mythical and metaphorical perspective on the performance of politicians is that it has by and large been applied to the stage of political activity and the associated news genres of the public and the popular stage (e.g., Carey, 1988). The performance requirements that emerge from celebrity culture and that are located primarily on the stage of private life have hardly received attention unless in the incidental treatment of exceptional political scandal (e.g., Lull and Hinerman, 1997; Thompson, 2000; and the Monica Lewinsky case). These are, however, mostly stories of adultery and sexual deviance, shedding little light on the mundane performance demands that celebrity culture poses to politicians. My own work about the representations of politicians and their families in the Dutch celebrity press may be helpful to explore these requirements in some general terms (van Zoonen, 1995, 1998b, 2000b; van Zoonen and Brants, 1995).

The Dutch celebrity press started in the mid-1970s with the weekly magazine *Story*, and now consists of weeklies, glossy monthlies, newspaper sections, and television magazines. From the start, the celebrity press has covered politicians and their private lives. While there has been one incident of outright partisanship with one magazine in particular crusading against the left-wing government of the 1970s, the Dutch celebrity press as a whole cannot be called partisan in its assessment of the private worth of politicians, unlike its British and American counterparts (e.g., Bird, 1992; Seymour-Ure, 1993). It is contextual rather than general in its assessment of politicians' private behavior. Politicians who proclaim the centrality of family life, like the Dutch Christian Democrats, should live up to their example; while politicians who favor sharing community resources and finances, like the Social Democrats, should not be found wasting public resources. Thus, while the love life of one of the single Dutch Social Democrat ministers was the center of favorable attention, she found herself in the middle of a "scandal" for having the lights in her house on all night. Throughout the years, however, the coverage of politicians has consisted first and foremost of anecdotes about cabinet members and political leaders who obviously have the most wide-ranging prominence, and who are thus most likely to fit the criteria for celebrity status. Family life is the second biggest category, and in this theme one can see most clearly how the stage of private life enables the performance of the political persona. The dominant angle in family stories is the opposition between the obligations of a political career and the possibility of having a fulfilling family life. A 1989 story about a female state secretary began: "Politics with its long working hours can break up even the best marriages, as some ministers and members of parliament have experienced. But AMOR can strike as well, and this is new!"[6] Another story covers the marital problems of a party leader by saying that they are caused by the great stress of his work and the absence of time to spend with "his beautiful wife." In more recent articles, the same frame appears in articles with headlines such as: "After Twenty Years Finally a Private Life!" or "Minister Sees Her Husband Only Once a Week." The opposition between family life and politics usually is packaged as a story about the price that politicians pay for their career and the sacrifice of their families, their wives in particular. It is a highly stable frame: the headline of an article about the 1977 prime minister's wife reads, "She Pays a Heavy Toll," while a story some fifteen years later, about another prime minister's wife, says, "Few women would like to change places with her." What does the celebrity press expect of the politicians, who are the husbands in these marriages? Their political career does not allow them much time for their family life; this is a given. Working 90 to 100 hours a week is portrayed as normal behavior, an undisputed duty. From that workload, a number of situations appear that are relevant for the celebrity press: not only politicians' marriages are in danger, but also their health and their safety. The politician and his family under siege is a small but significant topic over the years: "Lia Luns fears the kidnapping of her husband," "Anti-assault button for protection of ministers," "Frits Bolkestein harassed," "How safe are our politicians," and so on. The theme intensified, inevitably, after the assassination in 2002 of the immensely popular candidate Pim Fortuyn, a classic case of the exceptional outsider who challenged the Dutch political establishment with an unlikely combination of conservative populism and a gay lifestyle (see Pels, 2003, for more detail).

The discourse of sacrifice, whether it is through the forfeit of family life, health, or personal safety, connects well with the heroic role that the politician can build for himself from his performance on the political stage. He puts his personal well-being and safety at risk because of his public calling. This is the behavior expected by the gossip press; it should be supplemented by faithfulness and chivalry toward his family, which suffers for him. When he changes careers, he is expected to make up for lost time and return the investments his wife put into his political career: "Now that he is no longer minister, he can give more attention to his wife and children." The sexual scandal, so familiar in British and American politics (Thompson, 2000), is almost absent in the Dutch celebrity press. The occasional story of marital neglect or adultery, however, does again reveal the performance requirements of the sphere of private life: work hard, sacrifice your private interests, love and honor your family. When they are seen as adhering to these norms, the gossip press presents politicians as reliable and trustworthy people who are loved and respected by all. Celebrity coverage of the family is therefore an important genre for male politicians in which the virtue of their political personae can be performed. For female politicians the family frame works quite differently, as I shall discuss in the following chapter.

PERFORMANCE

The celebrity politician, then, is the successful embodiment of the concurrent constituents of the political field and the stage of private life. He emerges mainly from performance on television, because television and its many genres are the main source from which the majority of people learn about politics, with talk shows ranking high when it comes to influencing voting decisions. This has to do with the fact that politicians get to speak much longer in talk shows than the sound bites allowed to them in regular news and current affairs programs (Just et al., 1996; Patterson, 1993), which enables politicians to perform a more diverse and complete persona built from the performance requirements that emerge from the political *and* the private stage. Despite its large variety,[7] the talk show is typified as a "nexus of all sorts of talk—journalism, fiction, criticism, politics, research, Hollywood films" (Munson, 1993, p. 7). The politician appearing in these shows, therefore, must be able to switch easily from his position as a candidate, party leader, or minister to his status as a spouse, parent, or sports or movie fan. He must also master the language of the political field, characterized by an emphasis on relatively abstract social, political, and economic forces, and be able to speak in terms of his private experience and his individual achievements. A personal history of poverty, in other words, should come out as fluidly as a political assessment of the state of the economy.

Precisely this partiality toward private life has conferred much criticism on the talk show, which has regularly been described as antithetical to the political process: it would favor the therapeutic over the political, the sensational over the substantial, the personal over the social, and the emotional over the rational (e.g., Hirsch, 1991; Rapping, 2000). Also, talk shows are traditionally—within the industry—constructed as vehicles for the humor of the host, while the guest is the fall guy who must accept the role with grace. Yet, on the other hand, talk shows have been hailed as a new public sphere, creating a space for the experience and voice of ordinary people, calling attention to issues normally excluded from the public sphere, and allowing for a personal perspective on policy effects (Leurdijk, 2000; Livingstone and Lunt, 1994). According to Wayne Munson (1993, p. 3), talk shows offer politicians an improved political stage that they feel is less susceptible to the "manipulative, negative and 'soundbitten'" tendencies of news coverage. The hybrid nature of the talk show as a genre in which politicians have to draw from political and everyday experience, and in which they have to show their rational and emotional capacities, makes it the ultimate genre for the performance of the celebrity politician. Some concrete examples from the 2004 Democratic campaign for the presidential nomination will illustrate the variety of performance talents necessary in the entertainment-political complex.[8]

The television network MSNBC organized a series of live, hour-long interviews with the Democratic presidential candidates titled *Hardball: Battle for the White House*. Chris Matthews, a seasoned political interviewer, hosted the show, which took place in the John F. Kennedy Jr. Forum at Harvard University, in front of a live audience who could also ask questions. The host, format, and location of the show conveyed the aim of seriously presenting the Democratic candidates to a larger audience. That did not preclude the marketing of the show as a confrontational narrative specific to the spectacle of televised politics. The title of the show revealed as much, and on the website, host Chris Matthews was introduced with the line: "To get to the White House, they have to get past him." A further introduction read, "Chris is live from Harvard University, putting the Democratic presidential hopefuls on the hot seat like no one else can. From current campaign platforms, to past voting history, to those skeletons in the closet, *nothing is off the table*" (italics added).[9] Since "everything" is considered a possible subject, the candidate must be able to move through the various positions and styles that specific questions necessitate, and answer in ways that will put his persona across as the perfect embodiment of political and personal qualities. Although the interviews focused by and large on political issues, with the American presence in Iraq as a dominant issue, there were various fragments in the different episodes of *Hardball* that showed how the articulation of the political and the private has become a commonplace rhetorical move for political candidates. Sometimes that was the result of a direct question ("Could you open a window on your soul, could you tell us who is John

Kerry down deep?"). An audience member asks Senator John Edwards what his working-class background will bring to the presidency:

> *Edwards:* I didn't pay him to ask that question. . . . I know, from my own family, how big a deal it is to be able to buy your first home. How big a deal it is to actually save and invest. . . . If you grew up the way I did, it's very, very personal for you. You will fight your heart out for it. You have lived it.

Such evocations of personal biographies were run-of-the-mill for all candidates who appeared on *Hardball* and easily shifted from the political to the private. Senator Joe Lieberman said, for instance: "We have to set a standard that every child in America really does get a world class education. *Look, I'm the first in my family to go to college. I want every child in America to have that chance*" (italics added). This shows how the private functions easily as a resource for the performance of the political persona. Yet, as Corner (2003) has noted, the private also puts up a risk of various kinds, as is clear in a fragment from the interview with Governor Howard Dean, who is asked about his temper, although the example is relatively innocent:

> *Matthews:* But Wendell Holmes described Franklin Governor Roosevelt as a man possessed by a third-rate intellect, but a first-rate temperament. What do you think of that? And how would you rate yourself on those two scores?
>
> *Dean:* The temperament—We'll leave intellect out of it, but there temperament's fine most of the time. Most of the time.
>
> *Matthews:* If we elect you president, when can we count on the geyser going off?
>
> *Dean:* Probably not very actually. You know, I was re-elected five times as governor. If the geyser went off too long, I don't think I would have been re-elected five times.

The performance challenge for a candidate put on the spot for his private behavior or qualities is to bring it back to the stage of politics, which Dean tries to do by pointing at his reelections. The *Hardball* interviews show that today's candidates easily integrate the political and the private into a convincing performance. More specific performance demands come from the double location of the celebrity politician in the political field on the one hand and entertainment culture on the other. General Wesley Clark, for instance, was asked whether army leadership provided a better standard for the office than being elected.

> *Clark:* Running for office is—it's an art form. It's developed. And I'm doing it for the first time here. And it's been a lot of fun, it's been a real learning experience. And—and I've enjoyed it tremendously. But leadership,

working with heads of state, thinking about strategies, talking to members of Congress, that's something I've done for years and years and years, and I'm the only person in the race who's done it and had the practical leadership experience.

Reverend Al Sharpton was posed a similar audience question about his lack of political experience:

Man: Of all the candidates out there, why should I vote for the one with the least political experience?

Sharpton: Well, you shouldn't, because I have the most political experience. I got involved in the political movement when I was 12 years old. And I've been involved in social policy for the last 30 years. So don't confuse people that have a job with political experience. . . . As we have seen with the present occupant in the White House, George Bush was a governor, and clearly has shown he doesn't have political experience.

The performance demands that come from the celebrity dimension of the political persona are not often called upon in these interviews. In fact, only Reverend Sharpton ran a campaign in which entertainment culture had a part, through the endorsement of hip-hop stars and his previous alliance with soul artist James Brown. For some of the other candidates, even simple entertainment questions about their favorite movies produced too big a performance challenge. The quote is from the interview with John Edwards, but John Kerry ran into similar problems:

Matthews: What's your favorite movie? All time favorite movie. Don't say *Sound of Music.*

Edwards: I am not.

Matthews: Although I like it. Come on, that's the easiest question.

Edwards: It's been three years since I've seen a movie.

Matthews: Think of all the constituency groups in the Democratic Party. Think of how you can pander to them all right now. Which will it be? Favorite movie of all time, John Edwards? Hotline tomorrow. You're being hotlined.

Edwards: I'm thinking. I'm thinking. Let me think.

Matthews: You're like Jack Benny, "Your money or your life?" "I am thinking."

Edwards: I'm trying to come up with one.

Matthews: Come on. Your favorite movie. The buck stops here. You're the president. Somebody has asked you. You're the president and they ask you what your favorite movie is. You've got to answer this. You've got to look at Elisabeth [his wife in the audience]. You're looking for—that's your lifeline. She is your lifeline.

Edwards: It is in the back of my head. It's the movie where they're in prison and . . .

Matthews: Shawshank Redemption.

Edwards: Yes!

(APPLAUSE)

Other similarly personal questions about favorite books, philosophers, or musicians did not make any of the candidates stand out in particular, which made host Chris Matthews sigh at some point: "You are such a regular guy. It's a battle of regular guys."

THE POLITICAL PERSONA: A TYPOLOGY

The discussions in *Hardball* enable a further recognition of the kinds of personae that are available for the contemporary celebrity politician. The lament of *Hardball*'s host, Chris Matthews, that the candidates were all so "regular" points at a regularly identified dimension of celebrity, namely, that of proximity and distance. Celebrities come in various distinctions and degrees (e.g., Giles, 2000), but what qualifies the megastars is their paradoxical combination of being perceived as an "ordinary, regular" guy who is just like his fans ("she or he is one of us") and someone who is very special at the same time. This mixture of perceived proximity and distance has been noted as typical for the public admiration of royalty. The global appeal of Diana, princess of Wales and self-styled "Queen of Hearts," for instance, has been explained as her being both "one of us" and "one of them": "She perfectly embodied what has often been argued to be the central ambiguity necessary for the popular appeal of a modern, mediated royalty, indeed arguably to all celebrities, that they appear simultaneously ordinary and extraordinary" (J. Thomas, 2002, p. 46). What goes for royalty also counts for contemporary politicians: their appeal is simultaneously built on the impression that they are "just like us" (a regular guy) and thus deserving to represent "us," and on the idea that they must be more special and capable than "we" are and therefore also justifiably representing "us." The location of specific political personae on the continuum of proximity and distance depends as much on their personality, biography, and capacities as it does on the way "others"—the *Hardball* host, journalists, competitors, voters—perceive them as ordinary or special.

These are judgments, however, made against the stage of private life: in *Hardball*, favorite movies and books were the yardstick for the host to say "regular guy"; in the celebrity press, it is family life. The political stage offers another dimension on which the political persona can be located, that is the one of outsider versus insider. As discussed in chapter 1, the structural features of the political field in Bourdieu's terms tend toward exclusivity that blocks all people who do not or cannot conform to the political routines and mores. The resulting growing separation of the political field from everyday lives and experience makes politics susceptible to the intervention of outsiders whose promise invariably is that they will bring politics back to the "ordinary man." This is such a persistent cycle that it has been a common theme in popular fictional portrayals of politics since the 1930s, when Frank Capra produced *Mr. Smith Goes to Washington*, about a youth leader who naïvely goes to Washington and finds it to be a cesspool of dishonesty and corruption, with leaders only interested in their own fortune. With the help of a secretary converted to his idealism (not coincidentally a woman, as I will show in chapter 7), Mr. Smith brings virtue back to the capital (see Neve, 1992).

Since the celebrity politician is built from the *equal* contribution of elements from the political field and those of entertainment culture, the two dimensions together produce a typology that clarifies and explains the basic personae that celebrity politicians can perform, as shown in figure 5.1.

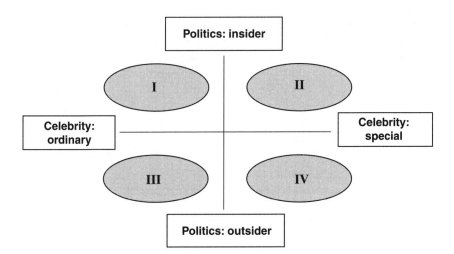

Figure 5.1. Typology of Basic Personae of Celebrity Politicians

This typology shows the different personae emerging from the concurrence of politics and celebrity. In category I, the run-of-the-mill politician appears; he is an insider to the political field and has few private qualities that make him stand out among ordinary people. Most of the contending Democrats appearing in *Hardball* qualify as such. One could also think of Al Gore, Bill Clinton's vice president, and John Major, the British conservative MP who succeeded Margaret Thatcher, as the quintessential examples. Jeffrey Archer, the British conservative, would qualify as belonging to category II: a seasoned Tory Party member whose title and exuberant lifestyle placed him at a fair distance from any of his supporters and who attracted an excessive amount of media attention for that (see Corner, 2003). One finds the outsider to the political process who operates as an "ordinary citizen" (category III) in the figure of the American independent candidate Ross Perot (although not ordinarily wealthy, of course). In the *Hardball* interviews, General Wesley Clark and Reverend Al Sharpton occupied that position, although the reverend is closer toward the outsider-special category because of his association with popular artists. Arnold Schwarzenegger, an outsider whose history, marriage, and physique separate him far from his fans, is the exemplary case of category IV. Each of the political personae covered by the casting scheme seem to have their deficiencies: the ordinary insider runs the risk of being considered boring (too ordinary) or an egocentric career politician (too much an insider); the extravagant insider may estrange his or her fellow politicians; the ordinary outsider misses the political experience and support coming from an inside path; and the exceptional outsider may raise expectations that will inevitably be disappointed. The ultimate celebrity politician, then, the one who is able to balance the contradictory requirements of politics and celebrity, is located right in the middle of the plot. He or she projects a persona that has inside experience with politics but is still an outsider; his (or, in some cases, her) performance builds on a unique mixture of ordinariness and exceptionality. It is a persona, for that matter, not restricted to any side of the political spectrum: Ronald Reagan was a political outsider when elected as governor of California, but an insider when he became president. He thus balanced an inside and an outside position. His history as a movie star positioned him as extraordinary: however, through his intimate communicative style, he performed the ordinary guy with ordinary preferences (see Morris, 1999). Bill Clinton's Arkansas origins enabled him to perform as an outsider to Washington politics, but he also managed to reconcile the many different interests and groups within the Democratic Party. While his sex appeal and charm seem to have been very special, his failure to control his drives invited the perception of him being a troubled ordinary man (Hamilton, 2003). Conservative Margaret Thatcher went all the way through the Conservative Party (insider) before she became its first female leader (outsider). She consciously used metaphors from "ordinary" women's daily lives (the family budget, for instance), but simultaneously operated as the strongest of men in her decision to go to war in the Falklands (Cradock, 1997). Tony Blair conquered the internal divisions of the Labour Party, but did so with a new, outsider program for New Labour. That he managed to survive and discipline the factions in the Labour Party made him inevitably stand out, and the birth of his son and especially his moving speech after the death of Diana, princess of Wales, made clear that he was also "one of us."[10] Yet, it would be a mistake to think that only politicians who perform a perfect blend of insider and outsider, and who create a convincing mixture of being ordinary and special at the same time, can be successful in the entertainment-political complex. The appeal of these different types is contingent upon the prevailing political climate: thus Jimmy Carter's campaign in the post-Watergate period was framed as meeting the general desire to have an ordinary man untainted by Washington's dubious morals as president (Jamieson, 1996). John Major, an ordinary insider, could take over Margaret Thatcher's position because her performance had become extravagant in the eyes of her opponents. Also, the course of political history itself may move politicians from one category to another. These are observations with the benefit of hindsight. For the future, the typology suggests that unless he builds an impeccable political track record, Arnold Schwarzenegger is very likely to be replaced by his absolute opposite in the typology: an ordinary insider candidate.[11]

NOTES

1. *The Governator*, documentary by Alex Cooke, broadcast on BBC Four, January 9, 2004.
2. It is no coincidence that "actor" has the double meaning of someone who is a professional performer and someone who is active in a particular field.
3. This research is revisited extensively in chapter 8.
4. I will come back to the predicaments and potentials of female politicians in more detail in the next chapter.
5. In a documentary about the 2003 election campaign of the Dutch Social Democrats, their leader is filmed preparing for a public appearance with a large live audience. When he is called to the stage, he sighs wearily: "Well, I better go out there and be myself again." *Wouter*, broadcast by VPRO television, 2003.
6. All translations from Dutch by the author.
7. Munson (1993), for instance, distinguishes between news/talk (*Today*, *Good Morning America*, *Meet the Press*), talk/variety (late-night shows), and talk/service (*Oprah*).
8. The approach is derived from a more systematic comparative analysis of the performance of politicians in Dutch and German talk shows (van Zoonen and Holzbacha, 2000).

9. Accessed at http://www.msnbc.com/modules/tvnews/Hardball_College Tour/ (January 4, 2004).

10. Much of that changed because of his support for the American war on Iraq and the subsequent Kelly affair. David Kelly was one of the British government weapons experts in Iraq who killed himself in the summer of 2003. He accused the government of exaggerating the presence of weapons of mass destruction in Iraq and got caught in a wave of publicity and governmental pressure.

11. The more difficult prediction involves the reelection of George W. Bush, a typical case of an ordinary insider, who is challenged by another ordinary insider, John Kerry.

6

⧢

Feminization? Female Politicians, Family, and Celebrity

In one of Barbara Cartland's hundreds of romantic novels, *The Enchanted Waltz* (1955), set in Vienna on the eve of the great peace conference of 1815, the heroine is told: "Women should stay out of politics and out of diplomacy too. At best it is dirty business" (p. 21).[1] In a Mills and Boon novel set in contemporary America, the heroine is asked, "Tell me what a nice girl like you is doing in a dirty business like politics?" (Hammond, 1993, p. 36). The man asking the question turns out to be the hero of the story, and some time later the heroine ponders that "he really seemed interested in her as a human being. That was something she wasn't used to in the hard chaotic world of politics where everyone just seemed to use each other" (p. 52).

In many other forms of popular fiction, politics and women are similarly constructed as the antithesis of each other. In movies, television series, and novels, it is common to see politics framed as a cesspit of dishonesty in which everyone looks out for one's (his) own interest and does not stop at blackmail, bribery, or corruption. Women, the traditional symbols of innocence and virtue, often figure to demarcate the opposition of self-centered politics with everyday humanity and morality (see van Zoonen, 1998a). Such popular images of women as virtuous outsiders are consistent with the existent secondary presence of women in politics: as I briefly indicated in the previous chapter, the number of women actually participating in politics is small, and they widely share an experience of difference and sometimes alienation. In this chapter, I will further discuss the position of women as outsiders to the political field, and examine their location on the celebrity dimension of contemporary politics. I will first

assess in general terms whether and how women in politics can draw
from the ingredients of politics and celebrity culture, and then look concretely at the way female politicians have constructed their personae, with
Hillary Clinton as the main example.

WOMEN ON THE POLITICAL-CELEBRITY AXES

Feminist philosophers, historians, and political scientists have minutely
explained the marginal participation of women in politics. In a discussion
of the political philosophies underlying Western liberal democracies, Susan Okin (1979) shows that most philosophers have excluded women from
the realm of politics, except for Plato, who allowed them a place among the
guardians in the republic. Yet, Plato wanted the guardians, responsible for
the safety and continuity of the republic, to forsake private possessions
and a private life. The qualification of both women and men for Plato's
guardian class was thus only possible because of the eradication of their
private lives; Plato and most other political philosophers considered
women as primarily responsible for and in the private domain. "In their
treatment of women," Ellen Kennedy and Susan Mendus write (1987, p. 3),
"otherwise diverse philosophers present a surprisingly united front." They
show how philosophers widely apart in time, space, and thought share the
conviction that women belong to the private sphere, because of their re-
productive functions and psychological dispositions. With women's monopoly of the private sphere comes—supposedly—a whole range of
attributes that philosophers like Adam Smith, Hegel, Rousseau, and Nietzsche have considered inappropriate for public life. They have all defined
friendliness, simplicity, love, hate, or other emotions; particularism; and
arbitrary inclinations as specific to women's functioning in the private
sphere and thoroughly at odds with the universal and rational approach to
justice and equality that public life allegedly requires. For Rousseau, this
dualism was a reason to elevate family life to a superior moral plane; for
Nietzsche, it was the basis to consider women "natural servants"
(Kennedy and Mendus, 1987). But both believed in the natural position of
men and women in respectively the public and private domain, and the
mutual exclusiveness of each domain's requirements. Feminist critics have
exposed in great detail the inconsistencies in political theories built on the
dichotomy between the public and the private (e.g., Pateman, 1989). They
have also pointed to authors like the nineteenth-century John Stuart Mill,
for whom the public-private distinction did not mean an exclusion of
women from politics; to the utopian socialists who denied a public-private
distinction altogether; and to other causes of women's oppression such as
patriarchy and capitalism (e.g., Elshtain, 1981; Jaggar, 1983).

Notwithstanding these and other criticisms of the public-private dualism (e.g., Garlick, Dixon, and Allen, 1992), family life still is a concrete barrier for women's participation in politics. The biographies of women who have held historical positions of great power show a remarkably similar absence of family life: many of them were unmarried or widows, and for most of them their image of chastity was one of their great virtues (cf. Fraser, 1988). Unmistakably, an epitome of such single female leadership is the sixteenth-century British queen Elizabeth I, who came to the throne when she was twenty-five and unmarried, and remained so until her death in 1603 at the age of seventy. Elizabeth and her council rejected successive suitors, all of whom failed to gather unanimous support in an era marked by factional, international, and religious divisions. Shimmering behind each dispute over the respective candidates was the fear that, as a woman, Elizabeth would be easy prey for the ambitions of English noblemen or foreign princes. The question of her celibacy dominated her domestic affairs for decades and has occupied historians ever since. Feminist historians have framed Elizabeth's decision to remain unmarried "as the deliberate, rational response of an intelligent woman to the practical problems of being a female ruler" (see Doran, 1996, p. 6). Others have held her troubled childhood responsible for her supposedly negative feelings about marriage.[2] Yet, although Elizabeth herself repeatedly expressed her lack of interest in marriage (cf. MacCaffrey, 1993), there are also signs of her desire for a companion and her frustration with celibacy, for instance in a poem she is held to have written in her fifties:

> When I was fair and young, and favor graced me,
> Of many was I sought their mistress for to be.
> But I did scorn them all, and said to them therefore,
> "Go, go, go, seek some otherwhere; importune me no more."
>
> How many weeping eyes I made to pine in woe;
> How many sighing hearts I have not skill to show,
> But I the prouder grew, and still this spake therefore:
> "Go, go, go, seek some otherwhere, importune me no more."
>
> Then spake fair Venus' son, that brave victorious boy,
> Saying: You dainty dame, for that you be so coy,
> I will so pluck your plumes as you shall say no more;
> "Go, go, go, seek some otherwhere, importune me no more."
>
> As soon as he had said, such change grew in my breast
> That neither night nor day I could take any rest.
> Wherefore I did repent that I had said before:
> "Go, go, go, seek some otherwhere, importune me no more."[3]

The historians' dispute over Elizabeth's desired or undesired celibacy need not be resolved in order to recognize how marriage and the prospect of family life posed a multiple dilemma to her, as it does today to other female leaders and politicians. Statistics about the marital status of female politicians show that, like high-status professional women in general, they tend to remain single or without children. Jamieson (1988, p. 85) adds that to have young children is a liability for female politicians, "because it reminds the public of a role that voters have been socialized to believe makes women less suitable and available for public office." Therefore, women candidates are often older than their male counterparts. It is telling, in this context, that the Dutch parliament does not have any kind of leave arrangements for pregnant politicians (see van Zoonen, 1998b). Yet there are indications that the public-private opposition is becoming less sharp, at least for male politicians. British prime minister Tony Blair's fourth child was born in 1999, while Blair was in office. Given his party's policies to advance child-care and parental leave arrangements, and considering that his wife was a high-profile lawyer, the obvious question to Blair was whether he would take parental leave (BBC, 2000). While Blair did not see how he could abandon his duties as PM for more than two days, the fact that the issue was raised at all suggests that political culture may be opening up to politicians' family responsibilities. Other male politicians have decided and managed to keep time for their families and take up their part in the family chores. However, the conclusion that public and private duties are no longer incompatible in the political field must be embraced with caution, if one considers what some male politicians reveal as sharing family responsibilities: "May I give an example?" a Dutch politician asked in a daytime talk show. "Sometimes you have to take some time for your children. On this coming Sunday, I go to a pop concert with my daughter" (quoted in van Zoonen, 1998b). In addition, while the integration of public and private life may become more common for male politicians, for women in politics it still presents a liability; this is at least suggested by the coverage of female politicians in the Dutch celebrity press (see Sapiro and Walsh, 2002, for more general evidence about the United States).

Family Life in the Celebrity Press

Female politicians occur relatively often in the celebrity press, primarily because of its large female readership. As in the coverage of their male colleagues, the main topics for female politicians are family life (for the married ones) and love affairs (for the singles). However, the celebrity press constructs the role of the family for female politicians—though not for their male colleagues—as distinctly problematic. The picture of sacrificing husbands waiting for their wives to come home after a long day in politics apparently does not accord with the prevalent gender norms in the celebrity press. Invariably, the absence of a "normal" family life is brought up. The treatment of one of the most popular Dutch female politicians, longtime minister of transport Neelie Smit-Kroes, is indicative: at the height of her career, the celebrity press covered her a number of times and had her admit that "her ambitions heavily hinder a 'normal' family life. Her husband and son do not see much of her." The family apparently suffered so much that years later, when internal party conflicts drove her out of politics, her then nineteen-year-old son sighed in one of the celebrity magazines: "Finally, I have my mother back." He was further presented as having suffered from his kindergarten years and hating politics: "I have learned to prepare my own meals!" Although the celebrity press often shows sympathy for the predicaments of female politicians in handling their double tasks, the unmistakable subtext of its coverage is stereotypical: the families of female politicians suffer because of their ambitions. The families of male politicians see similarly little of them; nevertheless, their plight is constructed as heroic and in support of the man's political career, as I showed in chapter 5. The current tendency of male politicians to explicitly and publicly claim time-outs for their family contributes to their overall image of integrity and adds a sense of them being modern men. By contrast, the families of female politicians, and female politicians themselves, appear as pitiable, for—as the celebrity press says—"it is not easy for women in politics," and "they know how sad a divorce can be." Thus, the celebrity press shows male politicians as living in an integrated world of public and private duties, while female politicians are presented as living in two conflicting worlds. Celebrity journalism evokes this picture of contradictory realms also by suggesting that the political persona of female politicians must be at odds with their private one. The confidence and determination that female politicians show in their political work is expected to disappear "behind the closed doors of the home." There, gentleness and leniency are prescribed as more appropriate (see van Zoonen, 1998b).

Female Politicians as Celebrities

While the celebrity dimension in current politics has positioned the private sphere as a typical stage for the performance of integrity, that stage is more favorable to men than to women: the celebrity treatment of the private lives of female politicians tends to exacerbate the public-private dimension on which women's marginal position in politics is built. Celebrity culture also poses another dilemma for female politicians, which has to do with the nature of celebrity itself. Looking up the word "celebrity" in any standard English dictionary generally produces a definition along the lines of "being famous," which moves the search to the meaning of fame. Fame is regularly described as "public estimation," "reputation," or "renown."[4] In the commonsense understanding that dictionaries reflect, fame and celebrity are thus considered to be dependent on the recognition of others and on a certain degree of public visibility. Thus fame and celebrity become unmistakably gendered qualifications, because public visibility is not evenly distributed among women and men, and because it does not carry the same meanings. In more theoretical understandings of fame and celebrity, the two are regularly defined as distinct from each other: "celebrity" is a product of the publicity produced by twentieth- and twenty-first-century mass media, whereas "fame" has a longer history as the typification resulting from outstanding and publicly recognized achievements (see Giles, 2000). Building on this distinction, one is tempted to suggest that fame is primarily a man's preserve, for it is built on public achievements, whereas celebrity would be a woman's domain because it is predicated on *being* (in the media) rather than *doing*. Although one does not find such a crude distinction in the celebrity literature, it is common to see the distinction between "fame" and "celebrity" described in the gendered terms of being respectively contingent on a culture of production versus a culture of consumption (e.g., P. D. Marshall, 1997). Yet, both fame and celebrity tend to exclude women from the political field, albeit in different ways. The public-private divide on which the exclusion of women from politics has been built has also prevented women's achievement of "fame."

P. D. Marshall (1997) describes how great achievement in premodern times resulted in public reputations of heroism and genius. The realms in which these could come about were religion, politics, and the arts, all fields not particularly open to women. In fact, as Kathleen Hall Jamieson (1988) shows in her history of public speech, women were actively excluded from achieving fame, not only because of their discursive and social position as private persons, but also because of vigorous restrictions on their speech. Jamieson goes through a variety of material and discursive means that were used to silence women: ducking stools, gagging, and the gossip's bridle were all physical measures exercised in public to enforce women's silence. "Long after ducking stools and gossip bridles had become curiosities in museums," Jamieson writes (p. 68), "the silence they enforced and the warnings they imposed continued to haunt women." The means to do so changed from physical to discursive: women engaging in speech acts considered inappropriate, especially those directed against institutional representatives like the clergy, science, or the law, were labeled *whores*, *hysterics*, or *witches*. They would, of course, be vulnerable to prosecution. As a result, Jamieson argues, a specific "feminine style" of speech developed that was consistent with women's role in the family and traditional notions of femininity. Although one would think these are processes of times gone by, Templin's (1999, p. 32) analysis of press cartoons about Hillary Clinton suggests that these mechanisms are still firmly in place:

> That the fantasy of silencing Hillary has great power is seen in the many cartoons . . . picturing a restrained and silenced Hillary—muzzled, a zipper for lips, in a box with air holes. The message is that the country would be better off if Hillary kept quiet.

"Fame," as the public recognition of exceptional achievements, is thus a quality that is difficult for women to obtain because of their historical exclusion from the public sphere. "Celebrity" is a no less problematic attribute, because it confines female politicians to notions of femininity that are not easily transposed to the political field. Celebrity refers to being well known because of mass media exposure. That exposure can be the result of extramedia fame, and in that case celebrity and fame collapse, but celebrity is also an independent product of the media themselves. The Hollywood star system is commonly seen as the historical source of celebrity culture. Biographies of stars and histories of studios have shown how Hollywood tried to transfer movie codes of masculinity and femininity onto male and female actors and their real lives (Dyer, 1979). Although not always successful, and although stories of actors trying to escape from their image abound, "celebrity" is structurally built on the confluence of media appearance with the real lives of performers. As a result, female celebrity is primarily articulated with the codes and conventions of media representations of women, of Hollywood conventions initially and an amalgam of television, pop music, and advertising images later. MacDonald (1995) argues that these representations can be brought back to four popular myths of femininity: femininity as enigmatic and threatening, femininity as nurturing and caring, femininity as sexuality, and femininity as a bodily practice. Female celebrities will inevitably be constructed from these mythologies. For Gledhill (1991, p. xv), who has the Hollywood cinema as her frame of reference, this means that the female star will necessarily become "a focus of visual pleasure for an apparently masculine spectator, the epitome of the male fetish." Taking a broader media ensemble as his departure, J. Gamson (2001) likewise argues that female sexuality and female celebrity are interlinked within an incessantly reworked "virgin-whore" discourse.[5] One might contend that recent female celebrities have subverted myths of femininity by explicitly playing with them and reinventing them. Madonna, the female megastar of the 1980s and 1990s, did not build her celebrity on a stable myth of femininity but on the continuous change of styles and performance

Chapter 6

(Schwichtenberg, 1993). In fact, contemporary femininity seems to have
become about the constant re-creation of the self through changing hair-
dos, dress, appearance, and—ultimately—plastic surgery (Davis, 1995).
Yet, however provocative such transgressions might have been, the
volatility of contemporary female celebrity does not offer a helpful cultural frame for female politicians any more than previous, more stable
models of female celebrity did. Female celebrity is still built primarily on
the appearance of the body, and the instability of changing appearances is
not the kind of reliable image that a politician would want to project for
herself. Most notions of female celebrity thus do not travel easily to the
political field. Schwartzenberg (1977), writing about political "superstars," therefore says that female politicians have only limited options in
celebrity politics. They need to mask their femininity and imitate men;
otherwise, accusations of being frivolous, coquettish, and—the worst—
loose will be their lot (p. 93).[6] As a result, Schwartzenberg continues,
charming leadership, a definite style for male politicians based on an understanding of politics as the art of seduction, is no option for women because of the sexual connotations. The only feminine model of celebrity
available to women in politics, according to Schwartzenberg, would be
that of the mother, tying in to myths of femininity as nurturing and caring. Yet it is highly unlikely that "motherhood" can be a building block
for the status of female politicians as celebrities: not only because it confines the politician in question discursively to the private sphere, but also
because real mothers in politics are not so simply worshipped, as was
clear in the previous section about the coverage of the celebrity press.

  Political philosophy, history, present-day politics, and celebrity culture
thus all tend to construct an opposition between family life and its associated qualities, and the requirements of a political life. As a result,
women in politics cannot escape the position of outsider in the political-
entertainment complex. Their fellow politicians and journalists often
frame them as such and imply that—therefore—they lack the necessary
experience and capacities for politics, even if their credentials prove otherwise (e.g., Norris, 2000). Female politicians have also defined themselves as outsiders, but some have turned this to their advantage:
Margaret Thatcher, for instance, who definitely made a long march
through the Conservative Party and was an insider by many criteria, portrayed herself as an outsider who was unintimidated by tradition and
unimpressed by reputations within the Conservative Party (Thatcher,
1993). More generally, however, women have played their private cards
by claiming that their position in the family provides them with the humanity and moral superiority usually absent but much needed in politics
(e.g., Ross and Sreberny, 2000). Yet their label as outsider remains un-
changed. Nor has celebrity culture modified this phenomenon: while the

opposition between the public and private lives of female politicians is often presented in a sympathetic and understanding way, as shown, celebrity coverage does not offer a stage where female politicians can perform a persona whose private and public life, and whose private and public talents, are integrated into a convincing totality. Rather, the celebrity attention for female politicians functions as a continuous reminder of their odd choices as women and their odd position in politics. Neither does celebrity culture offer an alternative frame for women to draw political capital from: apart from family life, female celebrity is predicated on appearance, sexuality, and—most recently—continuous experimentation with styles of femininity, all features that do not easily produce adequate ingredients for the performance of a convincing female political persona.

FEMALE POLITICIANS

Yet, even if political and celebrity culture together produce considerable barriers for female politicians, women have succeeded as politicians of various kinds, affiliations, and stature. How are their presence and achievements articulated with the political and celebrity expressions of traditional gender discourse? In some political systems, traditional family patterns have produced a way for women to enter politics, by enabling wives of deceased politicians to take their place. In the political history of the United States, for instance, forty-five women have been elected or appointed to fill congressional vacancies created by the deaths of their husbands, eight to the U.S. Senate and thirty-seven to the U.S. House of Representatives. As recent as 2002, Democrat Jean Carnahan was appointed to the Senate seat won posthumously by her husband (Center for American Women and Politics, 2003b). That particular route to a political position for women emerges from the fact that in U.S. politics, individual candidates campaign very much with the support and participation of their wives and families. Wives are therefore usually very visible in election campaigns and to a greater or lesser extent are part of the ticket. Bill and Hillary Clinton's 1992 campaign slogan, "Buy One, Get One for Free," may possibly be the most explicit example of this tendency, but is obviously not a unique case. The predicaments of such a traditional "wifely" route to political power have been most pronounced in the unending controversies around Hillary Rodham Clinton and her influence on her husband's politics, both when he was governor of Arkansas and when he was president of the United States. While a certain degree of influence from the first lady, whether gubernatorial or presidential, is expected and accepted in American politics, this is confined within traditional gender norms saying that influence should pertain to social and cultural issues, should be exercised modestly and implicitly, and should not overshadow the president himself (see *Social Science Journal*, 2000). Diverse first ladies have therefore taken up children's rights as their cause or the promotion of health issues or the arts (see Gould, 1996). Laura Bush, the wife of U.S. president George Bush Jr. and a former librarian, for instance, has taken the promotion of reading as one of her causes by organizing National Book Festivals (CNN, 2003). However, there is a fine line between Laura Bush–style "legitimate" first lady politics and unwanted activism. Controversial first ladies like Rosalynn Carter, Nancy Reagan, and—ultimately—Hillary Rodham Clinton have all been perceived as taking the center stage at the expense of the husband's position (Troy, 2000). Hillary Clinton's appointment, however, as a head of a presidential commission was unprecedented in its explicitness and in the amount of opposition it produced. Friend and foe have ascribed the failure of her efforts to reform the U.S. health care system as much to the result of adverse gender politics as to a lack of substantial support (e.g., Sheehy, 1999). Together with the Whitewater scandal, the unsuccessful health care reform program produced an all-time low in her popularity (Burden and Mughan, 1999; Burrell, 2000).[7] The controversies around Hillary Clinton have been perceived as the main threat to President Clinton's first term and the major cause of the Democrats' losses in the 1994 midterm elections (Winfield, 1997). True or not, these perceptions did cause her to withdraw from the overt political stage and focus on the more traditional concerns of first ladies, work on children's rights, and present a softer image (Blumenthal, 2003).

Often, the tensions around first ladies' political activities have been explained as being the result of their unclear status as unelected power holders. Whereas that indeed is a remarkable undemocratic strain in the U.S. system, many of the dilemmas that first ladies face have troubled independently elected women as well. Research has shown how voters perceive female candidates through a traditional gender lens; that means that they tend to consider women strong on issues that comply with women's customary role in the family, such as education and health care, while voters think men do better on issues such as crime and illegal immigration. As a result, the issue environment of particular elections will produce different opportunities for men and women: "A woman who calls for educational reform or more stringent enforcement of gender discrimination laws will be taken more seriously than a woman who calls for the death penalty or more aggressive monitoring of terrorist groups" (Iyengar et al., 1997, p. 97). Campaign managers and female politicians have been seen to conduct their strategies on the basis of these perceptions and other gender stereotypes. Kahn and Gordon (1997) examined three U.S. Senate campaigns and found that in the campaigns of female candidates, issues are more prominent than personal traits; also the kinds of issues women put forward differ from those of male candidates, with women predictably promoting issues that could be traced to their particular expertise in the family or the workplace. A further difference pertained to the ideological positions of women that were, on the whole, more liberal than those of men; attack ads and negative advertising were almost absent from women's campaigns because they were considered at odds with voters' stereotypes about "proper female behavior." Apart from that, Kahn and Gordon found that male and female candidates did not differ very much in their campaign strategies, which led them to conclude that "men and women present alternative agendas to voters, but they deliver these distinct messages in remarkably similar fashion" (1997, p. 74).

All these issues recurrently echo in concrete campaigns of female candidates, as a comprehensive example will show. Carol Mosely Braun, former senator for Illinois and former U.S. ambassador to New Zealand, ran for the Democratic nomination of 2004. With the war in Iraq hovering over the upcoming elections, the issue environment of war, terrorism, and security does not offer easy opportunities for women to excel. In an hour-long live television interview, an episode of the *Hardball* series on the Democratic candidates (see chapter 5), the first question of host Chris Matthews pertains to the war on Iraq.

Matthews: Senator?

Braun: Yes?

Matthews: Madam Ambassador?

Braun: Yes?

Matthews: Tomorrow morning you wake up, you're the president of the United States. What would you do in Iraq?

Braun: What would I do in Iraq? I would call the United Nations and I would call our allies around the world and offer them all Krispy Kremes and make up, and engage them in helping to—helping us to come out with honor.

One might read Braun's reference to Krispy Kremes as a woman's down-to-earth approach to diplomacy and international relations. However, as the host persists, Braun becomes much more hesitant with her answers, for instance when asked about the administration's motives to go to war: "You'd have to ask George Bush that"—"I don't know what their motive was. One can only speculate." Although, after a third prompt, she does get into a more in-depth discussion about the

Iraq policy, Braun's performance becomes much more convincing when asked about her policies for women, her ideas about affirmative action, and her goals for education.

> *Audience Question:* What issues in your campaign specifically target young women?
>
> *Braun:* Oh, specifically for young women, issues of equal pay for equal work. What [a] concept, huh? Women—young women make—women make
>
> (APPLAUSE)
>
> Women make 67 cents on the dollar. African-American women make 54 cents on the dollar. Hispanic women, Latinos, I'm sorry, make 54 cents on the dollar for every dollar that a man makes. That's just not right. And in addition to the pay disparity, there's disparity that carries over into pensions. Seventy-six percent of the elderly poor in this country are women. And there's a reason for it, because our work is not valued.

Besides the gendered articulations of issues, the position of women as outsiders to the political field is also reconstructed in this interview. In Carol Mosely Braun's case, her outsider position is even more salient because she is African American. Her status as a "first" and an outsider is highlighted throughout the interview and builds on the theme that ran through all her campaigns:

> *Braun:* When I first ran for office they told me that blacks won't vote for you because you are not a part of the Chicago Machine. The whites won't vote for you because you are black. And no one will vote for you because you are a woman.

In an exchange between Matthews and Braun that is atypical in comparison with the interviews with the other candidates, it shows how traditional codes of female celebrity are used to liven up the interview:

> *Matthews:* You danced with [fellow Democratic candidate] Howard Dean the other night; how is he?
>
> *Braun:* He is a pretty good stepper.
>
> *Matthews:* Is he really? What do you think it is that made his campaign sort of spark?
>
> *Braun:* Well, I make it a point not to really do commentary on other people's campaigns.
>
> *Matthews:* Come on!
>
> *Braun:* Well, I mean, come on. Why should I?

Matthews: I like this, a little gossip.

In this exchange, the celebrity dimension of politics becomes modestly manifest in the discussion of candidates dancing and the host's supposed desire for gossip. One can see the double bind in which the female candidate is put: expanding on her dance with Dean would open up the dangerous fields of sexual close encounters, whereas withdrawing from the topic makes her a spoiler of the host's longing for a little gossip.

Hillary Rodham Clinton

In the persona of Hillary Rodham Clinton, all the tensions and opportunities that women face in celebrity politics come together. She has been the focus of national and international attention from the election of her husband, Bill, as president of the United States in 1992 through the current moment of writing, when she is senator for New York.[8] Before that, she was already prominent as the governor's wife in Arkansas, and her preceding years in college and university have also regularly been described in terms of her central presence in the academic community (e.g., Warner, 1993). Unmistakably, she is one of the most described and researched politicians ever; she was the only first lady about whom a sustained series of public opinion polls was conducted (Burden and Mughan, 1999); authorized and unauthorized biographies were published while she was still in the White House (e.g., Warner, 1993; Sheehy, 1999); newspapers, glossies, and television alike have published an infinite number of stories, analyses, and cartoons about her and sought more and more access to the first lady (Winfield, 1997); academics have published monographs, edited collections, and articles about various aspects of her persona and position (e.g., Burrell, 1997, *Political Communication*, 1997; Winfield, 1994). Through this excessive publicity runs a consistent controversy:

> In the hands of conservative political cartoonists, talk show hosts and even respected columnists, Hillary Clinton seems to be a dangerously non-conformist first lady. To her admirers, on the contrary, Hillary Clinton represents a trailblazer who has, in the tradition of Eleanor Roosevelt reinvigorated the first lady role to include social activism. (Gardetto, 1997, p. 225)

The academic publications are no exception to this: conflicting interpretations and results are common. Burden and Mughan (1999), for instance, describe Hillary Clinton's position among the presidential advisors as "a seismic break" from the past (p. 238), whereas Troy (2000) sees it as one of the manifestations of a continuous feature in the U.S. presidency, that of wives operating as co-presidents. Likewise, Burden and Mughan (1999) attribute Hillary Clinton's nadir of popularity in 1996 to a combination of the Whitewater scandal and the decline of her health care initiative, whereas Burrell (2000) claims that the scandal was much more important than negative judgment of her overt policy advisory role. Clinton herself has always maintained that the amount and kind of publicity were not about her, but about what she represented. She has described herself as a symbol of transition on whom all tensions and anxieties about the new role of women are projected (Rodham Clinton, 2003).

Gardetto's (1997) research about *New York Times* coverage supports that thought in its conclusion that Hillary Rodham Clinton was more controversial as *wife* than as first lady:

> She represents a contemporary new woman—a married, middle class, career woman and mother, neither the emotional core of her family nor the subordinate of her husband—and, as such, she is potentially threatening to the social imaginary family and the gender inequality upon which it rests. (p. 236)

Winfield (1997) adds to that observation that the White House press office did not quite know how to handle her symbolic challenge to gender stereotypes. The decision to show as many of her diverse female and professional roles as possible resulted in a multidimensional image that was hard to fit into media and cultural conventions, and onto which each individual and social sympathy and antipathy could be projected (see also K. Campbell, 1998). As a result, the distance between Hillary Clinton's personally desired and experienced persona and the many public constructions has always been considerable, and this discrepancy was at its widest during the Whitewater scandal: "She did not recognize the picture that was being painted of her. She was revolted by the creation of her false persona. She believed it would be a long time before she could ever restore her reputation" (Blumenthal, 2003, p. 175). Whitewater, however, was only the extreme of the many occasions that forced her to change her style and performance, to reinvent her persona as it were, during her life as the wife of the governor and then the president. Every overt sign of independence, starting with her wish to maintain her own name after her marriage to Bill Clinton, was met with public controversy and disapproval and forced her to step back into an image of more traditional femininity. Probably the funniest, but still telling, episode in this oscillation between independence and tradition was her suggestion in the 1992 campaign that she could have stayed home to bake cookies, only to find herself some time later in a chocolate-cookie-baking contest with the incumbent first lady, Barbara Bush (see Warner, 1993). In the context of all controversy being about her unconventional, multidimensional performance as a "wife," it becomes understandable why her popularity reached its high during the Lewinsky scandal of 1998. Not only was her reaction to the whole affair considered to be of impressive dignity (Burrell, 2000), but also—finally—she fitted a conventional model of a wife, be it the sad one of the "wronged wife." Many an observer has claimed that the popularity gained from this position enabled her to run her own, independent campaign for the U.S. Senate (Tomasky, 2001). Yet what probably was the more important gain for Hillary Clinton from the Lewinsky scandal, however tragic in a personal sense, is that it removed the family dilemma from her political persona. As shown in this chapter, women in politics have persistently been framed as wronging their families, by political philosophy, history, and political and celebrity culture alike. Bill Clinton's adultery, and the public humiliation that it produced for his wife, made him into a nonentity for the performance of Hillary Clinton's new persona as a candidate for the U.S. Senate. With a grown-up daughter and a husband who lost his right to claim her attention, Hillary Clinton was able to construct a persona that has enabled women throughout the centuries to participate in politics: that of the woman who has fulfilled her motherly duties and who does not have a husband to look after anymore.

Hillary Clinton's campaign for the U.S. Senate required another reinvention of her persona that would articulate "female politician" with "New Yorker." As a visual image, that was relatively easy to achieve: out went the pastel lady's suits that signified her traditional role as wife to the president, in came the black trouser suits that accorded better with female independence and "New York" (Rodham Clinton, 2003). In her campaign, a fortunate match between her celebrity status and her personal preferences could be realized. The "listening tour" she organized to get to know the concerns of the New York voters drew out large crowds who merely came out to see this (in)famous curiosity, yet the tour provided Clinton with the thorough and perfectionist preparation that is said to have always characterized her professional style. It also allowed her to claim, later in the campaign, a New York identity by the oft-repeated sound bite: "I may be new to the neighbourhood, but I am not new to your concerns" (quoted in Cos and Snee, 2001). Her campaign focused on issues much more than the campaigns of her Republican opponents, who tried to mobilize the controversial images that surrounded her first ladyship and made her reliability and integrity an issue. While Clinton herself and campaign watchers (Tomasky, 2001) have presented her issue-driven campaign as the result of individual desires and style, the issue focus is a more general feature of the classic woman's campaign that Kahn and Gordon (1997) identified. In addition, the kind of issues that Clinton made central to her campaign are also not specific to Clinton—although they are in line with her long-term expertise—but have been seen to play well for women candidates in general. The following quote from her announcement to run for the Senate is in style and substance typical for the kind of rhetoric that is available to women in the public-private confines of celebrity politics:

> When I ate lunch with teachers at a school in Queens, I heard how hard it is to teach and learn. . . . When I visited businesses from Jamestown to Great Neck, I thought about my father, who ran a small business. . . . When I spoke with breast-cancer survivors at Adelphi University, I thought about Bill's mother and the courageous battle she fought. . . . You know, when I sat on porches and in backyards from Elmira to New Rochelle, I heard parents' concerns about the media's influence on their children. (Quoted in Cos and Snee, 2001, 2022)

Here a traditional female persona is performed through the allusion to domestic settings (porches and backyards), the reference to family members (her father, Bill's mother), and the particular substantial concerns: education, health, small business, parents' concerns about their children.

Yet her campaign also exploited and benefited from her celebrity status and the popularity acquired through the Lewinsky scandal. Television ads played on the many failed attempts to silence her, but the event that is considered to have turned the campaign around was one of the TV debates with Republican opponent Rick Lazio. First the host to the debate confronted her with Bill Clinton's misbehavior, accusing her of having embarrassed the country with her denials. Then, a little later, Lazio walked up to her and tried to force her to sign a campaign finance reform bill. Both actions were reminiscent of the invasion of her private space that were part of the Lewinsky scandal, and both turned public opinion toward her: "On this night, both moderator and opponent combined to make Hillary more sympathetic than she had ever managed to make herself during this campaign" (Tomasky, 2001, p. 39).

Another feature of Clinton's campaign, the mutual hostility between her and the press, has also been common in other women's campaigns (Witt, Paget, and Matthews, 1994). Although part of the negative press coverage resulted from her controversial celebrity status (Scharrer, 2002), the latter also attracted a relatively large amount of television coverage from which she may have benefited. Television is by its combination of visual and verbal information more open to diverging interpretations than print journalism (Fiske, 1987). In Hillary Rodham Clinton's case, both M. Brown (1997) and Burden and Mughan (1999) have suggested that therefore television coverage counteracted the negative verbal judgments that were expressed in the press and through television's voiceovers. That may explain why, in the face of tremendous uproar and opposition, she won the elections with a considerable lead: "She succeeded by ignoring the demands of the intelligentsia and the clamor of the media" (Tomasky, 2001, p. 288). Yet there is more to it than that; in the end, her persona harked back, in various ways, to traditional frames of women in politics, and she seems—finally—to have gained some benefit from her perilous celebrity status.

NOTES

The beginning of this chapter is taken from Sreberny and van Zoonen (2000), pp. 1–2.

1. I have translated these quotes back into English from the Dutch translation.

2. Being the daughter of Henry VIII, she witnessed the decapitation of her mother, the death of her stepmother, the removal of the following stepmother, and the decapitation of stepmother number three. Her stepfather, the husband to her fourth stepmother, is alleged to have sexually harassed her, having his eyes on the crown that he expected to be hers (see MacCaffrey, 1993).

3. "When I was fair and young," from Representative Poetry Online. Department of English, Toronto. http://eir.library.utoronto.ca/rpo/display/poem2565 .html.

4. All of these meanings are from www.dictionary.com.

5. Although Gamson uses the concept "female publicity," his arguments apply similarly to "female celebrity."

6. Paraphrase of the Dutch translation of Schwartzenberg (1977).

7. Although the pollsters differ in their appreciation of the main cause, Burrell (2000), for instance, says that it wasn't the overt policy advice but the Whitewater scandal, whereas Burden and Mughan (1999) claim the opposite.

8. June 2004.

7

❧

Dramatization:
Plots in Politics

Hillary Clinton's story could easily be read as a Movie of the Week (MoW), the single-episode, American-style, made-for-TV docudrama in which true stories of ordinary people (mostly women) conquering tremendous setbacks or even traumas are narrated. The genre covers themes like incest, domestic violence, rape, cancer, or AIDS, often from the perspective of women. According to Elaine Rapping (1992), it is television's way of telling the diverse stories of women's oppression that feminism brought out into the open, be it within the frame of individual suffering and survival, with clearly identified heroes and villains and with an imperative happy end, or at least an end with a "morally reassuring note" (Thorburn, 1994, in Sloniowski, 1996). Rapping (1992), one of the few authors to pay serious attention to the genre, claims that it offers a way to understand common cultural and political experiences for people with no other sources of information. The Movie of the Week has been said to be the successor of Hollywood's "women's weepies" and melodrama (Byars, 1991). Hillary Clinton's recurring struggles to maintain her independence, integrity, and dignity against the permanent onslaught of conservative patriarchal forces would fit the rules of the genre well, especially because after her ultimate humiliation as a wronged woman, a triumphant victory led her—independently—to her "destination": a seat in the Senate. Clinton's campaign managers framed her experience in a condensed story line for her ads that resonates with the codes of the MoW by stressing her vigorous resilience in the face of relentless opposition:

> They tried to get her to back down on teacher testing. She wouldn't. They tried to make her give up after the health care reform failed. She kept working. They

105

tried to silence her in China. But she spoke out for women's rights as human rights. They criticized her book about children. She took the proceeds, nearly $1 million, and gave it to children. All her life, Hillary has stood up for what she believes in. For better schools, better health care. Now she'll stand up for us. (Quoted in Cos and Snee, 2001)

Clinton's campaign managers have not been the first ones to recognize the relevance of narrative in presenting and promoting candidates; many political ads read as mini-stories working toward the happy end that only the candidate can realize (see Jamieson, 1996). Narrative, as discussed in chapter 4, makes the combination of people and places understandable. The actions and promises of politicians make more sense when they can be framed as part of a narrative that people are familiar with and to which they can relate. Such popular narratives invite expectations of possible actions, expected opposition, and likely outcomes, and thus suggest a sense of success and failure in the political process.

Consider, as an example, the typical story of heroic pursuit against all odds. Mythology, literature, and popular culture are full of such stories, ranging from the Argonauts' quest for the Golden Fleece to Rambo's attempt to single-handedly win the Vietnam War. In election times, it is the quintessential political story of the candidate going for the highest prize in a field full of competitors. To the dismay of many critics, the main concern of journalists covering campaigns has been said to be "who gets there first," at the expense of coverage of the substantial differences between the candidates (e.g., Broh, 1980). Winners and losers are the inevitable outcome of these "horse races": for winners a new story then begins, whereas the losers have to fight their way back in or disappear in the background. "Horse race journalism" is only one expression of how narrative frames the expectations and assessment of politics; politicians, journalists, and publics have used other frames to organize political understandings as well. In chapter 2, for instance, I discussed how the soap is used as a metaphor to denounce political misbehavior. Douglas Kellner (2002) has described successive American presidencies and administrations as good and bad movies respectively, depending on their degree of political success. He legitimizes this perspective by saying that "publics see presidencies and administrations in terms of narrative and spectacle, so that theorizing the cinematic and narrative nature of contemporary politics can help us understand, critique and transform our political system" (p. 485). Pomper (2003, p. 19) argues likewise, and claims that political storytelling, as found in the television series *The West Wing*, "can complement journalism by offering an entertaining and realistic view of the White House that sharpens images of the presidency and national politics." Both Kellner's and Pomper's approaches are in line with my own aim to articulate politics with the dominant cultural codes of entertainment that put stars and stories (character and narrative, as proposed in chapter 4) at the heart of everyday sense making. In this chapter, therefore, I will look at political stories through the four inter-textually connected frames of Quest, Bureaucracy, Conspiracy, and Soap. These frames organize the telling of real and fictional political stories alike, as I will demonstrate. Each of them invites another perspective on the motives and actions of politicians, the participation of women, the expected struggles, the role of citizens, and the "right" outcome; each of them—in other words—entertains citizenship differently. I will first explain why these four frames are the most relevant.

COMPETING STORIES

"Politics" is a small but perennial topic in all kinds of popular genres. In his history of popular culture, Peter Burke (1978) identifies a particular manifestation of "politics" as the exploitation of common people by the representatives of the king. Sometimes folk stories and ballads tell of the misdemeanors of the king himself, as a 1707 French song does ("Le Roi est un bougre et un voleur"),[1] but more often the objects of popular distrust are the king's men. For instance, in the story of Robin Hood, it is not King Richard the Lionheart who is to blame for the people's fate, but the deputy of his brother John, the sheriff of Notting-ham.[2] In the seventeenth-century rebellions of French farmers, the popular stories were not directed at the king but at his evil counselors: "Vive le roi, fie aux élus"[3] (Burke, 1978).

Current expressions of popular culture still address the theme of public officials usurping people's money. According to Elisabeth Bird (1992, p. 62), it is a fixed ingredient of the American supermarket tabloids: "A staple is the government waste story, in which Washington bureaucrats are shown to be pouring hardworking taxpayers' money down the drain." The quintessential story, according to Bird, involves the government's attempt to cover up its wrongdoings, and in that respect the theme of public officials wasting and abusing their mandate spills over into the excess of the conspiracy story. While Bird (1990) presents the Kennedy assassination as a continuing saga of conspiracy that pervades mainly popular journalism, Peter Knight (2000) sees it as a node around which an all-embracing culture of conspiracy has developed:

Following the assassination of President Kennedy in 1963 in particular, conspiracy theories have become a regular feature of everyday political and

cultural life . . . part and parcel of many people's normal way of thinking
about who they are and how the world works. (p. 2)

Knight suggests that the conspiracy theories about Kennedy's assassination were exacerbated in the wake of the Watergate scandal, which without doubt was a proven political scheme with a huge impact on successive political events. Afterward, every suspicion of a scandal and every
actual scandal in American politics has immediately received the suffix
"gate," as in "Iran-contragate," and "Monicagate" (see Schudson, 1992).
Yet, as Knight (2000) argues, it is not only the discovery of real machina-
tions and cover-ups that accounts for "conspiracy" as a dominant narrative in contemporary politics. Conspiracy has also become "an often un-
coordinated expression of doubt and distrust" (p. 44) as a result of
people's perceptions of governmental bureaucracies and the global economy developing beyond their understanding and control.

The frames of bureaucratic incompetence and its conspiratorial excess
commonly include more upbeat stories of individual efforts and success.
The sheriff of Nottingham was displaced by the individual actions of the
true hero of the story, Robin Hood. Watergate is as much a narrative of
conspiracy as it is the saga of the two journalists, Bob Woodward and Carl
Bernstein, following their self-assigned mission to find the truth. As stories, such quests for "justice" or "truth" have all the structural features of
popular narrative that folklorist Vladimir Propp (1923) identified. Each
story, he claimed, consists of a specific sequence of preparation, compli-
cation, transference, struggle, return, and recognition, which are carried
by the typical characters of heroes, villains, dispatchers, helpers, donors,
pretenders, and the princess/king. Fiske (1987) has applied a Proppian
perspective to news stories, and claims that they follow the particular narrative structure of social harmony disrupted by an external action (of a
villain or social process), followed by a struggle for resolution, which results in another, new state of equilibrium.[4] Politics, in this vein, can thus
also be approached as a field of competing stories about social harmony,
forces of disruption, and states of stability. The structure of these stories is
always the same, but what they tell is different: "The cultural specificity
or ideology of a narrative lies in the way this deep structure is transformed into apparently different stories, that is, in which actions and individuals are chosen to perform the functions and character roles" (Fiske,
1987, p. 138). In contrast with other popular stories, many political narratives do not have a definitive ending; old and new challengers always
contest seeming resolutions, and stability is always disrupted anew. Such
a neverending cycle of conflict and resolution adds an element of soap to
the quests, explaining partly why the soap metaphor is such a popular
frame to put on politics.

The four frames of Bureaucracy, Conspiracy, Quest, and Soap are alternately combined, extracted, and separated in specific political stories. It does not make much difference to the construction of the narrative whether these stories are real or fictional. Watergate, for instance, a story containing Conspiracy and Quest, has been told through press coverage, television journalism, documentary reconstructions, dramatized movies, TV series, (auto)biographies, cartoons, memorabilia, merchandising, and other cultural forms (see Schudson, 1992). In fact, political fiction and fact regularly converge: former political advisors or speechwriters have informed movie and television producers about how to make a convincing picture of politics. A former Democratic speechwriter who worked for Dukakis and Clinton wrote films like *Dave* and *Pleasantville* (1998) (see Neve, 2000). Politicians and journalists have made cameo appearances as themselves in political movies: Larry King, CNN's star host, for instance, appeared in *Primary Colors* (1997) to interview one of the key politician characters in the film. The presence of these people is commonly used as a marketing device to generate larger popular appeal. This also happens the other way around: political fictions have functioned to inform real politics. Ronald Reagan, for instance, has been said to have modeled his political persona on the Frank Capra movies, borrowing lines and themes from *Mr. Deeds Goes to Town* and *Mr. Smith Goes to Washington* (Rogin and Moran, 2003). As stories, therefore, politics, political journalism, and political fiction are hard to distinguish since they are intertextually connected through the same basic frames. I will demonstrate this in more detail by discussing the expressions of Quest, Bureaucracy, Conspiracy, and Soap. While these usually occur in some kind of combination, the different emphases in each represent different versions of the political process and citizenship.

THE QUEST

The quest is *the* frame through which to focus election stories: the term "quest" itself is often used as a synonym for campaign or race, as in "the quest for the White House." These stories have often been told quite literally as journeys, showing candidates traveling from one place to another by various means of transport, stopping only briefly in their pursuit for the final destination. Timothy Crouse's *Boys on the Bus* (1972), about the reporters following the 1972 presidential campaign trail, is the classic journalistic articulation of such an expedition. The book is as much about politics as it is about the journalists covering the campaign spending most of their time in the bus, waiting—amidst a treadmill of routine speeches, press releases, and unsubstantiated gossip—for the one-off quote or event that will make their scoop.

The campaign story, in fact, is built on a double quest: that of the candidate trying to reach his or her seat and of journalists trying to get hold of the candidate. That angle is also present in the documentaries about George Bush's 2000 campaign for the presidency and Arnold Schwarzenegger's 2003 pursuit to become California's governor. *Journeys with George* is the video diary of Alexandra Pelosi, a network news producer who spent one and a half years with George Bush's campaign.[5] The prevailing images in the documentary are of journalists in buses, packed and unpacked at regular intervals, waiting for the candidate to spend some time with them. While in Pelosi's movie, the candidate does occur once in a while, in *Arnold Schwarzenegger: The Governator*, director Alex Cooke only gets to see him from a distance, at staged spectacles and press meetings, and when getting back into his bus.[6] Campaigning, so these stories tell, is about driving, flying, and other means of travel. While *The Boys on the Bus*, *Journeys with George*, and *The Governator* all reveal image-making spectacles, spin doctoring, and press manipulations as part and parcel of election campaigns, the narrative frame of the election quest and its specific visualization also convey another message: in their literal representation of movement, these images produce a symbolic message about political energy, capacity, and desire for change. The pictures of landscapes coming by and candidates and journalists stepping out of the bus onto the ground do a similar symbolic trick, namely, that of connecting "politics" to the country and to "the people."

In a classic narration of the political quest, Frank Capra's *Mr. Smith Goes to Washington* (1939), a train journey provides the articulation between the country, the people, and politics. Jefferson Smith (played by James Stewart) is the protagonist of the story, a Boy Scout leader from a small town who is invited to fill the vacant seat for his state in the Senate. The connection between country and politics is first made through Mr. Smith's train journey to Washington: when he sees Capitol Hill and the Lincoln Memorial through the train windows, he decides he has to go see "the expressive symbols of American democracy" (Neve, 2000, p. 22) before he can go to his new office and start his work. Later in the film, Mr. Smith emerges as the icon of the common man, whose values are anchored in small-town America and whose ideal to represent "the people" of his state is frustrated by the private interests of his corrupt mentors and opponents alike. The conflict centers on a land deal, and it is only through the efforts of his Boy Scouts and the help of his secretary Clarissa Saunders that Mr. Smith manages to achieve political victory. Brian Neve (1992) has shown how Capra's depiction of the ordinary man, small-town values, and tainted political mores, also present in his other movies, is rooted in the late-nineteenth-century populist political tradition in the United States, built on agrarian protest and a more general construction of an opposition between elites and "the people." Many later Hollywood versions of politics have built on this populist tradition, with "the people" figuring prominently to authenticate the quest of the hero, who is portrayed as "the outsider, the man of the people, renewing American ideals and metaphorically bringing Washington practice in line with the classical form symbolised by the Capital Dome" (Neve, 2000, p. 27). This motif is the driving force in *Dave* (1993), a Hollywood comedy about the adventures of Dave Kovic (Kevin Kline) in the White House. Kovic happens to look exactly like the incumbent president and earns a bit of extra money by acting as the president at openings of shopping malls and retail centers. The film opens with a shot of Dave sitting on a pig and entering a car showroom. A speaker announces him as "the President of the United States." At that moment, two FBI agents spot him and invite him to stand in for the real president that night. Dave agrees but finds himself trapped in the role when the real president dies in the middle of an adulterous act. He is asked to stay on as long as necessary to prevent the country and Wall Street from panicking. The vice president, he is told, is a nut and cannot be trusted. Dave slowly discovers that, in fact, no one can be trusted except the vice president, and the story unfolds into a saga of the simple but goodhearted ordinary man fighting the foul and ubiquitous powers of self-interest and corruption. With the aid of the first lady, who likes her new husband much better than the old one, Dave wins his struggle and brings humanity and decency back into politics again.

In *Dave*, as in *Mr. Smith Goes to Washington*, the integrity of "the people" as opposed to the duplicity of politicians is embodied in the protagonist. In *Primary Colors* (1997), the movie based on the Clinton campaign with John Travolta impersonating Clinton (called Jack Stanton in the film), "the people" provide the background against which the candidate's sincerity comes into view. In the midst of a crisis around his sexual escapades, Stanton retreats in a doughnut bar run by an average American working man. The man's continuous offering of more doughnuts and coffee irritates Stanton's aide Henry, who is the character through which the story is told. Stanton, however, is shown as sincerely connecting to the man's concerns. In another scene in which he addresses a crowd of workers whose jobs are in danger, Stanton is similarly presented as in touch with "the people." In fact, Henry is asked to forgive Stanton his weaknesses and to ignore dirty campaign tricks because of his work for "the people." After a range of incidents culminating in the suicide of one of the campaign advisors, Henry decides he "does not like the game" and tells Stanton that he resigns. With a combination of charm, manipulation, and sincerity, Stanton asks Henry—and, through him, the audience—to stay because

> Who can do this better than me? Think about it, is there anyone else out there with a chance to actually win this election, who'd do more for the people than I would? Who'd even think about the folks I care about?

In the populist telling of the quest, "the people" are the source to which all actions of the hero can be traced. They are, in Propp's structuralist terminology, the dispatchers of the hero, the ones who send him on his mission. Women in these stories structurally function as decisive helpers: in *Mr. Smith Goes to Washington*, it is his secretary Saunders (played by Jean Arthur), who invigorates him with new energy when he has decided he cannot beat the Washington powers and wants to return home. She also comes up with the political, legal, and publicity strategies to win his case. In *Dave*, the first lady is the one to explain the workings of the White House to Dave. In *Primary Colors*, Mrs. Stanton is the one organizing the campaign when the candidate and his advisors are singing and socializing. The position of women in the quest, then, is very much like the one discussed in chapter 6, supporting but rarely independent movers of the story.

Female versions of the quest based on true stories have occurred, however. The life of Pamela Harriman, who changed from society wife to courtesan, Democratic fund-raiser, and finally U.S. ambassador to France, was made into a TV movie, *Life of the Party* (1998). The story of a working single mother's struggle against an energy company polluting the environment, retold in *Erin Brockovich* (2000) with Julia Roberts, may not be about politics in the sense used in this book, but is nevertheless another example of the few female representations of the political quest. Yet—tellingly—her boyfriend, who would have to be the main helper in the quest, cannot bear the demands of her pursuit on her private life and leaves before the happy end.

BUREAUCRACY

The heroes in the quest frames invariably find politics to be a strange disconnected field at best, or a quagmire of calculation, manipulation, and dishonesty at worst. In both cases, the hero and "the people" are portrayed as more sensible and ethical. In *Dave*, the stand-in president is confronted with budget measures he does not understand and agree with. In order to get a grip on the matter, he calls a friend who runs a small business. The following scene is typical:

Dave: You've got to help me cut the budget.

Friend: You have got to cut the budget?

Dave: Yeah, about $650 million.

Dave tells his secretary to get his friend fresh bratwurst and hot mustard (after all, they are ordinary people), and they delve into a pile of official documents. In line with the populist theme of the movie, Dave's friend then says: "I tell you Dave, I've been through this stuff a bunch of times and it just doesn't add up. Who does these books? If I ran my business this way, I'd be out of business."

Incompetence is one important background against which the political quest can be told, depravity another. Mr. Smith is elated to meet a much-admired senator in Washington, only to find out that he is part of Washington corruption. When the senator tries to explain that a certain amount of give and take, wheeling and dealing, is inevitable in politics, Mr. Smith gets totally depressed and wants to leave the capital. Jack Stanton's attempt, in *Primary Colors*, to keep his young aide Henry on his team represents a similar confrontation between the innocent virtue of ideals and the compromised pragmatism of politics. In *City Hall* (1996), Al Pacino gets to play the tainted politician, a mayor of a big city, whose young and idealistic assistant provides him with a moral mirror reminding him of his own past ideals gone lost. Yet, however bleak the context of the quest stories may be, they always contain the opportunity for change and a better world, albeit entirely dependent on the hero's individual worth and ability. Such possibilities of improvement are absent from political narratives in which bureaucracy is presented as a force beyond the individual's control. Neve (2000) has called these stories the "cynical" antidote to the naïve populism of the quest frame. Like the quest, the cynical political story has been told through various fictional and nonfictional genres, with "real" and "imaginary" regularly converging. Take, for instance, as the ultimate television account of bureaucracy, the British television comedy *Yes, Minister*, and its sequel *Yes, Prime Minister*. The key characters are Sir Humphrey Appleby, a top civil servant; Jim Hacker, minister and later prime minister; and Bernard Woolley, his private secretary. The motor to the events is the supposedly perennial battle between scheming, languid civil servants and passing, self-interested politicians. A quote from the 1982 episode, about Hacker and Sir Humphrey's attempt to keep one of the few women in the civil service from resigning, is typical for the kind of laugh the series aims at.

Sarah Harrison: Well quite honestly, Minister, I want a job where I don't spend endless hours circulating information that isn't relevant, about subjects that don't matter to people who aren't interested. I want a job where there is achievement, rather than merely activity. I am tired of pushing paper. I want to be able to point to something and say: *I did that.*

Sir Humphrey: I don't understand. . . .

Sarah Harrison: I know, that's why I'm leaving.

Jim Hacker: Surely you're not saying that the government of Britain is unimportant?

Sarah Harrison: No, it's very important. It's just that I haven't met anyone who is doing it.

The series was first broadcast on British television in 1980 and has remained immensely popular ever since.[7] Margaret Thatcher, then British prime minister, marked the series as utterly realistic: "Its closely observed portrayal of what goes on in the corridors of power has given me hours of pure joy."[8] Thus the articulation by the series of the relation between the civil service and politicians was no longer merely funny, but also projected as a close portrayal of reality. Thatcher was actually so fond of the series that she wrote a sketch herself that was played at the National Viewers and Listeners Awards in 1984.[9] In it, she appeared as the prime minister proposing to "abolish all economists . . . quickly." Such convergence of the fictional and nonfictional representation of the classic bureaucracy story is visible to this day in academic papers on governance that regularly evoke *Yes, Minister* to disqualify existing inefficient procedures and other red tape.[10] Unlike the quest stories, there is no character here that offers the slightest prospect of amendments to bureaucratic waste and incompetence. Even the structural position of the "wife," the woman's role in the narrative from which help and sensibility usually come about, does not really offer solace. Jim Hacker comes home and complains to his wife, Annie:

Jim Hacker: That is the last interview I give for a school magazine; she asked some very difficult questions.

Annie Hacker: Not difficult, just innocent. She was assuming there was some moral basis to your activities.

Jim Hacker: Well, there is.

Annie Hacker: Oh Jim, don't be silly.

In a discussion of television fiction about politics, John Street (2002, p. 16) says about *Yes, Prime Minister*: "The joke is not that funny things happen in politics, but that politics is laughable." That is a feature that the series has in common with satire, which is explicitly aimed at ridiculing politics to undermine its power (Keighron, 1998). Yet these seem to be features of the genres of comedy and satire, rather than of the frame of bureaucracy. Other famous frames of "bureaucracy," for instance, can be found in the work of the German-Jewish writer Franz Kafka, in whose novels the protagonists are subjected to the sinister forces of an impersonal government from which they cannot find an escape; *Der Prozess* (The Trial; 1925) is probably the best known. "Kafka" has become synonymous with rampant bureaucracy and a term of reproof rather than laughter. Frederick Wiseman's fly-on-the-wall documentary of the New York welfare system (*Welfare*; 1975) similarly recounts how workers and clients get caught in the maze of regulations and laws that govern social security, portraying a "bureaucracy pitted against people who are least fit to deal with it."[11]

CONSPIRACY

As Max Weber claimed in his classic treatment of bureaucracy, *Wirtschaft und Gesellschaft* (1921, pt. 3, chap. 6), one of its defining features is that it is impersonal; thus the suffocating effect of the Kafkaesque treatments of bureaucracy arises from the impossibility to find a single individual or group of people responsible for the fate of the story's victims. If there were such responsible agents, the narrative of bureaucracy would become a story of conspiracy. Michael Schudson (1992), for instance, analyzes different reconstructions of Watergate and shows how journalists told the discovery from the burglary to the impeachment of Richard Nixon as a detective story building up to the final disclosure of the villain. In comparison with the bureaucracy frame, the conspiracy frame thus offers the relative solace of a comprehensible origin. Knight (2000) says that the conspiracy theories about the Kennedy assassination have survived and intensified because the idea of a lone gunman more or less coincidentally hitting his target would be unbearable: "conspiracy theories provide a consoling sense of closure, gravity and coherence in the face of the seeming randomness of a disaffected loner killing the president" (p. 78). The detective dimension in the conspiracy frame makes the whodunit a recurring motif in both popular and political histories. There is, for instance, an ongoing popular controversy about the fifteenth-century British king Richard III, who is supposed to have killed his little nephews to keep his throne; that is at least how Thomas More and William Shakespeare have told his story. Both More and Shakespeare, however, were close to the Tudor kings who usurped the throne from Richard. Later historians have argued that Richard III was the victim of More's and Shakespeare's propaganda for the Tudors rather than a cold-blooded murderer. Even nowadays, there are still Richard III supporters who request the bodies of the two princes, alleged to be buried in the Tower, to be subjected to DNA analyses so as to free Richard of all charges.[12]

Conspiracy has thus been intricately tied to the retelling and spinning of history to the avail of the current power holders. It is therefore no surprise that "spin doctoring," as it is called today, is an important element in the conspiracy frame, a theme that has gained more prominence with the increased presence of mass media as a stage of politics. Allegations and counterallegations between journalists and politicians about rotating facts into sellable stories have become an integral part of political debate (e.g., Kurtz, 1998) and of popular culture. The American TV comedy *Spin City*, for instance, has a mayor and his press officer (Michael J. Fox) as the key characters, with much of the fun coming from the press officer's attempts to cover up his boss's childishness. A much more sinister picture is presented in the 1997 movie *Wag the Dog*, about the cover-up of a sexual harassment case against the American president days before the elections. Only a larger story, so the presidential staff thinks, will divert the attention, and thus a Hollywood producer is called in to make pictures that will convince journalists and audiences that the United States has invaded Albania. A few months after the film's release, both the Monica Lewinsky scandal and the American attacks on Afghanistan and Iraq broke loose, a parallel between script and reality that did not go unnoticed and made headline news all over the world.

A more detailed understanding of the conspiracy frame, and how it constructs the political process, can be extracted from an analysis of the Fox television series *24*, which first aired in 2001 and has won a number of awards since. The key characters are special agent Jack Bauer (played by Kiefer Sutherland), working for a CounterTerrorist Unit (CTU), and U.S. president David Palmer (played by black actor Denis Haysbert). In the first series, Palmer is still a presidential candidate who is subjected to an assassination plot from which Jack has to rescue him. Jack's efforts jeopardize his wife and children, so apart from the president he has to save his family as well. It is soon clear that there is a mole in the CTU. As it turns out in the final episodes, it is the woman with whom Jack once had an affair, Nina Meyers. Jack manages to save the president and his daughter, but Nina kills his wife in the end. A main feature of the series is that each weekly episode covers one hour of the full day (twenty-four hours) in which the whole sequence of events takes place. Invariably each episode opens, therefore, with Jack saying: "I am special agent Jack Bauer and this is the longest day of my life." After his first longest day, another one followed in 2002. In the second season, Palmer has been elected and is the first black president in American history. He is confronted with a terrorist threat to detonate a nuclear bomb above Los Angeles. Jack's guilt over the death of his wife has made him retreat in apathy, and he couldn't care less until the president personally calls him in. More ruthless than before, he goes after the terrorists, finds Nina on his path again, but also the president's wife, Sherry, who was shown to be unscrupulous in the first series. She teams up with forces in and around the government that secretly support the terrorist threat, expecting it to force the president to retaliate. As a result, the influence of the military and the arms industry would grow. Everything is more or less solved in the final episode, until the president shakes hands with an unknown and falls to earth immediately afterward, obviously infected by something through the handshake. This cliffhanger builds up to Jack's third longest day in his life; in the 2003 season, he and President Palmer take on bio-terror and Latin American drug cartels. The show is built on the unscrambling of multiple conspiracies in which no one can be trusted, whether it is one's family, one's colleagues, or one's aides. Reminiscent of the conventions of the film noir (see Krutnick, 1991), women in *24* are particularly devious; in the first two seasons, Jack's former mistress, the president's wife, and a young blond girl turn out to be key players in the terrorist plots, ridiculing, it seems, Jack's all-too-trusting masculinity. Plots and subplots are immensely complicated, but always tied to real political threats, fears, and contingencies, as political actors and audiences alike recognize. The following comment on rec.arts.tv, an Internet news group, after the last episode of the second season is typical:

My question though: Did the real-life Secret Service cringe upon seeing the episode? Particularly during election years, Presidents shake the hands of a LOT of people. Setting aside whether it would be fatal or not, isn't this a major problem?

*

I would think plot lines like this upset the Secret Service in general (and I guess I can't blame them), regardless of the specific mechanism used (in this case, toxic cooties).

*

Excitement always wins over reality, and the stuff on the glove will do whatever the writers need it to do—witness the 25th Amendment subplot. All Palmer had to do was WRITE A LETTER to the Congress and he's President again; every member of the Cabinet would have known this, and known that so long as Palmer could hold a pen he was President—any overnight vote in the face of his vigorous, coherent protest would have looked like a coup attempt as well—would any real-life cabinet have had the guts for that?[13]

The sole icon of virtue in *24*'s "tangled narrative hairballs" (Feeney, 2004) is President Palmer, who is relentless in his pursuit of the morally and politically right course. He even throws out his scheming wife in the middle of the elections of the first season, happily jeopardizing his chances of victory to maintain his integrity. Palmer's virtue, however, is built on Jack's vice. The president would no longer have his life (in the first season) or his office (in the second season) if it weren't for Jack hunting down all conspirators till their (often cruel) death. Although Jack obviously sides with the good guys, his actions compete in cruelty with those of his opponents. The subtext to *24*, therefore, is that the political front of moral virtue embodied in President Palmer is possible only because there is a hidden backstage in which intimidation, violence, torture, and killing are standard tools. In *24*, as in Conspiracy in general, no one can be trusted.

SOAP

President Palmer has found a strong rival outside of *24* in Josiah (Jed) Bartlet, another fictional president of American television, presiding in *The West Wing*, a weekly NBC drama series built around the political professionals in the White House. On the Internet, one can vote for Bartlet or Palmer as the best president;[14] *24* and *West Wing* story lines have been contrasted for their civic lessons (Rothman, 2003); and there has been strong competition among them for the Emmy Awards, the television industry's yearly awards. As "prime time presidents" (Rosenberg, 2002), both have been compared for their personalities and their views, both as television characters and in the context of current political issues (Hayton, 2003). When Martin Sheen, the actor who plays President Bartlet, publicly opposed the war against Iraq, the UK *Observer* published a piece claiming that Sheen's alter ego Bartlet and his colleague Palmer would have backed the real president George W. Bush: Bartlet's and Palmer's decisions in their respective television presidencies would divulge a similar unilateralism to that of Bush, and an evangelical liberalism close to that of Blair: "They would probably sell it better than President Bush has managed to achieve so far. They would sound more like Tony Blair. But back it they would" (Katwala, 2003). Such comparisons notwithstanding, *The West Wing* has been articulated with the real U.S. presidency much more than *24*. The show's dramatic structure revolves around the president, his chief-of-staff, and his communications staff. Although they are all shown working on various political story lines that are obviously connected to real political issues (gays in the military, the census, terrorist threats, gun control, and so on), the drama is in the personal motivations, the friendships and antagonisms, the love and occasional hate between characters, and the effect that politics has on private lives. The presence of a core location, the focus on a community of people trying to get by, the emphasis on the human side of public affairs, the multiple story lines, and—especially in the later seasons—the core tension between two "families," Republican and Democrat, are all narrative features that bring *The West Wing* into the realm of the prime-time soap opera. In this way, it produces a telling of politics that is closer to its inevitably collective nature of negotiation and compromise than the frame of the quest allows, which projects the individual hero as the single agent moving the story. That does not mean that "quest" is absent from *The West Wing*: in fact, the political story lines have been constructed as repetitive mini-quests of the staff, without the guarantee of a happy ending, however, and with a new challenge waiting after each precarious victory. This continuous frustration of the quest is epitomized in the first series when President Bartlet complains to his chief-of-staff that his ideals are continuously compromised by the anticipation of possible opposition, loss of electoral support, or a media showdown. The president and his aide decide on a more principled course and find the rest of the staff cheering behind them: "The episode represents politics as a melodramatically heroic struggle by those who forsake electoral calculation for principle" (Street, 2002, p. 19). But, as said in chapter 2, it is a melodrama for men: "The boys in the backroom at Pennsylvania Avenue have each other. And that's all that matters" (L. Smith, 1999). All women in the series appear in supporting roles to the men, as wife, daughter, girlfriend, or private or press secretary. Their function in the narrative is similarly predictable: they are the sources of moral insights and of everyday common sense. Lane (2003, p. 33) argues that the tensions between political considerations of the male characters and the everyday moralities of the women produce "moments that traverse power, privilege, and social categories of identity by rejecting hierarchical relationships between high level officials and low-level assistants." That is subversion, however, which is built on the maintenance of a rather traditional understanding of femininity, which has historically constrained women's agency in politics and which has provided only stereotypical openings for women in the narratives of politics. The male bonding that is central to the series has been criticized on other grounds as well. The loyalty of the staffers to each other and to the president has been considered one of the unrealistic strands, together with the high-paced walking around, in what otherwise has been called a convincing portrayal of the political process in the White House (Levine, 2003). Such criticism notwithstanding, the series has been immensely successful, in terms of ratings, critical acclaim, and political appreciation. Both Republicans and Democrats have praised the series for its positive portrayal of public service. Marlin Fitzwater, former White House spokesman for Presidents Reagan and Bush, considers the series "healthy, good for the country."[15] Clinton's press secretary Joe Lockhart is equally approving:

> There are thousands of people who work in this government who are either Democrats or Republicans who come to work every day because they care, and they are committed to promoting what they think is in the best interests in the country. . . . And this show, while not real gives you a flavour of these people. That has to be a positive.[16]

That "positive" is all the more exceptional in the context of the dominant narrative of politics, which seems to have become one of distrust and cynicism. Neve (2000), for instance, ends his review of 1990s Hollywood portrayals of politics with the conclusion that effective models of political participation and action have become rare; Patterson (1993) concludes similarly after his analysis of political journalism, and Knight (2000, p. 3) typifies both popular and political culture as built on "the default assumption in an age which has learned to distrust everything and everyone."

Both Street (2002) and Neve (2000) have concluded that the narratives of Quest and Soap open up more possibilities to envision political participation and change than the narratives of Bureaucracy and Conspiracy. Quest and Soap are about individuals, operating alone or in teams, for the greater good of society; Bureaucracy and Conspiracy are about the sinister forces that favor private interests and oppress individual choice. The first two would offer a position to audiences in which their actions were framed as relevant and possibly influential; the other two would invite passivity, if not fatalism. Yet, the four narratives seldom occur in their pure forms: almost every Conspiracy story contains a Quest, Soap has its Bureaucracy, and so forth. In the BBC drama *The Project*, based on the rise to power of New Labour, the two protagonists and their friends are working toward the liberation of Labour from decades of opposition in Parliament. The first episode opens as a classic quest story with the key actors getting into a (mini)bus to move to the center of power, London. Along the way, love interests, personal and political betrayals, and other ingredients of melodrama are inserted into the story, as are conspiracies against Tory candidates and—in the second and final episode—against New Labour dissidents themselves. While the mixture of narrative ingredients in *The Project* may be extreme and a possible cause for its relative lack of audience appeal (see Kibble-White, 2002), a certain amount of polysemy, of multiple meanings, is inherent to all media texts and thus also to the fictional and fantasy stories of politics discussed in this chapter. The question of whether a particular narrative frame of politics opens up the imagination of participation and change, and what kind of imagination that is, can only be answered by looking at the way audiences make sense of these narratives and of the people featuring in them. The next chapter looks, therefore, at the way in which audiences construe political stars and stories.

NOTES

1. Translation: "The king is an egg and a thief." Translation by the author.
2. Legend and reality are probably quite far apart, with Richard the Lionheart less brave and his brother John less evil than commonly presented: see *Legends of the Isles*, Discovery Channel, Valkieser Publishing, 2000, video.

3. Translation: "Long live the King, down with the tax collectors." Translation by the author.

4. Fiske in fact uses Todorov's (1977) social interpretation of Propp in this respect.

5. 2002, directed by Aaron Lubarsky and Alexandra Pelosi.

6. BBC Four, Friday, January 9, 2004.

7. It was rereleased on DVD in 2003 and was short-listed by British audiences as one of the ten best British comedies ever (accessed at www.bbc.co.uk/sitcom/top10.shtml).

8. Accessed at www.yes-minister.com/introduc.htm.

9. Accessed at www.yes-minister.com/thatcherscript.htm.

10. For example, Cairney (1997), Hoopes (1997), Garret (2002), and Letwin (2003).

11. Accessed at http://film.guardian.co.uk/Century_Of_Films/Story/0,4135,401800,00.html (February 9, 2004).

12. See www.richard111.com.

13. See rec.arts.tv, "How Dead Is President Palmer?" (May 23, 2003), accessed at http://groups.google.nl/groups?q=president+palmer&hl=nl&lr=&ie=UTF-8&selm=b0uza.697532%24OV.650859%40rwcrnsc54&rnum=1.

14. For example, www-personal.umich.edu/~bgoodsel/post911/2003_02_16_arch.htm.

15. Accessed at www.pbs.org/newshour/media/west_wing/fitzwater.html.

16. Accessed at www.pbs.org/newshour/media/west_wing/lockhart.html.

8

⊰⊱

Presentations: Popular Resources for Citizenship

The modernist concern about entertainment in politics is built on the assumption that it has detrimental effects. However, as I discussed in chapter 1, video or television malaise is a contested thesis about media effects around which supportive and counteracting research has been produced. To understand and pursue the relevance of entertainment to politics, a different angle than the one of "effects" is necessary. In the context of citizenship, the first issue is not what entertaining politics does to citizens, but what citizens do with entertaining politics, for citizenship is not something that pertains if it is not expressed in everyday talk and actions, both in the public and the private domain. Citizenship, in other words, is something that one has to do, something that requires performance. The issue in this chapter is therefore whether and how entertaining politics enables people to perform as citizens. Consider, for instance, the following comment of an avid *West Wing* fan that was posted on the Internet Movie Database (IMDb):

> The West Wing *is the best television show I've ever seen. I'm required to watch it for my Introduction to Political Science class this semester, and I thank God all the time for that. The new episodes aren't enough for me; I watch the reruns on Bravo at 7 and 11 every weeknight, and my roommate is hopelessly hooked now too. I like a million things about* The West Wing. *It's astonishingly smart and informative—I know that it is not an exact representation of what goes on, but as far as I can tell a lot of it is very realistic. The characters, their relationships, and their dialogue are smart; the sets are detailed and well maintained; and the plots go through the whole range of the situations and the emotions that the real inhabitants of the West Wing are likely to experience.* The West Wing *is fast-paced and each episode is made like a short movie. The production values, and the scripts*

are fantastic. If only the real White House was full of people as smart as these guys, we might be in a better shape as a country.

This quote is telling for various reasons: it undermines the stereotype, common in the modernist discourse of politics, that popularization and personalization provide overly simplistic clues to people without much education and without much political interest. Here is a person with much the opposite qualifications—a political science student—who uses *The West Wing* to make a comment on the political process ("the plots go through the whole range of the situations and the emotions that the real inhabitants of the West Wing are likely to experience") and to imagine better political conditions ("if only the real White House was full of people as smart as these guys, we might be in a better shape as a country"). The quote thus also shows that the popular and the personal in politics, as constructed through *The West Wing*, can function as resources for discussing, criticizing, and imagining politics for the performance of citizenship. One might contend that the comment contains all the flaws that are feared in modernist political discourse: a superficial focus on the qualities of people instead of issues, and a confusion of reality and fiction. Yet those may be much more the result of the particular context of the Internet Movie Database, which is not a political setting and which assumes rather short statements, than a typical example of this student's understanding of politics (if the latter were the case, one might want to doubt the teaching).

In this chapter, I will discuss in more detail how the personalization and popularization discussed in the previous chapters facilitate people to perform as citizens. The chapter draws from an exploratory analysis conducted for this book about people's interpretation of fictional political leaders and narratives. For the latter, I collected the user comments on an array of political texts that were posted on the Internet Movie Database, and on a limited number of Internet discussion groups. These data were used to reconstruct the variety of civic performances enabled by the personal and the popular in politics. They do not produce a representative picture of how the different reactions are distributed among audiences; in analogy with qualitative research designs, the results are aimed to be representative for kinds of civic performance rather than for kinds of people. I will first review how people judge political leaders ("the personal") and what kind of performance they expect of them; then I will discuss what people do with political narratives ("the popular").

THE PERSONAL

Three American political scientists—Miller, Wattenberg, and Malanchuk (1986)—opened their highly influential article on the way people assess the personal characteristics of politicians with the following quote: "Candidate evaluations are one of the most important but least understood facets of American voting behaviour" (p. 521). They ascribe the dearth of research in this area to the dominance of the political discourse that considers voting on the basis of personality characteristics as irrational. Yet, although in the wake of their article many more studies on the effects of political leadership have appeared, most authors apparently still feel the need to justify their projects against the allegation that an assessment of the personal qualities of politicians before or instead of considering policies and issues is an impoverished way of making sense of politics. Bean and Mughan (1989, p. 1175), for instance, write that critics find that "personalisation trivialises democracy as individuals are encouraged to make their voting decisions on the basis of ill-informed judgments about the idiosyncratic personality characteristics of individuals who rise and fall from the political stage." Ohr and Oscarsson (2003, p. 23) make a similar comment when they say that "in public discussions of the personalisation of politics and voting behaviour it is often feared that citizens increasingly base their political judgments and their eventual voting decision on superficial, media built images of political leaders." Cutler (2002) also refers to the supposed irrationality and lack of knowledge of "personal voters."

As a result of the common prejudice against personalization, there are still many uncertainties as to how, when, and why personal characteristics of politicians matter to citizens. The research of Miller and his colleagues (1986) produced five enduring categories that people use in their perception of political candidates: competence, integrity, reliability, charisma, and personal traits. These categories precede the performance of individual candidates: citizens fit the candidates into their existing ideal structures, so to speak. The five categories persist over time, as does the relative importance of the categories; from the 1950s onward, the perception of a candidate's competence appears as the most important dimension of people's judgments of candidates, followed by integrity and reliability. These are three performance-related indicators, according to Miller and his coauthors, which suggests that, in fact, a political evaluation is hidden in the personalized assessments. Charisma and personal traits, in contrast, are entirely based on the perception of private features and have become mentioned less and less in American election studies, regardless of people's level of education and political interest. Counter to the modernist concerns with personalization, the results of this research show that the higher people's education and their level of political interest, the more likely they are to express comments on the personality traits of candidates, which is the reason why Miller et al. typify elections as "personality contests for college-educated voters" (p. 527).

Cutler's (2002) work on the way in which the sociodemographic characteristics of candidates and voters interact in electoral choice can be seen as a more detailed analysis of the fifth category of Miller's candidate schemata, the personal traits. But even in this least political category of judgment, it appears that *all voters*, regardless of partisanship, knowledge of issues, and other measures of political sophistication, assess candidates on the basis of their personal features and tend to appreciate candidates who are more like themselves in terms of gender, ethnicity, religion, or geographical background. A discussion that arose around the depiction of a black U.S. president ("David Palmer") in the television series *24* shows that such identifications on the basis of shared demographics are not simplistic one-to-one connections, but part of a composite reaction in which several other considerations are weighed. Actor Denis Haysbert, playing President David Palmer, for instance, claimed that he likes the idea of playing an African American president and the idea of actually having an African American president. Yet he also has been quoted as wanting to play a president for all the people: "I don't think it should matter to the American people what colour skin is on their president. What should matter is the content of their character" (quoted in Waxman, 2002). Reactions to the role of Palmer on Internet news groups show similar ambiguities. One fan provoked a discussion on the Internet news group rec.arts.tv:

> *In the first episode of last season's* 24, *Jack's boss pointed out that it was absolutely imperative that they save Palmer's life, because if Palmer were assassinated it would have caused a race war that would have split the country apart. I wonder if one reason the show isn't big with many Afro-Americans is that Palmer seems to be, in my opinion a conservative and not a liberal. He's more Colin Powell than Jesse Jackson.*
> ≥ *For one thing, Palmer seems to be a centrist, if anything.*
> ≥ *Unless you define a conservative Democrat as "doesn't scream that Republicans want to kill children and enslave minorities," I don't think we have seen enough of Palmer's policies to define him.*
> ≥ *I see Palmer as being more his own man than Colin Powell would be as President of the United States, but the first comment on Powell appears to be on-point.*
> ≥ *I can't see this making a bit of difference.*[1]

Here, in only five brief comments, one sees a number of judgments secreted below the surface: assessments of personal traits of a fictional politician are articulated with real politicians and with a cursory evaluation of their respective political positions. A similar, but more heated, discussion emerged in another news group:

> *Tonight on* 24 *they revealed that David Palmer was a Democrat but there is no way he is a Democrat. I know it's politically correct to say that all blacks are Democrats, but he is not a whining, race-hustling, welfare-protecting, reparations-seeking liberal*

like most black democrats are wont to be. He is a Republican and we all know it!
Democrats don't have that much integrity.
   ≥ *Somebody gives a damn I guess.*
   ≥ *It is clear that you are a racist as you are generalizing black men and Democrats*
and you are basing much of your opinion on the man's race.[2]

In these discussions, however cursory and fast-paced they are, one can recognize how people use the assessment of political performance and of personality traits together to evaluate candidates and articulate them with ideological standpoints. The combined political leadership studies have provided more general evidence of these mechanisms and also suggest— very forcefully—that level of education, political sophistication, and political interest do not produce a different degree or kind of assessment. In fact, Elisabeth Gidengil's (2003) comparison of leader effects and voter characteristics in nine Western democracies suggests that the *more* politically involved people are and the *better* they know who they want to vote for, the *more* leadership evaluations matter to them. That pattern occurs often enough for Gidengil to suggest a general pattern that occurs regardless of the varying weight of political leadership across different political systems. Ohr and Oscarsson (2003) conclude the same on the basis of an explicit comparison of leadership effects in presidential systems versus party systems. Some of the results suggest, in addition, that if levels of education and political sophistication matter to leadership evaluations, it is primarily because they produce a more extensive range of considerations that stretch beyond "mere" candidate judgments (e.g., Cutler, 2002; Miller, Wattenberg, and Malanchuk, 1986). Other data, however, propose that the emphasis on personal qualities that is so explicit and excessive in campaign times produces a priming effect on all voters: amidst all of the different considerations they can evoke to make their electoral choices, campaigns summon leadership assessments primarily (see Mendelsohn, 1996; Venturino, 2002).

If, then, the criteria with which to judge politicians exist before the performance of specific candidates, and these criteria pervade the whole citizenry of different electoral systems, the question of relevance is: where do these schemata come from? The leadership literature is not very clear about the origins of candidate schema. Miller and his research group (1986) claim that people deduct them from their experience with past presidents; the media obviously are an important intermediary in such a process, but Mendelsohn (1996) adds that interpersonal communications can act against media frames. Probably the fullest treatment of the resources people use to make sense of politics in general, including candidates and leaders, comes from William Gamson (1992). He makes a distinction between media discourse, experiential knowledge, and popular wisdom. The popular representation of politics and politicians in the various forms of fiction discussed in the previous chapter—books, television, movies—cuts across these three resources; evidently they are part of media discourse about politics, especially because of the many explicit articulations with the reality of politics (cf. chapter 7 of this book); however, the particular realistic codes and conventions of popular culture also provide a vicarious sense of experiential knowledge. Gamson describes experiential knowledge as stories based in direct familiarity and in the more distant experiences of others—friends, family, friends of friends, and people one hears on the radio or sees on television. By extension, the realistic style inherent to popular accounts of politics enables the parasocial interaction with popular protagonists that allows people to "transcend their personal experience and to imagine how they would feel in another person's situation" (W. Gamson, 1992, p. 123). Gamson's third resource, popular wisdom, is articulated with particular subcultures and finds its expression in rules of thumb, a proverb, or an analogy with everyday life situations. As became clear in the previous chapter, such popular wisdom is a central part of the popular representations of politics, as appeared, for instance, in the scene from the movie *Dave* in which Dave, the impersonator of the American president, and his friend compare the national budget with the books of a small business.

What kind of resource does popular culture's combination of media discourse, experiential knowledge, and popular wisdom produce to evaluate politicians? It is a multifaceted resource; that much is apparent in the variety of audience comments on Jack Stanton, the Clintonesque candidate in *Primary Colors*. Many viewers put the main tension in the film, between Stanton's political ideals and capacities and his private misbehavior, in the forefront of their reaction, be it in different kinds of accounts. A relatively straightforward description of the dilemma reads:

> *Stanton really wants the best for the people but in his private life he has done some stupid things.*[3]

Some people said that the movie produced an understanding of politics and Bill Clinton that was useful to them, but for one person that involved a reflection on his dilemmas, whereas it produced a stark judgment for the other.

> *This story does an amazing job of explaining the unexplainable Bill Clinton. Can a good politician who cares about the people, win without doing some amoral things? Does being an unfaithful husband mean that someone is a bad man or candidate? The story brilliantly goes over such things without ever being preachy, and it is also very funny.*[4]
>
> *
>
> *The film is at its most captivating when it puts the hero and his colleagues against a moral dilemma. Take a certain route and increase the chances of winning . . . but at the cost of someone else's career, family, entire life. Is it worth it?*[5]
>
> *

This film made me think about Clinton as well as politicians in general. What is admirable, what is not acceptable, what is it we really "want" in our public officials?[6]

The judgments deliver differently:

The movie is key, KEY, to understanding our most recent criminal president, Slick Willy. They should show it on the History Channel![7]

*

But the funny things is, the main Pro-Clinton message that it ultimately delivers is "Gee, he may have done all these terrible things, but he says he cares about the people, so it's ok."[8]

*

Let's face it: Clinton might have had private problems, but he was a GREAT president.[9]

From this brief, first analysis, three different kinds of accounts can be detected: descriptions, reflections, and judgments. Whether the comments are descriptive, reflective, or judgmental, they all involve an explicit or implicit discussion of the tension between "integrity" as a moral category to evaluate the private behavior of politicians, "reliability" as the political category to think about what a politician will do for the public, and "competence" as the category indicating whether a politician will be able to operate successfully in the context of office.

In the case of *Primary Colors*, the sources that people use to comment on integrity, reliability, and competence are obviously much wider than the story and the qualities of the film itself. They must have drawn from media discourse to compile their opinion of Bill Clinton, they appeal to popular wisdom ("In real life, there are no good guys. There are no bad guys. There are just guys"),[10] and they use the film to express their ideological stance. The film seems to expand the resources that people already have to make sense of politicians, rather than alter what they thought already. As one viewer said: "I don't think *Primary Colors* will change anyone's opinions of the Clintons."[11]

Audience reactions to the protagonist in *Mr. Smith Goes to Washington* constitute a less complex assessment of the political character played by leading actor James Stewart. The 1939 film is still repeatedly shown on cable and network television, and is used in classrooms of various kinds. The comments on the Internet Movie Database demonstrate that the film provides contemporary audiences with material to think about politics. The story constructs a more dichotomous struggle between good and evil than *Primary Colors*, which many viewers recognize. They present *Mr. Smith* as part of a general narrative tradition and of Frank Capra's work in particular:

Mr. Smith goes to Washington is a timeless, brilliant parable of Good versus Evil, played against the backdrop of the U.S. Senate.[12]

*

I like movies like this with an oppressed person who stands up for what they believe in.[13]
*

Very like Mr. Deeds goes to town in a lot of ways—hick gets a position of power and then attempts are made to discredit him.[14]

As a result of the clear-cut boundaries in the film, the reflection on candidate qualities that *Primary Colors* evoked is rare in audience comments on *Mr. Smith*. Many viewers *want* to believe in the message of the film, although they simultaneously indicate the fantasy of that desire:

The idealism of Jefferson Smith might feel a bit anachronistic today, but, and I know this is a cliché, the world could use more people with his values.[15]
*

Nowadays it is more likely to be the case that the depiction of only ONE politician as "in bed with business" or "remote from the people" makes it look like a fantasy. But it is a fantasy—an ode to the American dream.[16]
*

After all, who doesn't wait for a Jeff Smith to come around and win us the America we wish we had?[17]

Jefferson Smith apparently embodies an ideal of integrity that contemporary audiences cannot find in real politics. But at the same time they recognize it as a dream, as a utopia that does not comply with the everyday requirements that politicians face. Whether that recognition takes the form of cynicism ("it is hard to accept that politicians are basically good people")[18] or of a kinder mollification ("this film is so sweet in it's [sic] belief that one man can shake the system")[19] does not make much difference; it is a strong undercurrent in the general reverie about integrity. Predictably, *Dave*, a film much like *Mr. Smith*, evokes similar evaluations of the presidential character played by actor Kevin Kline. Integrity is the main feature that makes his persona appealing to audiences who—again—at the same time label the story as completely unrealistic ("it's a totally unbelievable story";[20] "the basic premise is nonsense").[21] The most explicit expression of this balance of reality and fantasy in the appreciation of fictional presidents is in a comment on the president of *The West Wing*, Jed Bartlet:

There will never be a real president like Jed Bartlett [sic] in the White House, but every American can get a healthy dose of inspiration from fictional Jed Bartlett [sic], "man of the people."[22]

Audience reactions to the politicians in *Primary Colors*, *Mr. Smith*, *Dave*, and *The West Wing* suggest that fictional politicians are not simple yardsticks to compare the qualities of real politicians; fictional politicians are subjected to the same categories of judgments that people use to evaluate real politicians. Both real and fictional politicians thus seem to function in the continuous (re)construction and expression of people's evaluative schemata. People use their evaluation of both fictional and real politicians to make clear to others what they think are appropriate modes of conduct in office. Their comments display how popular culture can be called upon to express civic values and perform citizenship. Their comments also suggest that different styles of performance allow for different positions: the simple descriptive style seems only to put forward what the film is about, but implicitly contains a priority of what is important. It makes a difference whether one describes *Dave* as a vehicle for actor Kevin Kline or as a movie about integrity. "Integrity" is expressed in the style of fantasy by dreaming about utopian ideal politicians, but also in reflective mode by contemplating the dilemmas of a fallible character like Jack Stanton (or, for that matter, like Jim Hacker, the minister in *Yes, Prime Minister*).[23] The latter is in sharp contrast with the judgmental style in which the fictional politicians are used to condemn or praise their real-life counterparts, mainly because of the political side they embody. How do these four styles—description, utopia, reflection, and judgment—come out in the reaction to the fictional stories of politics?

THE POPULAR

Before discussing people's reaction to the stories of politics in more detail, it is important to note that a sizeable 40 percent of the comments on the movies used for this analysis did not address political themes at all, but mainly contained an endorsement of script, acting, visuals, or whatever other features that make good movies or television. Even explicit reconstructions of political events, like *All the President's Men*, evoke such nonpolitical notes, both to advise for and against the film:

> *Everything about this film is top notch. The acting, photography, art direction, everything. I can't recommend it too highly.*[24]
> *
> *O man, I am sorry, I have seen this film twice. And it is boring, boring, boring. 2 and half hours of two guys asking questions on the phone or in person. Sometimes they get answers, sometimes they don't. Rinse and repeat.*[25]

Description and Realism

The other 60 percent that do refer to politics in their feedback often do so in a rather general manner. "Realism" appears as a strong anchor for people to comment on the texts. *Wag the Dog*, for instance, received as fierce comments on its realism[26] as on its lack of credibility.[27] Usually, comments on the (lack of) realistic depiction of politics are based on a hunch of how things go in politics. *Yes, Prime Minister* drew remarkable kinds of real-life comparisons:

> *I watched this programme with my parents who are civil servants (in India) and they tell me every bit is true.*[28]
> *
> *From first hand experiences not with the British but the European administration and from my studies of political science I can pledge the satire to be really, really sharp.*[29]

The use of realism as a criterion to assess the qualities of fictional political texts resembles the way in which experiential knowledge, as identified by William Gamson (1992), is brought into play when people talk about real politics. Both real and fictional politics seem weighed against what people know (or think they know) about politics: "This documentary [*Journeys with George*] shows nothing new or exciting about Bush junior."[30] Sometimes the result is more cynical:

> *I couldn't follow any of it. I gathered that most of the pols involved were liars and cheats, but what else was new?*[31]
> *
> *One does get the drift of how decisions are reached, the chain of command, the coddling up to congress and the public at large, and of course the power play and influence peddling, the continual spin doctoring of public opinion, and of course the perennially cynical but necessary White House press corps.*[32]

In the latter comment, a double descriptive take is at work: the commenter describes what politics is about through his assessment of the descriptive qualities of the program. There is a clear element of learning involved in these kinds of comments. Because texts are taken as realistic depictions, it becomes possible for audience members to express and endorse new perspectives:

> *Watching TV news footage has become different after this movie.*[33]

Such a learning element is enhanced because many of these texts have been used in educational settings; read, for instance, a student's comment on *Mr. Smith*:

> *This movie was da bomb! we watched it in social studies and im like oh great here is a boring ol' black and white movie. But I watched it and really got into I! Frank Capra was cool. It teaches you a lot about the House of Representatives and the Senate and Fillibusters [sic].*[34]

From such learning experiences, recommendations and encouragements ensue to see a particular movie or series. A common remark, for instance, is "if you ever had any interest in politics, this is the show for you."[35] Another reviewer calls upon politicians to learn from *The West Wing*:

> *I've read that Mafioso study mob movies to learn how to behave. If politicians do the same with political shows, maybe* The West Wing *could make a contribution beyond mere entertainment.*[36]

Judgment

Comments like these show that "description" and "realism" involve other kinds of assessments that are more specific about a reviewer's political position. The above comments on what politicians could learn from fiction imply, for instance, a criticism of politicians that is based in distrust (as in the *Wag the Dog* statement), or in a disapproval of their behavior (as in the *West Wing* comment). Such verdicts also come in the form of explicit ideological judgments about the politics as represented in the text. An unambiguous current in these comments is a critique on the overall liberal perspective of Hollywood—as a shortcut term for film and television.[37] IMDb users have presented *The West Wing* in particular as Hollywood's answer to the presidency of George W. Bush:

> *The producers of the show should keep on dreaming, presumably it acts as some type of therapy so that they can come to terms with a Texan like Bush as president, who knows?*[38]
> *
> *It really is liberal Hollywood's answer to being shut out of Washington on almost every front.*[39]

Predictably, *The West Wing* has attracted reverse support from liberals:

> *It is unabashedly—dare I say in these reactionary times—ultra-liberal and proud of it.*[40]
> *
> *I'm proud to be a liberal and it's nice to see a popular television program keeping the philosophies that I espouse in the forefront of millions of Wednesday night television viewers.*[41]

Such an identification of the politics of Hollywood is obviously not reserved for *The West Wing*. Other films have attracted parallel conservative critique and liberal support:

> All the President's Men *is a bad movie glorifying the no-good Commies who helped to bring down the greatest President of all time, Richard Nixon.*[42]
> *
> *Well, perhaps I'm biased. I enjoy films that have Republicans getting their just desserts. Especially "Tricky Dicky."*[43]

Such remarks fit easily into existing political oppositions and confirm a truism in media effects research, namely, that people selectively perceive media offerings and mold them into their own—in this case ideological—frameworks. A comment on *Wag the Dog* identifies the same mechanism:

> *How many movies play both sides of the fence so well. Rabid conservatives should enjoy the movie's slaps at Hollywood; rabid liberals should enjoy the movie's slaps at win-at-all-costs politicians.*[44]

Yet other comments indicate a much more complex process and demonstrate that resentment or appreciation of a film's or series' ideology is not by definition simply predicated upon one's own views. A viewer of *Dave*, for instance, who considers himself "a liberal of sorts" was somewhat turned off by its partisan stance:

> *It's pretty obvious where the movie's politics lies—there is no ambiguity of purpose, no voice for any other view. . . . I'm an American Liberal of sorts and moments in this movie made me wince because of their obvious propaganda.*[45]

A conservative viewer of *Dave*, nevertheless, liked the movie despite its politics:

> *Yes, the movie arguably has a liberal slant, but I was an avid Rush Limbaugh fan when I, along with two other super-conservatives, first saw this movie, and we all three loved it. If your political ideology is the only thing keeping you from enjoying this movie, then I mourn for you.*[46]

Similar comments were posted for *The West Wing* with conservatives expressing their appreciation of the show, despite its politics. Obviously, for such viewers the appeal of fiction like this is located on another plane than ideology. In fact, a common observation is that one is to be pitied if ideology guides one's pleasure:

> *If you let your political viewpoint or your demand for reality get in the way of enjoying it, so much the worse for you.*[47]

Reflection

The reflective style in the IMDb comments involves the presentation of the political stories as a series of dilemmas and compromises. This style is apparent in the gratification that people derive from seeing politicians portrayed as people of "flesh and blood," who suffer from human frailties like the rest of "us." It was especially visible in the discussions of Jack Stanton. It also comes about in the comments on the story qualities of political texts. It entails people who reflect on what they have seen, and who stress that one has to reach one's own conclusions. It is sometimes presented as a battle between contradictory forces: a *West Wing* viewer summarizes it as "how idealism has to meet reality,"[48] a fan of *Yes, Prime Minister* labels it as "the eternal fight between progress and reaction."[49] A typical comment of this kind is on *All the President's Men*:

> *It is far more than one of the essential conspiracy films. It is about politics, life, how we deal with things, the quest to find what's wrong, to weed out those who cannot meet the challenge!*[50]

A different person uses almost similar kinds of words to describe *Primary Colors*:

> *This film says something about life, compromises, ambition and what doing good means.*[51]

The West Wing evokes such comments as well:

> *It paints a fair and critical picture of the American society and it's [sic] place in the world. The show salutes certain aspects of American life while not being afraid to criticize others.*[52]

But the archetypal reflection was made in a comment on *Dave*:

> *It's a genuinely heart warming political fairy tale that leaves you with both a glimmer of hope and a sense of desperation. We're exposed to a White House resident who is decent and good and above the burdensome, prohibitive game of politics, while we simultaneously realise that whomever we in the real world put in the Oval Office, while he or she may be a genuinely decent human being, that person will always be answerable to the power and influence of campaign funds that are the currency and commodities in Washington.*[53]

The desire for a fairy tale is explicit in this comment, but it is modified by a pragmatic, almost cynical recognition of real political processes.

Utopia

In the full utopian style, political fictions seem to be used to muse about the uncontested existence of a perfect society and an ideal political process that surpasses partisan and ideological oppositions. Such fantasies pertain to the virtues of ordinary human beings and to the country itself and they include—often—a critique of prevailing cynical attitudes. One viewer, for instance, loved *Dave* because of the way the film suggests "that the common man makes for a better politician."[54] In the utopian comments, the common man is presented as possessing the common virtues ("helping others," "honesty") that politicians seem to lack. "There is good in mankind," one viewer comments, after having watched *Mr. Smith Goes to Washington*.[55] A fan of *The West Wing* says:

> It makes me wonder if there might be merit and value in politics after all . . . if only because the people behind the politics might be genuinely motivated people and not the ego-maniacs they sometimes appear to be.[56]

Apart from the American people, American institutions and the country itself are the subjects of hope and dreams. *The West Wing*, one viewer says, "compels you to believe in your government despite all the reasons it gives you to despair of it."[57] The American press is the institution receiving a boost as a result of *All the President's Men*,[58] and if one wants sustenance of American politics in general, *Mr. Smith*, a reminder of "the greatness of our nation,"[59] is offered as the cure:

> The film is good tonic for anyone who has doubts about the truth in government and what a meritorious service it is to serve one's country at the highest levels. I strongly recommend this film to anyone wanting a good dose of old-fashioned American politics.[60]

What is interesting is that the comments on the American institutions come from non-American as well as from American viewers of these texts. An Edinburgh fan of *The West Wing* assumes that it is "the White House as I'm sure, most Americans and we would like it to be,"[61] and an Australian viewer calls it "emblematic of the America you desperately wish to believe in."[62] Foreign viewers, in particular, however, heavily judge the series precisely for what they feel is American propaganda. An Argentinean viewer says:

> They show you what they want and make the presidency look good, which doesn't exist in any country. Don't buy it especially nowadays with that prehistoric ape in the White House.[63]

The utopian style obviously is an optimistic one. It collides with cynical accounts of politics. *Mr. Smith*, for instance, is presented as "the triumph of optimism over world-weary cynicism"[64] and a "non-cynical heart-warming message."[65] *The West Wing* is equally appreciated:

> NBC has risen above the bad jokes or rips on our political system, and created a television show that provides us hope and comfort in the belief that those in government service and politics truly do care about the "man or woman" on the street.[66]

As they do in the wishful comments on the political heroes in these stories that I discussed earlier in this chapter, viewers anchor their utopias in firm ground; they recognize and label them as dreams, as in one comment on *Dave*: "my favourite of the White House wishful fantasy genres";[67] or they present them in an ironic way, as one viewer does in his presentation of the leading journalists in *All the President's Men*: "the dynamic duo is our only hope."[68]

THE MISSING

The analysis until now has shown how diverse movies and series like *Mr. Smith Goes to Washington*; *Dave*; *Primary Colors*; *Yes, Prime Minister*; *Wag the Dog*; *All the President's Men*; and *Journey with George* enable people to think about the dilemmas that politicians and politics face (reflection), criticize or praise politicians for their morals and stories for their ideology (judgment), and express their hopes and ideals (utopia). In addition, some stories give their viewers the feeling that they have acquired new knowledge about specific elements of politics, which provides them with means to describe what they see as politics (description and learning). Although large numbers of the analyzed comments did not address politics at all, there were enough that did to warrant the conclusion that popular culture does indeed function as a source of gaining insight in politics and as a means to perform citizenship by presenting one's ideas in a public setting. It does not seem to matter much whether the popular text in question is based on true or fictional politics, because fictions like *Mr. Smith*, *Dave*, *The West Wing*, or *Yes, Prime Minister* are thoroughly researched and built on knowledge and the advice of insiders to true politics; because both fiction and nonfiction of politics draw from the same popular codes about character and narrative (see chapter 7); and because people seem to apply the same frames to make sense of fictional and true politics. As will have become clear from the extensive presentation of comments, this merger of fiction and reality does not produce an impoverished process of political sense making: superficial and profound, serious and comical, brief and elaborate, ideological and matter-of-fact comments alternate on this platform. Nor does it lead to an apolitical kind of sense making, because different ideologies and partisanships were presented through the comments. The question of whether the particular frames of Quest, Bureaucracy, Conspiracy, and Soap that were discussed in the previous chapter evoke particular responses can only be answered tentatively; the quest frame in films like *Mr. Smith* and *Dave* seemed especially helpful to fantasize about "the people," "human virtues," and "America." Judging from the comments, utopia seems easier to nourish from this kind of popular culture than from everyday political journalism, which some deem as unpleasantly cynical. Yet the quest did also invite the descriptive, reflective, and judgmental styles, as the diversity of comments has shown. The soap frame in *The West Wing* and *Primary Colors* seemed especially fertile for people reflecting on the moral and political dilemmas that they consider part and parcel of the political process, although (Prime) Minister Jim Hacker, framed in bureaucracy, also got a statement on the continuous tension between ideals and human flaws.[69] The conspiracy frame was not simply related to a particular kind of reaction, although *Wag the Dog* did seem to produce a platform for cynical judgment. That did not seem the case for *All the President's Men*, which, despite the strong presence of the conspiracy frame, could also be read as a successful quest of two journalists.

What is it that people do *not* do with these texts, and possibly do not do with other popular cultural renditions of politics? In other words, what kind of citizenship is not performed through the reactions to these texts? There are very few specific references to concrete political issues and events in the 546 IMDb comments that were analyzed. In the ninety-two reactions to *The West Wing*, for instance, that range from the beginning of the series in 1999 into its fifth season in 2004, only two episodes received comments that were anchored in real political issues: the episode that was made right after the 9/11 attacks attracted both a positive statement ("amazing") and a negative one ("terrible"),[70] and an episode from the first series about the death of a homeless man who turned out to be a decorated Vietnam veteran caught praise from several people for being so moving. One statement on *Mr. Smith* read that the plot was unbelievable because "I can't find the part in the Constitution that empowers the federal government to loan money to build a boys camp,"[71] while another discussed recent behavior of "Bush and Blair stampeding through the UN with total disregard for democracy."[72] These were the only two reactions of seventy-five (from August 1998 to November 2003) that made a connection with concrete political events. Dave's struggle to find room in the budget to maintain funding for homeless shelters did not evoke a flicker of reflection on policies for the homeless, nor did *Primary Colors* invite anyone to express a position on Jack Stanton's ideas about the economy and employment policy. Some IMDb commentators did summarize *Wag the Dog* in terms of its coincidence with the Monica Lewinsky scandal, but in a descriptive way. There were some politicized comments about the relevance of the movie for understanding the Iraq war:

> This movie is far more relevant than when it first appeared because it understands the politics of terrorism, suitcase bombs, the increased role of the CIA and, at the end, the need to go back to Albania (nee Iraq) and finish up the job. It is definitely a far more relevant film to view today than it was in 1997.[73]

One may contend that the lack of political specificity in the reaction to these films is the result of the fact that the films themselves focus in a rather general way on politicians and the political process, and much less on concrete political issues. Such an explanation is supported by the fact that—as said before—some 40 percent of the reviews did not mention anything political at all; as one reviewer of *The West Wing* said:

> *Trust me, it's not all about boring politics. There are enough non-political plots to keep your interest.*[74]

If the political generality of the texts were indeed the source of the rather broad focus of the comments, one would expect that a film that does zoom in on a specific issue would receive more detailed comments. Yet, if one considers *Erin Brockovich* as a movie about industrial policy versus environmental and health concerns, that film also did not produce highly detailed comments on these issues. Commentators summarized the film as a story of a single mum working herself up to a better future, or as a general David versus Goliath story, or as an example of legal drama like *A Class Action*. Actress Julia Roberts, who plays the lead role, is the focus of many comments, and only rare observations place the politics of the movie at its heart:

> *Should the big corporations be sued for trying to cut costs and therefore provide a cheaper product [or make more profits if you are a cynic] for the consumer? Or produce at a higher cost and keep the consumer safe? Erin thinks she has the answer; watch and see her in action. 5 stars.*[75]

The analyses in this chapter thus demonstrate that popular representations of politics, in which character and narratives are central, provide people with an opportunity to pick up and confirm a broad sense of politicians and the political process, and enable them to express general political reflections and judgments. It is unlikely that people will use these kinds of texts for their understanding and evaluation of concrete political issues; it seems that they take them up to sharpen their overall angle on politics and express an overall sense of utopia rather than a detailed picture of it.

NOTES

1. rec.arts.tv, "24's Black President Poorly Marketed?" Thread (13 contributions), June 6, 2002–November 8, 2002.

2. soc.culture.African.American, alt.politics.democrats, alt.politics.usa.republican, "NO WAY DAVID PALMER IS A DEMOCRAT," April 2, 2002–April 5, 2002.

3. IMDb, August 4, 2003.

4. IMDb, September 17, 2003.

5. IMDb, February 9, 2000.

6. IMDb, May 25, 2000.

7. IMDb, April 29, 2002.

8. IMDb, December 27, 2003.

9. IMDb, March 2, 2002.

10. IMDb, February 9, 1999.

11. IMDb, May 25, 2000.

12. IMDb, August 16, 2003.

13. IMDb, August 16, 2002.

14. IMDb, May 6, 2003.

15. IMDb, May 16, 2003.

16. IMDb, April 1, 2003.

17. IMDb, July 20, 2002.

18. IMDb, February 11, 2003.

19. IMDb, August 22, 2000.

20. IMDb, March 12, 2003.

21. IMDb, September 24, 2002.

22. IMDb, January 4, 2004.

23. IMDb, October 16, 2002: "Eddington plays a cabinet minister who is the perfect embodiment of the modern politician. High in ideals, but forever made human by ambition, partisan backbiting, concession making and opinion poll obsession."

24. IMDb, August 3, 2002.

25. IMDb, February 20, 2002.

26. IMDb, June 20, 2003.

27. IMDb, May 30, 2002.

28. IMDb, September 7, 2001.

29. IMDb, January 20, 2004.

30. IMDb, February 9, 2003.

31. Comment on *All the President's Men*, IMDb, August 5, 2002.

32. Comment on *The West Wing*, IMDb, January 12, 2001.

33. Comment on *Wag the Dog*, IMDb, August 1, 2003.

34. IMDb, November 2, 2002.

35. Comment on *The West Wing*, IMDb, August 3, 2000.

36. IMDb, March 29, 2001.

37. In the IMDb comments, this is not a dominant perspective in numerical terms; that may be the result of the particular texts that were selected for the analysis, as well as of the particular platform that the IMDb constitutes. It cannot be taken as indicative of the prominence of this perspective in other contexts.

38. IMDb, August 21, 2003.

39. IMDb, February 13, 2004.

40. IMDb, December 5, 2003.

41. IMDb, November 12, 2002.

42. IMDb, May 27, 2002.

43. IMDb, April 17, 2002.

44. IMDb, August 11, 2003.

45. IMDb, March 20, 2000.

46. IMDb, February 25, 2001.
47. IMDb, September 25, 2003.
48. IMDb, January 15, 2004.
49. IMDb, July 3, 1999.
50. IMDb, September 14, 2001.
51. IMDb, July 3, 2003.
52. IMDb, August 23, 2003.
53. IMDb, February 25, 2001.
54. IMDb, September 1, 2000.
55. IMDb, July 17, 2000.
56. IMDb, August 18, 2002.
57. IMDb, August 27, 2003.
58. IMDb, December 13, 2002.
59. IMDb, January 27, 1999.
60. IMDb, April 1, 2003.
61. IMDb, August 19, 2001.
62. IMDb, January 15, 2004.
63. IMDb, September 30, 2002. Similar comment from Hungary on July 16, 2003.
64. IMDb, March 15, 1999.
65. IMDb, June 2, 1999.
66. IMDb, February 16, 2000.
67. IMDb, February 20, 1999.
68. IMDb, February 21, 2003.
69. *Yes, Prime Minister* also provoked relatively few comments on the IMDb, which makes it hazardous to generalize from them.
70. October 3, 2001, and December 4, 2001, respectively.
71. IMDb, May 20, 2003.
72. IMDb, April 1, 2003.
73. IMDb, August 16, 2002; similar comment made on January 28, 2003.
74. IMDb, September 30, 2003.
75. IMDb, April 8, 2002.

9

⊰⊱

Reflections: Populism, Deliberation, and Diversity

Let me end this book with some reflections on its connection to core issues in political theory: populism, deliberation, and diversity. They are meant as an agenda rather than a full-fledged discussion. First, however, here is a brief summary of the preceding argument.

The citizen can very well be entertained, but not within the limited space that modernist understandings of politics produce. In that space, entertainment and its popular genres are actively ignored, invalidated, or exploited. Academic critics have produced extensive expositions and research results, and they claim that a range of detrimental effects result from entertainment in politics. Their language is ridden with captivating watchwords like "video malaise," "mediacracy," "dumbing down," "sound bite politics," or "celebrity politics." Terms like these function as shortcuts to extensively elaborated dismissals of all elements in politics that fall outside the serious realm of information, deliberation, and policy formation. These terms are also put forward as markers of eminence: by no measure can the writers be caught showing a superficial, frivolous attitude toward politics and the performance of civic duties. On the contrary, what they proclaim is "better education," a "new Puritanism," or even "the elimination of television" in order to produce better citizens, citizens who are more like themselves. A specific variety of that discourse is produced by journalists who use the metaphor of the popular soap opera to denounce all political developments that do not fit the modernist frame. These include a mixture of public and private processes like sexual and financial abuse, incompetence, spin, and political conflict. As a result, journalists too construct a wide gap between politics and popular culture, with the latter miles beneath the status and relevance of the former.

The distance of popular culture from modern politics is a product of the two contradictory social traditions in which they are rooted: popular culture builds on oral tradition and folklore, whereas politics draws from literacy and modernity. To a degree, that antagonism runs parallel to the opposition between people and elites, and the dismissal of the popular functions partly as an instrument for the maintenance of elite dominance. Yet, most political elites in democratic societies recognize the relevance of "the people" as the source of legitimate representation, and thus they exploit—especially in campaign times—popular means of communication, assuming that they will therewith reach citizens who would otherwise be cut off from politics. While the narrative frame of the soap opera has been used to convey what politicians and parties stand for, a major popular vehicle in these efforts is popular music. The encounters between popular music and politics are probably the most schizophrenic of all articulations of politics and popular culture. For sure, much, if not most, popular music has nothing to do with politics, nor do its fans want any kind of tie. Nevertheless, there are enough performers and bands that regularly use their music to express their political views. While politicians do eagerly seek associations with popular music to endorse their positions and policies, they hardly ever consider the politics of popular music as valid, nor do they perceive popular musicians as legitimate representatives in political debate. Popular music is routinely approached as an object for politics, to be used and controlled at will, rather than a subject, an actor to be taken seriously. That situation is exemplary: submission, exploitation, or at best benign neglect characterize the position of all popular culture in modernist political discourse. The effects are twofold: people for whom popular culture provides their main everyday perspectives on politics and society are excluded from the political field and denied the possibility to perform as citizens, because their style and frame of reference do not fit the prescribed requirements. Instead of requesting more and better education, modernists would do well to consider whether and how politics can be transformed into a more inclusive practice. This is all the more pressing because people who do manage to live up to the modernist constraints are faced with a highly demanding, hardly pleasurable notion of citizenship that does not easily compete with the other kinds of roles and identities that people want to perform. Although, again, the media are often blamed for making civic performance an unattractive option amidst all their entertainment showers, other responsibilities such as work and family seem to produce equally important competitors to citizenship (e.g., Bellah et al., 1986). These two effects exacerbate the structural tendencies in the political field that tend to shrink it to a playground of expert elites.

The search for entertaining citizenship is therefore in a sense at par with the attempts of social movements to open up the political field to a wider group of actors. To explore the entertainment of/in citizenship—to examine, in other words, the relevance of popular culture to open up the political field—makes sense only if the routines of the popular parallel the practices of the political. On the surface, this parallel is there: the current successful wave of participatory multimedia entertainment like *Big Brother* or *Pop Idol* in which audiences can partake in the course of events by voting for or against their favorite candidates has inspired academics, television executives, and political actors alike to think about formats for "reality politics" that would invigorate a citizenry that is—so they feel—increasingly alienated from politics. There are, however, more fundamental and helpful similarities between the active fans of participatory multimedia entertainment and the committed citizen that political parties and politicians look for. Both fans and citizens emerge as a result of performance, of pop-cultural and political actors respectively; both fans and citizens seek information about their objects, talk and discuss, try to convince others of their preferences, and propose alternatives; both fans and citizens have a necessary emotional investment in their objects that keeps their commitment going. Thus, the way fans are positioned, the activities they undertake, and the relation they have with their objects is not fundamentally different from what is expected from good citizens in modernist discourse of politics. And thus it would not have to be a problem if politics were more like popular culture, because it still would be capable of attracting the same kind of desirable civic/fan activity. If that is a valid assumption, it becomes justifiable to examine whether and how the defining paradigmatic and syntagmatic features of popular culture—a focus on individuals and a preference for narrative—are present in politics and how they entertain the citizen; in other words, how they make it pleasurable to engage in politics, and how they maintain the idea that politics is important. "Personalization" and "dramatization" are the key terms here, referring to the prominence of individual politicians and the framing of their ideas and action in coherent story lines.

Personalization is a problematic component in modern politics, because it negates its premise that the force of ideas instead of the weight of individual politicians should drive the democratic process. As a result, personalization is often mistaken as nonpolitical and as an easy way to escape the more difficult discussion of issues. That seriously underestimates the intricacies of personalization in two ways: it underrates the challenges that current-day politicians are faced with, and it fails to appreciate the complex assessments people make of the performance of individual politicians. From the intersection of a politician's performance and the appreciation of it by his or her fans/citizens emerges the political *persona*: the political self as revealed to and perceived by others, a composite product of the politician's biography, track record, actions, and personality on the one hand and the responsibilities, failures, and features that the politician's everyday observers project onto him or her on the other. For such a political persona to be successful in the entertainment of citizenship, the politician has to operate with equal accomplishment in the fields of politics and popular culture; he or she has to act a convincing political celebrity, so to speak. That does not mean that celebrities per se make good politicians, as somber modernists would fear, but nor does it mean that politicians per se make better politicians; they are both specific types of political personae whose success will be contingent on the prevailing political *and* popular culture.

The female celebrity politician meets specific trials that have to do with women's historical and cultural monopoly in the private sphere and their exclusion from the public sphere. As a celebrity and as a politician, the female persona therefore has to project a culturally satisfactory articulation of contradictory public and private demands: the allegedly soft qualities of femininity need to be reconciled with the hard behavior supposed to generate political vigor, a demanding public career needs to be in balance with a stable private life, and the visual and physical codes of feminine celebrity need to be in accordance with cultural models of political ability. How these tensions play out has been publicly visible in the many controversies around the persona of Hillary Clinton. Her case also demonstrates that on top of personal and political features, the political persona acquires meaning through the specific stories in which he or she is framed. After the Lewinsky scandal and Hillary Clinton's selection as Democratic candidate for the U.S. Senate elections in New York, Clinton's persona fell neatly in the classic narrative of "wronged woman overcoming her ordeals."

The more general frames that underlie the stories (both the fictional and the true stories of politics) are those of the quest, bureaucracy, conspiracy, and soap. Each frame seems to invite different understandings of political causes and events, different strategies for political action and policy, and different opening for civic involvement; in other words, each frame seems to entertain citizenship differently. Actual audience reactions, however, to popular films and television series built from these frames show that they all function as occasions for people to perform as citizens: watching these texts stimulates many people to describe what politics is about, reflect about the dilemmas in politics and of politicians, express their ideological judgments, and fantasize about a utopian politics. Although these civic commentaries are rarely very specifically anchored in concrete political issues or events, they do demonstrate a willingness to articulate one's views on politics in a public setting.

The conclusion to the original question put forward in chapter 1, then, must be that citizenship can be entertained through the popular vocabularies offered by personalization and dramatization. On the simplest level, these vocabularies are entertaining in the sense that they make citizenship simply more pleasurable for more people, but they also offer instruments to think about what citizenship should mean, and they invite a hospitable surrounding for the performance of citizenship.

POPULISM

For some readers this may be a problematic conclusion, as this may have been a problematic book overall. In the course of writing and discussing these issues, I have on occasion been accused of naïvely advancing a dubious kind of populism. Twice, in different contexts, fellow scholars even felt the need to remind me of the propaganda of the Third Reich as evidence of the way in which popular codes of communication will manipulate citizens into the mindless state of "fans," erase democratic procedures, and bring evil leaders to power. Comments like these necessitate a specific examination and articulation of *Entertaining the Citizen* with current discussions around populism. The critiques testify of the bad reputation that populism has acquired as a result of World War II and, more recently, of the revival of right-wing extremism in several Western democracies. Mazzoleni, Stewart, and Horsfield (2003) have brought together research about a number of these "neo-populist" movements and concluded that the media do play an indispensable role in their rise to power. For sure, mass media and "the popular" can form dangerously intolerant alliances, but that is not by definition the case.

In their extensive studies of populism, both Margaret Canovan (1981) and Michael Kazin (1995) point out the historical existence of democratic and antidemocratic types of populism that have mobilized left-wing as well as right-wing sentiments.[1] "In both cases," Canovan (1999, p. 4) says, "what was involved was the mobilization of interests and opinions that were perceived by their adherents as being neglected by those in power despite being the concerns of the mainstream." Populism always involves a protest or policy on account of "the people" who fall outside the reach of the political system. As discussed in chapter 1, from Bourdieu's proposition that the political field is structurally inclined to withdraw into an ever-smaller group of expert representatives, it follows that a populist reaction is an inevitable counterforce to the structural contraction of the political field. De Haan (2000) connects populism to the classical republican ideology of the Italian city-states, which proclaimed an inexorable cycle of politics, in which professionalization is followed by popular reaction, a change of power, and—inevitably—a new cycle of professionalization, re-action, and change. Therefore, he argues, "populism is first and foremost opposed to a political division of labour; populist resentment is aimed primarily at political professionals" (de Haan, 2000, p. 34). One of the Hol-lywood presentations of politics as a story of an individual hero out on a quest to replace a self-serving political elite—think of *Dave* and *Mr. Smith*—is thus not simply a product of the romantic individualism that is thought to sell best to audiences, but also the outcome of an unshakable tradition in political history and theory. That tradition also explains why the persona of the political outsider is such an attractive option for con-tending candidates: it builds on a notion of the political process that has both popular and political appeal. Nevertheless, all this does not mean that "the people" will necessarily enjoy and follow populism. One of the things that chapter 8 showed is that audience reactions to different kinds of political personae and stories often strike a balance between utopian desire and pragmatic realism. A series like *The West Wing* seems at the same time to be appreciated for its presentation of politics and public ser-vice as a worthwhile endeavor aimed at improving the world, and for its realistic depiction of politicians squabbling, compromising, and settling for the pragmatic rather than the "best" solution. But audience reactions to other stories and politicians contained a similar mixture of fantasy and common sense. Such double-edged perspectives resemble what Canovan (1999) has called the "redemptive" and "pragmatic" faces of democracy; faces that are inextricably linked and cannot exist without the other. In fact, Canovan argues that populism emerges mainly if the gap between "promise" and "performance" becomes too big: a space for populism emerges if politicians live on their promises without delivering, but also when politicians merely manage problems without providing a vision of a better world. In that respect, several popular political characters, narra-tives, and reactions discussed in the previous chapters must be reassuring for the contestants of populism, for they both present and evoke the even-handed merger of faith and skepticism necessary for democracy to thrive.

DELIBERATION

As much as my project has been framed in terms of populism, as little has it been connected to theories of deliberation.[2] This is, of course, because theories of deliberative democracy are the modernist response to the gap between political elites and everyday citizens, and modernism has a blind spot for the relevance of pleasure, entertainment, and fun—as will be clear from the previous chapters. Yet, if one takes the writings of "delib-erationists" at face value, ignores their modernist constraints, and stretches their ideas just a little, their search is much the same as the one I conduct in this book. The key issue in theories of deliberation is whether and how "difference," "otherness," "multiplicity," "heterogeneity," "diversity," or "fragmentation" can come and be held together in a democratic entirety. Allison Jaggar (1999, p. 308), a feminist political philosopher, investigates, for instance, "how cultural heterogeneity may be compatible with social stability and civic solidarity." Chambers and Costain (2000) put it similarly and propose that the communicative prerequisite for democracy entails an acknowledgment of the diversity of actors, their particular idioms, and their power differentials.

"Culture" in most theories of deliberation has to do with the differences resulting from the identity politics of the new social movements (e.g., gender and sexuality) and with the diversity in the multicultural societies that emerged out of widespread migration patterns. Rarely does "culture" include popular culture or entertainment as something that needs to be recognized and acknowledged. What happens when one reads "popular culture" into the recommendations for deliberative democracy? Jaggar (1999) identifies three key civic virtues as a prerequisite for deliberative democracy. The first is multicultural literacy (i.e., learning to understand the meaning of other groups' or individuals' words, "even if they are delivered in a halting or unorthodox style or express ideas incompatible with dominant views"; p. 42); the second is moral deference, which implies an active evaluation of an individual's or group's credibility and a willingness to let experiences of subordination realign one's emotional constitution. Such openness to "emotional reconfiguration" forms Jaggar's third civic virtue. If one reads "popular culture" into Jaggar's virtues, that means that virtuous citizenship can also be built on the political expressions that are presented as popular culture (for instance, in personalized and dramatized politics), just like it can be built from the political expressions that are present in popular culture genres, whether they are tabloid media, popular series, rap music, or heavy metal. My point in relation to deliberative democracy is not that the deliberative modernist style of presentation and argumentation should be replaced with a popular mode; rather, a variety of discourse is more inclusive than the prescriptions of deliberation allow. Valid knowledge and arguments in deliberations of political issues should come from a range of different sources. My point is also not that popular culture provides a good source of deliberation by definition of its being popular. As there is good political journalism and bad political journalism, there are good and bad expressions of politics in popular culture. The good ones may achieve a political awareness that other means of communication rarely produce. Oxford fellow Timothy Garton Ash claims, for instance, that national traumas have been more easily told through the format of a moving soap opera than through the factual means of journalism. He mentions *Roots*, about the repressed history of slavery in the United States, and recommends the format to the Serbians to come to terms with the atrocities of their recent regimes (see chapter 4).

One final example seems hard to dismiss, even for the purest of deliberationists. Consider a typical comment on the widely praised 1988 debut album of black singer Tracy Chapman:

> The lyrics resonate with messages about inequality and exploitation and particularly the violence endemic between racial groups. Who could fail to recognise the haunting truths so melodically portrayed in *Across the Lines*? . . . She sings of domestic violence in Behind the Wall, a well constructed a cappella that highlights the number of women killed by their husbands and portrays the frustration of being powerless to stop it. (Hackwriters.com/Tracy Chapman, 2002)

This demonstrates how a deliberation of women's experience with domestic violence could be based not only on government investigations, investigative journalism, or feminist advocacy groups, but also on a tabloid tale, a TV movie "based on a true story," or a popular song.

DIVERSITY

I have claimed that the style of popular culture typified by personalization and dramatization may offer a way into politics for people otherwise excluded or bored. I have also claimed that popular fictions of politics enable people to perform as citizens. That is, of course, all very respectable, but it should not make one blind to the sexist, racist, and other antidemocratic tendencies that also exist in popular culture. I have not focused on those much, because they are so much part of the common academic and political discussions of popular culture (e.g., Lester, 1996; Dines and Humez, 1995). Nevertheless, even if one wants to hold up the munificent face of popular culture, as I have chosen to do in this book, there still seems no escape from gender and ethnic stereotypes. In all the popular stories of politics discussed in this book, whether framed in a campaign message or a work of fiction, the public-private distinction appeared to constrain women's options and strategies: it produces a limited expectation of the areas in which women are competent, it limits the communicative styles available to women, it directs them into supportive rather than into independent roles as politicians, and it positions them as outsiders to the political field. The confinement of political personae from minority ethnic groups is similar, although their numbers are even smaller, both in real and in fictional accounts of politics. Yet, if one wanted to bring that up against the relevance of popular culture as a resource for the performance of citizenship, one would have to recognize that in that respect popular culture is not so different from other means and genres of political communication.

There is an impressive body of literature that has revealed sexism and racism as inherent to day-to-day print and television journalism (e.g., Carter, Branston, and Allen, 1998; Law, 2002). While some authors ascribe this to the dominance of white men among professional journalists and others suggest that news values and organizational routines make the reliance of journalism on cultural stereotypes inevitable, the outcome is nevertheless the same. There is a quickly growing amount of feminist work that reveals the ways in which gender stereotypes inform regular policy documents and that recommends the subjection of mainstream policy preparation, discussion, and implementation to norms of gender equality (e.g., Pollack and Hafner, 2000). Sexism and racism, therefore, are not sufficient allegations to exclude popular culture from the political field, for one would have to exclude much run-of-the-mill "serious" journalism and policy documents as well. C. Campbell (1995) even concludes, after having analyzed hours of television news, that television fiction provides a more accurate picture of race in America than the news media do. In that context, it is telling that the first realistic mainstream summoning of a black president in the United States appeared in a prime-time television series. Yet, as it was not my purpose to present the popular style as a better means of political exchange than the modernist style, it is not my aim to hold up popular culture as more democratic or inclusive than other forms of political communication. Just as the exclusive modernist understanding of politics is limiting, an exclusive popular understanding of politics would be limiting. Popular culture does have its flaws, but it needs to be acknowledged as a relevant resource for political citizenship: a resource that produces comprehension and respect for popular political voices and that allows for more people to perform as citizens; a resource that can make citizenship more pleasurable, more engaging, and more inclusive. In other words, a resource that can entertain the citizen.

NOTES

1. Canovan also typifies an "agrarian" populism based in a romantic appreciation of "the land," which does not directly bear on the discussion here.
2. Dryzek (1990) is the common reference here.

References

Aalberts, C., and L. van Zoonen. 2001. Politics in popular music. Paper presented at the Annual Conference of the Society for the Advancement of Social Economics (SASE), June, Amsterdam.

Abercrombie, N., and B. Longhurst. 1998. *Audiences: A sociological theory of performance and imagination*. London: Sage.

Adorno, T., et al. 1950. *The authoritarian personality*. New York: Harper.

Ahmed, K. 2000. Seven days that spun out of Blair's control. *Observer*, July 9. Accessed at http://observer.guardian.co.uk/politics/story/0,6903,341392,00.html (June 14, 2004).

Algemeen Dagblad. 2001. Politici Delfzijl hebben ruggengraat van vanillevla. September 11.

All hail "The American Candidate." 2003. *Electronic Media*, January 27. Accessed at www.tvbarn.com/archives/009242.html.

Ang, I. 1985. *Watching "Dallas": Soap opera and the melodramatic imagination*. London: Methuen.

Armstrong, E. G. 1993. The rhetoric of violence in rap and country music. *Sociological Inquiry* 63(1): 64–83.

Ash, T. G. 2000. A reality show that is riveting the world. *New York Times*, November 28, 2000.

———. 2002. A nation in denial. *Guardian*, March 7. Accessed at www.guardian.co.uk/comment/story/0,3604,663017,00.html (June 13, 2004).

Ayres, B. D. 1999. Political briefing: Political soap opera rivets Mississippi. *New York Times*, June 11, 1999.

Baker, K. 1993. *The turbulent years: My life in politics*. London: Faber and Faber.

Bare, J. 1993. The role of non-traditional news sources in the 1991 presidential campaign. Paper presented at the annual conference of the American Association of Public Opinion Research, May, St. Charles, Illinois.

Barnhurst, K. G. 1997. Media democracy: How young citizens experience the news in the United States and Spain. Ph.D. diss., University of Amsterdam.

———. 1998. Politics in the fine meshes: Young citizens, power and media. *Media, Culture and Society* 20:201–218.

Barnhurst, K. G., and E. Wartella. 1991. Newspapers and citizenship: Young adults' subjective experience of newspapers. *Critical Studies in Mass Communication* 8:195–209.

Baskaran, S. 1981. *The message bearers: The nationalist politics and the entertainment media in South India, 1880–1945.* Madras (Chennai), India: Cre-A.

Baxter, R. L., C. de Riemer, A. Landini, L. Leslie, and M. W. Singletary. 1986. A content analysis of music videos. *Journal of Broadcasting and Electronic Media* 29:333–340.

Bayles, M. 1994. *Hole in our soul: The loss of beauty and meaning in American popular music.* New York: Free Press.

Baym, N. 2000. *Tune in, log on: Soap, fandom and online community.* London: Sage.

BBC. 2000. Blair baby sparks leave debate. May 21. Accessed at http://news.bbc .co.uk/1/hi/uk/757698.stm (March 18, 2004).

Bean, C., and A. Mughan. 1989. Leadership effects in parliamentary elections in Australia and Britain. *American Political Science Review* 83(4): 1165–1179.

Beavers, S. 2003. *The West Wing* as pedagogical tool: Using drama to examine American politics and media perceptions of our political system. In *"The West Wing": The American presidency as television drama,* edited by P. C. Rollins and J. E. O'Connor, 175–186. New York: Syracuse University Press.

Bellah, R., R. Madsen, W. Sullivan, A. Swidler, and S. Tipton. 1986. *Habits of the heart: Individualism and commitment in American life.* Berkeley: University of California Press.

Bennett, H. S., and J. Ferrell. 1987. Music videos and epistemic socialization. *Youth and Society* 18:344–362.

Bennett, S., S. Rhine, R. Flickinger, and L. Bennett. 1999. "Video malaise" revisited: Public trust in media and government. *Harvard International Journal of Press/Politics* 4(4): 8–23.

Berger, A. A. 1982. *Media analysis techniques.* London: Sage.

Berk, P. 1997. Getting down to business in Moliere's "Le Bourgeois Gentilhomme" (French theater). *Contemporary Theatre Review* 6:57–76.

Binder, A. 1993. Constructing racial rhetoric: Media depictions of harm in heavy metal and rap music. *American Sociological Review* 58:753–767.

Bird, E. 1990. The Kennedy story in folklore and tabloids: Intertextuality in political communication. In *Politics in familiar contexts: Projecting politics through popular media,* edited by R. Savage and D. Nimmo, 247–268. Norwood, N.J.: Ablex.

———. 1992. *For enquiring minds: A cultural study of the supermarket tabloids.* Knoxville: University of Tennessee Press.

Black Public Sphere Collective, eds. 1995. *The Black Public Sphere.* Chicago: University of Chicago Press.

Blackhurst, C. 2001. Hamilton: A man clinging to his tattered reputation. *Independent,* August 11.

Blumenthal, S. 2003. *The Clinton wars: An insider's account of the White House years.* London: Viking Books.

Blumler, J. 1999. Political communication systems all change: A response to Kees Brants. *European Journal of Communication* 14(2): 241–249.

Boggs, C. 2001. Social capital and political fantasy: Robert Putnam's *Bowling Alone. Theory and Society* 30(2): 281–297.

Boorstin, D. 1972. *The image: A guide to pseudo-events in America.* New York: Atheneum.

Bourdieu, P. 1984. *Distinction: A social critique of the judgment of taste.* Cambridge, Mass.: Harvard University Press. Translation of *La distinction: critique sociale du jugement.* Paris: Les Éditions de Minuit, 1979.

———. 1991. *Language and symbolic power.* Cambridge: Polity Press.

———. 1998. *On television.* New York: New Press.

Branigan, T. 2002. George Michael video rages at US policy in Middle East and attacks "poodle" Blair. *Guardian,* July 2.

Brants, K. 1998. Who's afraid of infotainment? *European Journal of Communication* 13(3): 315–335.

Broek, M. van den. 2000. Sporen onder een vergeten viaduct. *Volkskrant,* December 23.

Broh, C. 1980. Horse-race journalism: Reporting the polls in the 1976 presidential elections. *Public Opinion Quarterly* 44(4): 514–529.

Brooks, J. 2001. Millbankers. *Guardian Unlimited,* June 5. Accessed at http://politics .guardian.co.uk/news/story/0,,502030,00.htm.

Brown, A. 1998. *Fanatics! Power, identity & fandom in football.* London: Routledge.

Brown, J. D., and K. Campbell. 1986. Race and gender in music videos: The same beat but a different drummer. *Journal of Communication* 36(1): 94–106.

Brown, M. 1997. Feminism and cultural politics: Television audiences and Hillary Rodham Clinton. *Political Communication* 14: 255–270.

Brown, M. E. 1990. *Television and women's culture: The politics of the popular.* London: Sage.

Brown, M. E., and D. C. Gardetto. 2000. Representing Hillary Rodham Clinton: Gender, meaning and news media. In *Women, politics and communication,* edited by A. Sreberny and L. van Zoonen, 21–53. Cresskill, N.J.: Hampton Press.

Brownstein, R. 1992. *The power and the glory: The Hollywood-Washington connection.* New York: Vintage Books.

Bryant, J., and S. Thompson. 2002. *Fundamentals of media effects.* Boston: McGraw-Hill.

Buckingham, D. 2000. *The making of citizens: Young people, news and politics.* London: Routledge.

Burden, B., and A. Mughan. 1999. Public opinion and Hillary Rodham Clinton. *Public Opinion Quarterly* 63(2): 237–250.

Burke, P. 1978. *Popular culture in early modern Europe.* Aldershot, UK: Wildwood House. Dutch translation, *Volkscultuur in Europa, 1500–1800.* Amsterdam: Agon.

Burrell, B. 1997. *Public opinion: The first ladyship and Hillary Rodham Clinton.* New York: Garland.

———. 2000. Hillary Rodham Clinton as first lady: The people's perspective. *Social Science Journal* 37(4): 519–546.

Byars, J. 1991. *All that Hollywood allows: Re-reading gender in 1950s melodrama.* London: Routledge.

Cairney, P. 1997. Advocacy coalitions and policy change. Paper presented to the 1997 Annual Conference of the Political Studies Association, April, Jordanstown.

Calhoun, G., ed. 1992. *Habermas and the public sphere*. Cambridge, Mass.: MIT Press.

Campbell, A., P. Converse, W. Miller, and D. Stokes. 1960. *The American Voter*. New York: Wiley.

Campbell, C. 1995. *Race, myth and the news*. London: Sage.

Campbell, K. 1998. The discursive performance of femininity: Hating Hillary. *Rhetoric and Public Affairs* 1:1–19.

Canovan, M. 1981. *Populism*. New York: Jovanovich.

———. 1999. Trust the people: Populism and the two faces of democracy. *Political Studies* 17:2–16.

Carey, J. W., ed. 1988. *Media, myth and narrative: Television and the press*. Beverly Hills, Calif.: Sage.

Carmines, E., and J. Stimson. 1980. The two faces of issue voting. *American Political Science Review* 74:78–91.

Carter, C., G. Branston, and S. Allen, eds. 1998. *News, gender and power*. London: Routledge.

Cartland, B. 1955. *The enchanted waltz*. Magna Large Print Books.

Censorship Alert. 1986. Rock music & videos under attack. April. Accessed at www.freedomparty.org/issupapr/ca_o8.htm (September 16, 2002).

Center for American Women and Politics (CAWP). 2003a. Women and politics. Accessed at www.cawp.rutgers.edu (March 2004).

———. 2003b. Women who succeeded their husbands in Congress. Fact sheet. Accessed at www.cawp.rutgers.edu (January 14, 2004).

Cernetig, M. 2002. *American Idol* meets *The West Wing*. *Globe and Mail*, September 21. Accessed at www.theglobeandmail.com/servlet/ArticleNews/printarticle/gam/20020921/UTVTVN.

Chambers, S., and A. Costain, eds. 2000. *Deliberation, democracy and the media*. Lanham, Md.: Rowman & Littlefield.

Chastanger, C. 1999. The Parents' Music Resource Center: From information to censorship. *Popular Music* 18(2): 179–192.

Chen, D. 2000. In Dutchess, politics, sex, suicide and a big man behind the curtain. *New York Times*, February 4.

Christenson, P. 1992. The effects of parental advisory labels on adolescent music preferences. *Journal of Communication* 42(1): 106–113.

Christenson, P. G., and D. F. Roberts. 1998. *It's not only rock and roll: Popular music in the lives of adolescents*. Cresskill, N.J.: Hampton.

Clarke, H. D., and M. C. Stewart. 1998. The decline of parties in the minds of citizens. *Annual Review of Political Science* 1:367–378.

Clinton, Hillary Rodham. *See* Rodham Clinton, Hillary.

Cloonan, M., and R. Garofalo. 2003. *Policing pop (sound matters)*. Philadelphia: Temple University Press.

Cloonan, M., and J. Street. 1997. Politics and popular music: From policing to packaging. *Parliamentary Affairs* 50:223–234.

CNN. 2002. George Michael faces public test. Accessed at www.cgi.cnn.com/2002/SHOWBIZ/Music/07/29/george.song/ (September 4, 2002).

———. 2003. Interview with Laura Bush. *Larry King Live*, December 21.

Cohen, M. 1988. *The Sisterhood: The true story of the women who changed the world.* New York: Simon and Schuster.

Coleman, S. 2003. *A tale of two houses: The House of Commons, the Big Brother House and the people at home.* London: Hansard Society.

Corner, J. 2003. Mediated persona and political culture. In *Media and the Restyling of Politics*, edited by J. Corner and D. Pels, 66–84. London: Sage.

Corner, J., and D. Pels, eds. 2003. *Media and the Restyling of Politics.* London: Sage.

Cos, G., and B. Snee. 2001. "New York, New York": Being and creating identity in the 2000 New York State Senate Race. *American Behavioral Scientist* 44(12): 2014–2029.

Cradock, P. 1997. *In pursuit of British interests: Reflections on foreign policy under Margaret Thatcher and John Major.* London: John Murray.

Creech, K. 2001. The Internet goes to court: A Napster case study. Paper presented at Broadcast Education Association Annual Convention, April 20. Accessed at www.business.uiuc.edu/gebauer/Courses/Readings/InternetGoesToCourt_NapsterCase_Creech.doc (March 11, 2004).

Crouse, T. 1972. *The boys on the bus.* New York: Random House.

Cutler, F. 2002. The simplest short cut of all: Sociodemographic characteristics and electoral choice. *The Journal of Politics* 64(2): 466–490.

Dahlgren, P. 1995. *Television and the public sphere: Citizenship, democracy and the media.* London: Sage.

Dalton, R. J. 1996. *Citizen politics: Public opinion and political parties in advanced Western democracies.* Chatham, N.J.: Chatham House.

———. 2000. The decline of party identifications. In *Parties without partisans: Political change in advanced industrial democracies*, edited by R. J. Dalton and M. Wattenberg, 37–63. New York: Oxford Press.

Damasio, A. R. 1995. *Descartes' error: Emotion, reason and the human brain.* New York: Avon Books.

Davis, K. 1995. *Reshaping the female body: The dilemmas of plastic surgery.* London: Routledge.

Dayan, D. 2001. The peculiar public of television. *Media, Culture and Society* 23(6): 743–767.

Deen, F. 2001. Borst wil vooral jeugd redden met kruistocht tegen roken [Borst wants to save youth in particular with crusade against smoking]. *Volkskrant*, February 20.

De Haan, I. 2000. From Moses to Maggie: Popular political wisdom and the republican tradition in political thought. *Javnost/The Public* 7(2): 33–45.

De Vos, H. 1978. *Inleiding tot de wijsbegeerte van de Grieken en de Romeinen.* Baarn, the Netherlands: Het Wereldvenster.

Dillon, J. 2001. Labour sets out its (tele)vision for Britain. *Independent*, May 20. Accessed at www.independent.co.uk/story.jsp?story=73491.

Dines, G., and J. Humez, eds. 1995. *Gender, race and class in media.* London: Sage.

Dor, M., and R. Federman. 1964. *Der politische Witz* [The political joke]. Munich: Verlag Kurt Densch.

Doran, S. 1996. *Monarchy & matrimony: The courtships of Elizabeth I.* London: Routledge.

Dowd, M. 2000. Liberties: Tin cup couple. *New York Times,* September 24.

Dryzek, J. 1990. *Discursive democracy: Politics, policy and political science.* Cambridge: Cambridge University Press.

Durlauf, S. 2002. *Bowling Alone:* A review essay. *Journal of Economic Behavior & Organization* 47(3): 259–273.

Dyer, R. 1979. *Stars.* London: British Film Institute.

Edelman. M. 1964. *The symbolic uses of politics.* Urbana: University of Illinois Press.

Elchardus, M. 2002. *De dramademocratie.* Antwerp, the Netherlands: Lannoo.

El fracaso, el bochorno y la frase del año. 2003. January 10. Accessed at www4.terra.com.ar/canales/cgi-bin/imprimir.pl?noticia_id=60879&canal_id=2.

Eliasoph, N. 1998. *Avoiding politics: How Americans produce apathy in everyday life.* Cambridge: Cambridge University Press.

Elshtain, J. B. 1981. *Public man, private woman: Women in social and political thought.* Oxford: Martin Rovertson.

Etzersdorfer, I. 1997. "Personality" and "politics": Concerning the interaction of political and psychological factors related to interdisciplinary approaches of "political leadership" research. *Österreichische Zeitschrift für Politikwissenschaft* 26(4): 377–391.

Faber, M. J. 2000. Srebenica: de soap na het fiasco. *Trouw,* May 27.

Feeney, M. 2004. Torture chamber. Accessed at http://slate.msn.com/id/2093269 (February 9, 2004).

Fennema, M. 1982. Tussen vierde en vijfde macht [Between fourth and fifth estate]. In *Het politicologendebat: wat is politiek?* [The political science debate: What is politics?], edited by M. Fennema and R. van der Wouden, 17–35. Amsterdam: Van Gennep.

Fisher, R., and J. Kling. 1993. *Mobilizing the community: Local politics in the era of the global city.* Thousand Oaks, Calif.: Sage.

Fiske, J. 1987. *Television culture.* London: Methuen.

——. 1989. *Understanding popular culture.* London: Unwin Hyman.

——. 1992. Popularity and the politics of information. In *Journalism and popular culture,* edited by P. Dahlgren and C. Sparks, 45–63. London: Sage.

Fox, W. S., and J. D. Williams. 1974. Political orientation and music preferences among college students. *Public Opinion Quarterly* 38: 352–371.

Franklin, B. 1994. *Packaging politics: Political communication in Britain's media democracy.* London: Arnold.

Fraser, A. 1988. *Boadicea's chariot.* London: George Weidenfeld & Nicholson.

Freedland, J. 2001. The right is left bereft. *Guardian,* August 22. Accessed at www.guardian.co.uk/comment/story/0,3604,540515,00.html.

Freedman, J. 2002. *Media violence and its effect in aggression: Assessing the scientific evidence.* Toronto: University of Toronto Press.

Freeman, J., ed. 1983. *Social movements of the sixties and seventies.* New York: Longman.

Fried, C. B. 1996. Bad rap for rap: Bias in reactions to music lyrics. *Journal of Applied Social Psychology* 26(23): 2135–2146.

——. 1999. Who's afraid of rap: Differential reactions to music lyrics. *Journal of Applied Social Psychology* 29(4): 705–721.

Frith, S. 1978. *The sociology of rock*. London: Constable.

Frith, S., and J. Street. 1992. Rock against racism and red wedge: From music to politics, from politics to music. In *Rockin' the boat: Mass music and mass movements*, edited by R. Garofalo, 67–80. Boston: South End.

FX won't elect perfect candidate. 2003. Accessed at http://tv.zap2it.com/tveditorial/tve_main/1,1002,271%7C81377%7C1%7C,00.html (June 13, 2004).

Gaffney, J. 2001. Imagined relationships: Political leadership in contemporary democracies. *Parliamentary Affairs* 54(1): 20–29.

Galston, W. A. 2001. Political knowledge, political engagement, and civic education. *Annual Review of Political Science* 4:217–234.

Gamson, J. 2001. Jessica Hahn, media whore: Sex scandals and female publicity. *Critical Studies in Media Communication* 18(2): 157–173.

Gamson, W. 1992. *Talking politics*. Cambridge: Cambridge University Press.

Gardetto, D. 1997. Hillary Rodham Clinton, symbolic gender politics, and the *New York Times*: January–November 1992. *Political Communication* 14(2): 225–240.

Garlick, B., S. Dixon, and P. Allen, eds. 1992. *Stereotypes of women in power: Historical and revisionist views*. Westport, Conn.: Greenwood Press.

Garofalo, R., ed. 1992a. *Rockin' the boat: Mass music and mass movements*. Boston: South End Press.

———. 1992b. Understanding mega-events: If we are the world, then how do we change it? In *Rockin' the boat: Mass music and mass movements*, edited by R. Garofalo, 15–35. Boston: South End Press.

Garret, P. 2002. Yes minister: Reviewing the "looking after children" experience and identifying the messages for social work research. *British Journal of Social Work* 32:831–846.

Geraghty, C. 1990. *Women and soap opera*. Cambridge: Polity Press.

Gidengil, E. 2003. Voter characteristics and leader effects. Paper delivered at the 2003 Meeting of the European Consortium for Political Research, September, Marburg, Germany.

Gidengil, E., and J. Everitt. 1999. Metaphors and misrepresentation: Gendered mediation in news coverage of the 1993 Canadian leadership debates. *Harvard International Journal of Press/Politics* 4: 48–65.

Giles, D. 2000. *Illusions of immortality: A psychology of fame and celebrity*. London: Macmillan.

Gitlin, T. 2002. *Media unlimited: How the torrent of images and sounds overwhelms our lives*. New York: Henry Holt.

Gledhill, C., ed. 1991. *Stardom: Industry of desire*. London: Routledge.

Godschalk, B. 1999. Wat valt er nog te kiezen. *Trouw*, February 27.

Gordon, M. R. 1999. On Russia's far east fringe, unrealpolitik. *New York Times*, February 14.

Gould, L., ed. 1996. *American first ladies: Their lives and their legacy*. New York: Garland.

Grice, A., and D. Macintyre. 1999. I think this government is trying to conduct politics as a soap opera. *Independent*, December 23. Accessed at www.independent.co.uk/story.jsp?story=1451 (September 6, 2001).

Gripsrud, J. 1998. Cultural studies and intervention in television policy. *European Journal of Cultural Studies* 1(1): 83–96.

Grossberg, L. 1992. *We gotta get out of this place: Popular conservatism and postmodern culture.* London: Routledge.

Guardian. 2000. Another blow for trust. October 17. Accessed at www .guardian.co.uk/leaders/story/0,3604,383561,00.html.

Gumbel, A. 2001. Dark days for the blue-eyed boy of Condit County. *Independent,* July 15. Accessed at www.independent.co.uk/story.jsp?story=83560.

Haberman, C. 2000. NYC: Inviting an invasion of privacy. *New York Times,* July 8.

Habermas, J. 1989. *The structural transformation of the public sphere.* Cambridge: Polity Press.

Hagedorn, J. 2001. Another chance for people power. *New York Times,* March 16.

Hageman, E. 2000. Gewoon een uitglijer. *Trouw,* January 15.

Hague, W. 2000. Keynote address to the Conservative Party Conference 2000. Edited version in *Independent,* October 6. Accessed at www.independent.co.uk/story.jsp?story=10969 (September 6, 2001).

Hall, S. [1973] 1980. In *Culture, Media, Language: Working Papers in Cultural Studies, 1972–79,* edited by Centre for Contemporary Cultural Studies, 128–138. London: Hutchinson.

———. 1991. Over postmodernisme en articulatie: Een interview met Stuart Hall [On postmodernism and articulation: An interview with Stuart Hall]. In *Het minimale zelf en andere opstellen* [The minimal self and other essays], translated and edited by Anil Ramdas, 19–43. Nijmegen, the Netherlands: SUN.

Hall, S., and T. Jefferson, eds. 1980. *Resistance through rituals: Youth subcultures in post-war Britain.* London: Hutchinson.

Haller, M. 1991. Policy gambling, entertainment and the emergence of black politics: Chicago from 1900 to 1940. *Journal of Social History* 24:719–739.

Hallin, D. 1996. Commercialism and professionalism in the American news media. In *Mass media and society,* 2nd ed., edited by J. Curran and M. Gurevitch, 243–265. London: Arnold.

Hamilton, N. 2003. *Bill Clinton: An American journey.* London: Century.

Hammond, R. 1993. *The power of love.* London: Mills and Boon. Dutch edition, *Uitverkoren liefde.* Amsterdam: Harlequin Holland.

Harris, J. 2003. *The last party: Britpop, Blair and the demise of English rock.* London: Fourth Estate.

Hart, R. 1994. *Seducing America: How television charms the modern voter.* New York: Oxford University Press.

Hartley, J. 1992. *The politics of pictures: The creation of the public in the age of popular media.* London: Routledge.

Hayton, H. 2003. The king's two bodies: Identity and office in Sorkin's *West Wing.* In *"The West Wing": The American presidency as television drama,* edited by P. C. Rollins and J. E. O'Connor, 63–79. New York: Syracuse University Press.

Hermes, J. 1995. *Reading women's magazines.* Cambridge: Polity Press.

Hicks, J. P. 2000a. Bitter primary contest hits ethnic nerve among blacks. *New York Times,* August 31.

———. 2000b. Vitriol flows in race for Congress. *New York Times,* September 8.

Hill, A., and G. Palmer, eds. 2001. *Big Brother. Television and New Media* (special issue, August).

Hills, M. 2002. *Fan cultures.* London: Routledge.

Hirsch, A. 1991. *Talking heads: Political talk shows and their star pundits*. New York: St. Martin's Press.

Hirsch, P. 1980. The scary world of the non-viewer and other anomalies: A re-analysis of Gerbner et al.'s findings on cultivation analysis, part I. *Communication Research* 7(4): 403–456.

———. 1981. On not learning from one's own mistakes: A re-analysis of Gerbner et al.'s findings on cultivation analysis, part II. *Communication Research* 8(1): 3–37.

Hobson, D. 1989. Soap operas at work. In *Remote control: Television, audiences and cultural power*, edited by E. Seiter, H. Borchers, G. Kreutzner, and E. Warth, 150–167. London: Routledge.

Hodge, R., and G. Kress. 1988. *Social semiotics*. Cambridge: Polity Press.

Hoedeman, J., and L. Nicolasen. 2000. Van Hees vergat in PvdA gezag te verwerven. *De Volkskrant*, November 15.

Hoge, W. 1999. London journal. *New York Times*, December 23, sec. A, 4.

Hollander, B. 1995. The new news and the 1992 presidential campaign: Perceived vs. actual political knowledge. *Journalism and Mass Communication Quarterly* 72: 786–798.

Hoopes, S. 1997. Reforming the public sector: The British case. Paper presented to the Annual Conference of the Political Studies Association, April, Jordanstown.

Independent. 2000. Stop acting like a soap star. July 18. Accessed at www.independent .co.uk/story.jsp?story=41040 (September 6, 2001).

International Movie Database (IMDb). 2001. User comments for "West Wing, The." Accessed at http://us.imdb.com/commentsshow?0200276 (November 22, 2001).

Iyengar, S., and D. Kinder 1987. *News that matters: Television and American opinion*. Chicago: University of Chicago Press.

Iyengar, S., and W. McGuire. 1993. *Explorations in political psychology*. Durham, N.C.: Duke University Press.

Iyengar, S., N. A. Valentino, S. Ansolabehere, and A. F. Simon. 1997. Running as a woman: Gender stereotyping in political campaigns. In *Women, media and politics*, edited by P. Norris, 77–98. New York: Oxford University Press.

Jaffee, L. 1987. The politics of rock. *Popular Music and Society* 11(4): 19–30.

Jaggar, A. 1983. *Feminist politics and human nature*. Totowa, N.J.: Rowman and Allanheld.

———. 1999. Multicultural democracy. *Journal of Political Philosophy* 7(3): 308–329.

Jamieson, K. H. 1988. *Eloquence in an electronic age: The transformation of political speechmaking*. New York: Oxford University Press.

———. 1996. *Packaging the presidency: A history and criticism of presidential campaign advertising*. New York: Oxford University Press.

Jenkins, H. 1992. *Textual poachers: Television fans and participatory cultures*. London: Routledge.

Jobes, D., A. Berman, P. O'Carroll, S. Eastgard, and S. Knickmeyer. 1996. The Kurt Cobain suicide crisis: Perspectives from research, public health and the news media. *Suicide and Life-Threatening Behaviour* 26:260–271.

Johnson, T. J., M. A. M. Braima, and J. Sothirajah. 1999. Doing the traditional media sidestep: Comparing the effects of the Internet and other nontraditional media with traditional media in the 1996 presidential campaign. *Journalism and Mass Communication Quarterly* 76:99–123.

Jones, S. 1991. Ban(ned) in the USA: Popular music and censorship. *Journal of Communication Inquiry* 15(1): 73–87.

Joseph, J. 2000. Yesterday's viewing: The prime time ministers. [London] *Times*, December 12. Accessed at www.newsint-archive.co.uk/pages/main.asp (October 2001).

Just, M., A. Crigler, D. Alger, T. Cook, M. Kern, and D. West. 1996. *Crosstalk: Citizens, candidates and the media in the presidential campaign*. Chicago: University of Chicago Press.

Kafka, F. 1925. *Der Prozess* [The trial]. Reprint, New York: Everyman's Library, 1992.

Kahn, K., and A. Gordon. 1997. How women campaign for the US Senate. In *Women, media and politics*, edited by P. Norris, 59–77. New York: Oxford University Press.

Kalshoven, F. 1999. De herfstdip van Gerrit Zalm. *De Volkskrant*, October 2.

Katwala, S. 2003. Sorry Martin, President Bartlett would back this war. *UK Observer*, March 16. Accessed at http://bartlet4america.org/news/000381.html (February 9, 2004).

Katz, E., and P. Lazarsfeld. 1964. *Personal influence: The part played by people in the flow of mass communications*. New York: Free Press.

Katz, E., and T. Liebes. 1990. *The export of meaning: Cross cultural readings of "Dallas."* New York: Oxford University Press.

Kazin, M. 1995. *The populist persuasion: An American history*. New York: Basic Books.

Keighron, P. 1998. The politics of ridicule: Satire and television. In *Dissident voices: The politics of television and cultural change*, edited by M. Wayne, 127–145. London: Pluto Press.

Kellner, D. 1999. The X-Files and the aesthetics and politics of postmodern pop. *Journal of Aesthetics and Art Criticism* 57(2): 161–175.

———. 2002. Presidential politic: The movie. *American Behavioral Scientist* 46(4): 467–486.

Kennedy, E., and S. Mendus. 1987. *Women in Western political philosophy*. New York: St. Martin's Press.

Kennedy, R. 2000. The mayor's separation: The reaction. *New York Times*, May 12.

Kibble-White, J. 2002. Partly political broadcasts. Accessed at http://offthetelly.users.btopenworld.com/drama/political.htm (February 9, 2004).

Kielinger, T. 2000. Indiskretionen aus dem Inneren Kreis der Downing Street. *Die Welt*, October 19.

King, P. 1990. *Sex, drugs & rock 'n' roll: Healing today's troubled youth in the 90s*. Deerfield Beach, Fla.: Health Communications.

Kington, M. 2000. That old game show called politics. *Independent*, August 31. Accessed at http://argument.independent.co.uk/regular_columnists/miles_kington/story.jsp?story=43313.

Kleinrensink, J. 2001. Partijen zonder ideologie geven LN de ruimte. *Volkskrant*, June 12.

Knack, S. 1997. The reappearing American voter: Why did turnout rise in '92? *Electoral Studies* 16(1): 17–32.

Knight, P. 2000. *Conspiracy culture: From Kennedy to "The X-Files."* London: Routledge.

Krauss, C. 2000. Fujimori's fall: A nation's lion to broken man. *New York Times*, December 3.

———. 2001. An upriver battle for votes in Peru. *New York Times*, June 2.

Krutnick, F. 1991. *In a lonely street: Film, noir, genre, masculinity*. London: Routledge.

Kurtz, H. 1998. *Spin cycle: Inside the Clinton propaganda machine*. New York: Free Press.

Landale, J. 2001. Soap stars help Blair woo young vote. [London] *Times*, June 4. Accessed at www.thetimes.co.uk/article/0,,640-2001191070,00.htm.

Lane, C. 2003. The White House culture of gender and race in *The West Wing*: Insights from the margins. In *"The West Wing": The American presidency as television drama*, edited by P. C. Rollins and J. E. O'Connor, 32–42. New York: Syracuse University Press.

Lanting, B. 2000. Van Amerikanen mag de soap nog wel even duren [Americans would like this soap to last]. *Volkskrant*, November 17. Accessed at www.volkskrant.nl/zoek (September 6, 2001).

Lasswell, H. 1948. *Power and personality*. New York: W. W. Norton.

Law, I. 2002. *Race in the news*. Basingstoke: Palgrave.

Leijenaar, M. 1992. *Women and decision making in the late twentieth century*. Leiden: Martinus Nijhoff.

Lester, P., ed. 1996. *Images that injure: Pictorial stereotypes in the media*. Westport, Conn.: Praeger.

Letwin, O. 2003. Perspectives in criminal justice. Working paper no. 10. Faculty of Law and Social Sciences, University of Central England, Birmingham.

Leurdijk, A. 2000. Should I maybe perform striptease? Gendered representations of race relations and multicultural society in American and Dutch talk shows. In *Gender, politics and communication*, edited by A. Sreberny and L. van Zoonen, 251–274. Cresskill, N.J.: Hampton Press.

Levine, M. 2003. *The West Wing* (NBC) and the West Wing (DC): Myth and reality in television portrayal of the White House. In *"The West Wing": The American presidency as television drama*, edited by P. C. Rollins and J. E. O'Connor, 42–62. New York: Syracuse University Press.

Lewis, L. 1992. *The adoring audience: Fan culture and popular media*. London: Routledge.

Lichfield, J. 2001. Fugitive in Dumas affair confronts accusers in court. *Independent*, February 8.

Livingstone, S., and P. Lunt. 1994. *Talk on television: Audience participation and public debate*. London: Routledge.

Lodge, M., and K. McGraw 1995. *Political judgment: Structure and process*. Ann Arbor: University of Michigan Press.

Lont, C. 1992. Women's music: No longer a small private party. In *Rockin' the boat: Mass music and mass movements*, edited by R. Garofalo, 241–255. Boston: South End Press.

Lull, J., and S. Hinerman, eds. 1997. *Media scandals: Morality and Desire in the Popular Culture Marketplace*. Cambridge: Polity.

Lynxwiler, J., and D. Gay. 2000. Moral boundaries and deviant music: Public attitudes toward heavy metal and rap. *Deviant Behavior* 21:63–85.

MacCaffrey, W. 1993. *Elizabeth I*. London: Edward Arnold.

MacDonald, M. 1995. *Representing women: Myths of femininity in the popular media*. London: Edward Arnold.

MacGinniss, J. 1969. *The selling of the president 1968*. Harmondsworth, UK: Penguin Books.

Macintyre, D. 2000a. Mr. Mandelson is more than a star in a soap opera. *Independent*, October 19.

———. 2000b. The furore over Mr. Portillo proves the Tories are in crisis. *Independent*, November 30. Accessed at www.independent.co.uk/story.jsp?story=42253 (September 6, 2001).

———. 2001. The iron law of politics dictated that he had to go. *Independent*, January 25.

Maguire, K. 2001. Masters of the political black arts go to war. *Guardian*, March 10. Accessed at www.guardian.co.uk/guardianpolitics/story/0,3605,449373,00.html.

Mander, J. 1977. *Four arguments for the elimination of television*. New York: Morrow Quill Paperbacks.

Manin, B. 1997. *The principles of representative government*. Cambridge: Cambridge University Press.

Marcus, G. E. 2002. *The sentimental citizen: Emotion in democratic politics*. University Park: Pennsylvania State University Press.

Marcus, G. E., W. R. Neuman, and M. MacKuen. 2000. *Affective intelligence and political judgment*. Chicago: University of Chicago Press.

Marelli, S. 2002. El candidato de la TV: Videopolitica o chunga. Accessed at www.etcetera.com.mx/pag73ne25.asp.

Marshall, P. D. 1997. *Celebrity and power: Fame in contemporary culture*. Minneapolis: University of Minnesota Press.

Marshall, T. H. 1950. *Citizenship and social class and other essays*. Cambridge: Cambridge University Press.

Martin, L., and K. Segrave. 1993. *Anti-rock: The opposition to rock 'n' roll*. New York: DeCapo.

Martinez, T. 1997. Popular culture as oppositional culture: Rap as resistance. *Sociological Perspectives* 40(2): 265–286.

Mattelart, M. 1986. *Women, media, crisis: Femininity and disorder*. London: Comedia.

Mazzoleni, G., J. Stewart, and B. Horsfield, eds. 2003. *The media and neo-populism*. Westport, Conn.: Praeger.

McCain, Robert Stacey. 2003. Obituary for Neil Postman. *Guardian*, November 4. Accessed at http://education.guardian.co.uk/print/0,3858,4789048-110843,00.html (November 26, 2003).

McDonald, J. R. 1988. Censoring rock lyrics: A historical analysis of the debate. *Youth and Society* 19(3): 294–313.

McElvoy, A. 2001. How will the New Labour family recover from its tiff? *Independent*, April 4. Accessed at www.independent.co.uk.

McLaren, M. 2000. Ignore these nasty politicians, London needs an independent voice. *Independent*, February 8. Accessed at http://news.independent.co.uk/uk/politics/story.jsp?story=9816.

McNair, B. 2003. *Introduction to political communication*. London: Routledge.

McSmith, A. 2000. Is Big Brother watching you watching the soaps? *Observer*, January 30. Accessed at http://politics.guardian.co.uk/news/story/0,,456981,,00.htm.

Meijer, F. 2002. *Keizers sterven niet in bed: Van Caesar tot Romulus Augustus 44 v. chr.– 476 n. chr* [Emperors do not die in their beds]. Amsterdam: Van Gennep.

Melucci, A. 1988. *Nomads of the present: Social movements and individual needs in contemporary society.* London: Hutchinson Radius.

Mendelsohn, M. 1996. The media and interpersonal communication: The priming of issues, leaders and party identification. *Journal of Politics* 58(1): 112–123.

Meyer, T. 2002. *Media democracy: How the media colonize politics.* Cambridge: Polity Press.

Miles, M. B., and M. Huberman. 1984. *Qualitative data analysis: A sourcebook of new methods.* Beverly Hills, Calif.: Sage.

Miller, A., M. Wattenberg, and O. Malanchuk. 1986. Schematic assessments of presidential candidates. *American Political Science Review* 80:521–540.

Miller, T. 1998. *Technologies of truth: Cultural citizenship and the popular media.* Minneapolis: University of Minnesota Press.

Miller, T., and A. McHoul. 1998. *Popular culture and everyday life.* London: Sage.

Modleski, T. 1984. *Loving with a vengeance: Mass produced fantasies for women.* London: Methuen.

Morris, E. 1999. *Dutch: A memoir of Ronald Reagan.* New York: Random House.

Mouffe, C. 2000. *The democratic paradox.* London: Verso.

Mulgan, G. 1994. *Politics in an anti-political age.* Cambridge: Polity Press.

Munson, W. 1993. *All talk: The talkshow in media culture.* Philadelphia: Temple University Press.

Negus, K. 1996. *Popular music in theory: An introduction.* Cambridge: Polity.

Neve, B. 1992. *Film and politics in America: A social tradition.* London: Routledge.

———. 2000. Frames of presidential and candidate politics. *Javnost/The Public* 7(2): 19–33.

Newman, B. 1999. *Handbook of political marketing.* Thousand Oaks, Calif.: Sage.

Newton, K. 2003. May the weak force be with you: The role of mass media in modern politics. Keynote Address to the European Consortium for Political Research, September, Marburg, Germany.

Norris, P. 1996. Women politicians: Transforming Westminster? *Parliamentary Affairs* 49(1): 89–102.

———. 1997a. Women leaders worldwide. In *Women, media and politics,* edited by P. Norris, 149–166. New York: Oxford University Press.

———. 2000. *A virtuous circle: Political communication in postindustrial societies.* Cambridge: Cambridge University Press.

———, ed. 1997b. *Women, media and politics.* New York: Oxford University Press.

Oberdeck, K. 1999. *The evangelist and the impresario: Religion, entertainment, and cultural politics in America, 1884–1914.* Baltimore: Johns Hopkins University Press, 1999.

O'Brien, M. 2004. *Nazi cinema as enchantment: The politics of entertainment in the Third Reich.* Rochester, N.Y.: Camden House.

Ohr, D., and H. Oscarsson. 2003. Leader traits, leader image and vote choice. Paper delivered at the 2003 Meeting of the European Consortium for Political Research, September, Marburg, Germany.

Okin, S. 1979. *Women in Western political thought.* Princeton, N.J.: Princeton University Press.

Oliver, P. 1970. *The blues tradition.* New York: Oak.

O'Rourke, P. J. 1991. *Parliament of whores: A lone humorist attempts to explain the entire US government.* New York: Vintage Books.

Parenti, M. 1998. *Make-believe media: The politics of entertainment*. New York: St. Martin's Press.

Pateman, C. 1989. *The disorder of women*. Stanford, Calif.: Stanford University Press.

Patterson, T. 1993. *Out of order*. New York: Knopf.

Pels, D. 2003. Aesthetic representation and political style: Re-balancing identity and difference in media democracy. In *Media and the restyling of politics*, edited by J. Corner and D. Pels, 41–66. London: Sage.

Peterson, J. B., and P. G. Christenson. 1987. Political orientation and music preference in the 1980s. *Popular Music and Society* 11(4): 1–17.

Political Communication. 1997. *Hillary Rodham Clinton* 14 (special issue).

Pollack, M., and E. Hafner. 2000. Mainstreaming gender in the European Union. *Journal of European Public Policy* 7(3): 432–456.

Pomper, D. 2003. *The West Wing*: White House narratives that journalism cannot tell. In *"The West Wing": The American presidency as television drama*, edited by P. C. Rollins and J. E. O'Connor, 17–31. New York: Syracuse University Press.

Postman, N. 1985. *Amusing ourselves to death*. New York: Viking.

Pratt, R. 1990. *Rhythm and resistance: Explorations in the political uses of popular music*. New York: Praeger.

Prinsky, L. E., and J. L. Rosenbaum. 1987. "Leer-ics" or lyrics: Teenage impressions of rock 'n' roll. *Youth and Society* 18:384–397.

Propp, V. 1923. *Morphology of the folk tale*. English translation, 1958. Bloomington: Indiana University Press.

Putnam, R. 2000. *Bowling alone: The collapse and revival of American community*. New York: Simon and Schuster.

Radway, J. 1984. *Reading the romance: Women, patriarchy and popular literature*. Chapel Hill: University of North Carolina Press.

Rapping, E. 1992. *The movie of the week: Private stories, public events*. Minneapolis: University of Minneapolis Press.

———. 2000. US talk shows, feminism and the discourse of addiction. In *Gender, politics and communication*, edited by A. Sreberny and L. van Zoonen, 123–251. Cresskill, N.J.: Hampton Press.

Rawnsley, A. 2000. Tony's still winning the ratings war. *Observer*, July 9. Accessed at http://observer.guardian.co.uk/comment/story/0,6903,341470,00.html (June 13, 2004).

Reality TV search for Argentine politician. 2002. September 13. Accessed at http://news.bbc.co.uk/2/hi/entertainment/tv_and_radio/2255546.stm (March 17, 2003).

Rich, F. 2000. What's love got to do with it? *New York Times*, May 20.

Richards, S. 2000. We've had enough of the soap opera, now what about policy? *Independent*, October 22. Accessed at http://argument.independent.co.uk/commentators/story.jsp?story=40721.

Richardson, D. 2001. Extending citizenship: Cultural citizenship and sexuality. In *Culture and Citizenship*, edited by N. Stevenson, 153–167. London: Sage.

Roberts, S. L., and C. Lundin. 2001. College students, comedy and campaigns: Where American undergraduates get their political news and views. Paper presented at the WAPOR-conferentie, May, Rome.

Rock the Vote. 2002. *Mission statement: Rock the vote*. Accessed at www.rockthevote.org (October 4, 2002).

Rodham Clinton, H. 2003. *Living history.* New York: Simon and Schuster.

Rodman, G. B. 1996. *Elvis after Elvis: The posthumous career of a living legend.* London: Routledge.

Rogin, M., and K. Moran. 2003. Mr. Capra goes to Washington. *Representations* 84 (fall). Accessed at www.representations.org (February 3, 2004).

Rose, T. 1994. *Black noise: Rap music and black culture in contemporary America.* Hanover, N.H.: Wesleyan University Press.

Rosenberg, H. 2002. Prime-time presidents: It's wit versus grit. *Los Angeles Times*, November 25. Accessed at http://b4a.healthyinterest.net/news/000185.html (February 9, 2004).

Ross, K., and A. Sreberny. 2000. Women in the House: Media representation of British politicians. In *Gender, politics and communication*, edited by A. Sreberny and L. van Zoonen, 79–101. Cresskill, N.J.: Hampton Press.

Rother, L. 2000. Sao Paulo journal: What mayor's wife saw: A tangled tale of graft. *New York Times*, May 5.

Rothman, R. 2003. "West Wing," "24" provide civics lesson. *Charlotte Observer*, June 20. Accessed at http://bartlet4america.org/news/000544.html (February 9, 2004).

Sacket, R. 1982. *Popular entertainment, class, and politics in Munich, 1900–1923.* Cambridge, Mass.: Harvard University Press.

Sapiro, V., and K. Walsh. 2002. Doing gender in congressional campaign advertisements. Paper for delivery at the annual meeting of the International Society for Political Psychology, Berlin, July.

Scammell, M. 2003. Citizen consumers: Towards a new marketing of politics? In *Media and the restyling of politics*, edited by J. Corner and D. Pels, 117–137. London: Sage.

Scharrer, E. 2002. An "improbable leap": A content analysis of newspaper coverage of Hillary Clinton's transition from first lady to Senate candidate. *Journalism Studies* 3(3): 393–407.

Scheuer, J. 2001. *The sound bite society: How television helps the right and hurts the left.* New York: Routledge.

Schudson, M. 1992. *Watergate: How we remember, forget and reconstruct the past.* New York: Basic Books.

———. 1998. *The good citizen: A history of American civic life.* New York: Free Press.

———. 1999. Good citizens and bad history: Today's political ideals in historical perspective. Keynote lecture delivered at the conference on the Transformation of Civic Life, Nashville, Tennessee, November 12. Accessed at http://communication.ucsd.edu/people/f_schudson_nashville.html.

Schwartzenberg, R. G. 1977. *Politieke superstars: Vedettencultus in de politiek.* Antwerp: Standaard Uitgeverij. French Translation, *L'état spectacle* [The spectacle state]. Paris: Flammarion.

Schwichtenberg, C. 1993. *The Madonna connection: Representational politics, subcultural identities and cultural theory.* Boulder, Colo.: Westview Press.

Seiter, E., H. Borchers, G. Kreutzner, and E. Warth, eds. 1989. *Remote control: Television, audiences and cultural power.* London: Routledge.

Sennett, R. 1974. *The fall of public man.* New York: W. W. Norton.

Seymour-Ure, C. 1993. Campaign strategies: The challenge of the tabloids. Paper presented at the ECPR Joint Session of Workshops, Leiden, April 2–8.

Sheehy, G. 1999. *Hillary's choice*. New York: Random House.

Simmons, B. K. 1992. The effect of censorship on attitudes toward popular music. *Popular Music and Society* 16(4): 61–68.

Simon, Z. 2001. *The civil corporation: The new economy of corporate citizenship*. London: Earthscan.

Simonton, D. K. 1987. *Why presidents succeed: A political psychology of leadership*. New Haven, Conn.: Yale University Press.

Skanse, R. 2003. Chicks boycott overblown. *Rolling Stone*, March 19. Accessed at www.rollingstone.com/news/newsarticle.asp?nid=17757&cf=3566.

Sloniowski, J. 1996. Violations: The boys of St. Vincent. *Canadian Journal of Communication* 21(3). Accessed at www.wlu.ca/~wwwpress/jrls/cjc/BackIssues/21.3/sloniows.html (June 13, 2004).

Smillie, D. 1992. Madonna, the Red Hot Chili Peppers . . . and Bill Clinton. In *The homestretch: New politics, new media, new voters?* edited by M. Fitzsimon and E. C. Pease, 21–29. New York: Freedom Forum Media Studies Center.

Smith, J. 2000. Hague issues poll challenge at Blair. *Independent*, October 5. Accessed at www.independent.co.uk/story.jsp?story=10973 (September 6, 2001).

Smith, L. 1999. *The West Wing*: Reigning men. *Pop Matters*. Accessed at http://popmatters.com/tv/reviews/w/west-wing.shtml (November 22, 2001).

Social Science Journal. 2000. *First Ladies* 37 (special issue, 4).

Soetjipto, T. 2000. Suharto land to be searched for son. *Independent*, November 8. Accessed at www.independent.co.uk/story.jsp?story=20491 (September 10, 2001).

Sparks, C. 1992. Popular journalism: Theories and practice. In *Journalism and Popular Culture*, edited by P. Dahlgren and C. Sparks, 24–44. London: Sage.

Sprague, R., and K. Turner. 1990. Diary of a generation: The rhetoric of 1960s protest music. In *Politics in familiar contexts: Projecting politics through popular media*, edited by R. Savage and D. Nimmo. Norwood, N.J.: Ablex.

Sreberny, A., and L. van Zoonen, eds. 2000. *Gender, politics and communication*. Cresskill, N.J.: Hampton Press.

Stapleton, K. R. 1998. From the margins to mainstream: The political power of hip-hop. *Media, Culture and Society* 20:219–234.

Stephanopoulos, G. 2000. So how will history judge President Clinton? *Independent*, August 18. Accessed at www.independent.co.uk/story.jsp?story=40641 (September 10, 2001).

Stevenson, N., ed. 2001. *Culture and citizenship*. London: Sage.

Stop acting like a soap star. 2000. *Independent*, July 18. Accessed at www.independent.co.uk/story.jsp?story=41040 (September 6, 2001).

Street, J. 1986. *Rebel rock: The politics of popular music*. Oxford: Basil Blackwell.

———. 1997. *Politics & popular culture*. Cambridge: Polity Press.

———. 2000. "Prime time politics": Popular culture and politicians in the UK. *Javnost/The Public* 7(2): 75–90.

———. 2001. *Mass media, politics and democracy*. Basingstoke, UK: Palgrave Macmillan.

———. 2002. Cultures of cynicism: Popular television drama and antipolitics. Paper presented to the ECPR Joint Sessions, panel "Antipolitics and the media," April, Turin.

———. 2003. The celebrity politician: Political style and popular culture. In *Media and the restyling of politics*, edited by J. Corner and D. Pels, 85–99. London: Sage.

Szostak-Pierce, S. 1999. The power of subcultural style in techno culture. In *Appearance and power*, edited by K. K. P. Johnson and S. J. Lennon, 141–151. Oxford: Berg.

Templin, C. 1999. Hillary Clinton as a threat to gender norms: Cartoon images of the first lady. *Journal of Communication Inquiry* 23(1): 20–36.

Ter Bogt, T., R. Engels, B. Hibbel, F. Van Wel, and S. Verhagen. 2002. Dancestasy: Dance and MDMA use in the Netherlands. *Contemporary Drug Problems* 29:157–181.

Thale, M. 2001. Deists, Methodists and papists at London debating societies, 1749–1799. *History* 86: 328–347.

Thatcher, M. 1993. *The Downing Street years*. London: Harper Collins.

Thomas, J. 2002. *Diana's mourning: A people's history*. Cardiff: University of Wales Press.

Thomas, L. 2002. *Fans, feminisms and quality media*. London: Routledge.

Thompson, J. 2000. *Political scandal*. Cambridge: Polity.

Todorov, T. 1977. *The poetics of prose*. Oxford: Blackwell.

Tomasky, M. 2001. *Hillary's turn: Inside her improbable, victorious Senate campaign*. New York: Free Press.

Troost, N. 2001. Canada in de ban van politieke soap [Canada under the spell of political soap]. *Volkskrant*, July 21. Accessed at www.volkskrant.nl/zoek (September 6, 2001).

Troy, G. 2000. Mr. and Mrs. President? The rise and fall of the co-presidency. *Social Science Journal* 37(4): 591–600.

Turner, B., ed. 1993. *Citizenship and social theory*. London: Sage.

Turner, B. S. 2001. Outline of a general theory of cultural citizenship. In *Culture and citizenship*, edited by N. Stevenson, 11–32. London: Sage.

Van Holsteyn, J., and G. Irwin. 1998. *De frisheid van wilde limoenen: Studies over politici in de ogen van kiezers* [Politicians in the eyes of voters]. Leiden: DSWO Press.

Van Zoonen, L. 1988. Rethinking women and the news. *European Journal of Communication* 3(1): 35–53.

———. 1994. *Feminist media studies*. London: Sage.

———. 1995. Haagse Geheimen? Politiek en politici in de populaire pers. In *Communicatiewetenschappelijke Bijdragen 1994/1995*, edited by K. Renckstorf, P. Vettehen, Y. Need, and L. van Snippenburg, 119–140. Nijmegen, the Netherlands: ITS, Katholieke Universiteit Nijmegen.

———. 1998a. A day at the zoo: Political communication, pigs and popular culture. *Media, Culture and Society* 20(2): 183–200.

———. 1998b. Finally I have my mother back. Politicians and their families in popular culture. *Harvard International Journal of Press/Politics* 3(1): 48–64.

———. 2000a. Popular culture as political communication. *Javnost/The Public* 7(2): 5–19.

———. 2000b. The personalization of politics: Opportunities for women? *International Journal of Political Psychology* 9(3–4): 19–35.

———. 2000c. Book review: *Tune in, log on. European Journal of Communication Research* 25(2): 210–212.

———. 2001. Desire and resistance: *Big Brother* and the recognition of everyday life. *Media, Culture and Society* 23: 669–677.

———. 2004. Imagining the fan democracy. *European Journal of Communication* 19(1): 39–52.

Van Zoonen, L., and K. Brants. 1995. Ria Lubbers wil vervroegde verkiezingen: de politieke logica van de roddelpers. In *Verkoop van de politiek: De verkiezingscampagne van 1994* [Selling politics: The national election campaign of 1994], edited by K. Brants and P. van Praag, 111–128. Amsterdam: Het Spinhuis.

Van Zoonen, L., and C. Holzbacha. 2000. Personalization in Dutch and German politics: The case of the talk show. *Javnost/The Public* 7(2): 45–57.

Van Zwol, C. 1994. Groen Links gelaten over pilletjes op eigen feestje. *NRC Handelsblad*, April 25, 3.

Venturino, F. 2002. Personalization and electoral appeal: Berlusconi and Rutelli in the 2001 campaign. Paper delivered at the ECPR Joint Session of Workshops, April, Turin, Italy.

Wahl-Jorgensen, K. 2000. Constructing masculinities in the US presidential campaigns: The case of 1992. In *Gender, politics and communication,* edited by A. Sreberny and L. van Zoonen, 53–78. Cresskill, N.J.: Hampton Press.

Wallis, R., and K. Malm. 1992. *Big sounds from small peoples: The music industries in small countries.* New York: Pendragon Press.

Ward, L. 1999a. In true soap style, Hague's kitchen table couple stick the breadknife into Labour. *Guardian Unlimited,* April 15. Accessed at http://politics.guardian.co.uk/news/story/o,,455432,00.htm.

Ward, L. 1999b. Hague urged to back sex advice campaign. *Guardian,* May 13.

Warner, J. 1993. *Hillary Clinton: The inside story.* New York: Signet/Penguin.

Waxman, S. 2002. Haysbert: Role model and president. *Washington Post,* November 8.

Wayne, M., ed. 1998. *Dissident voices: The politics of television and cultural change.* London: Pluto Press.

Weber, M. 1918. Politics as vocation. Speech given at Munich University. Published in 1921 in *Gesammelte Politische Schriften,* Munich. Accessed at www2.pfeiffer.edu/~lridener/DSS/Weber/polvoc.html.

———. 1921. *Wirtschaft und Gesellschaft.* English translation accessed at www2.pfeiffer.edu/~lridener/DSS/Weber/BUREAU.HTML.

Weimer, W. 1999. Politik als soap. *Die Welt,* September 17. Accessed at www.welt.de/daten/1999/08/30/0830fo127318.htx?search=soap (June 15, 2004).

Wermuth, M. *No sell out: De popularisering van een subcultuur* [The popularization of a subculture]. Amsterdam: Aksant.

White, M. 1999. Don't edit politicians, Campbell tells BBC. *Guardian Unlimited,* February 10. Accessed at http://politics.guardian.co.uk/news/story/0,,455510,00.htm (September 6, 2001).

Widgery, D. 1987. *Beating time.* London: Chatto & Windus.

Winfield, B. H. 1994. Madame president: Understanding a new kind of first lady. *Media Studies Journal* 8(2): 59–71.

———. 1997. The making of an image: Hillary Rodham Clinton and American journalists. *Political Communication* 14:241–253.

Wintour, P. 1999. Blair scorns Fleet Street "soap opera." *Guardian Unlimited,* January 31. Accessed at http://politics.guardian.co.uk/news/story/0,,457215,00.htm (September 6, 2001).

Witt, L., M. Paget, and G. Matthews. 1994. *Running as a woman: Gender and power in American politics*. New York: Free Press.

Witteveen, W. 1992. *Het theatre van de politiek*. Amsterdam: Amber.

Young, I. 1980. Socialist feminism and the limits of dual systems theory. *Socialist Review* 50:169–188.

———. 1990. *Justice and the politics of difference*. Princeton, N.J.: Princeton University Press.

Zillman, D., and J. Bryant. 1994. Entertainment as a media effect. In *Media effects*, edited by J. Bryant and D. Zillman, 447–459. Hillsdale, N.J.: Erlbaum. Reprinted in D. McQuail. 2002. *McQuail's reader in mass communication*. London: Sage, 406–417.

Zipper zappt. 2001. Die Leute vom Reichstag—Die politische Daily Soap. *Die Welt*, January 11.

Zuckerman, A. S., L. A. Kotler-Berkowitz, and L. A. Swaine. 1998. Anchoring political preferences: The structural bases of stable electoral decisions and political attitudes in Britain. *European Journal of Political Research* 33:285–321.

Index

British Labour, 19–21, 27, 31, 45–47, 85, 120
British Tories, 20, 28–29, 31, 84, 120
Britpop, 45–47
Brown, James, 46, 81
bureaucracy, 17, 33, 107, 109, 112–15, 120, 137–38, 146
Bush, Barbara, 100
Bush, George, Jr., 33, 38, 46, 52n6, 81, 86n11, 96–97, 110, 118, 132–33, 138
Bush, George, Sr., 44, 46, 119
Bush, Laura, 96

Caetona, 39
Camel, 46
campaign, 14, 16, 20, 22, 26, 31, 38, 43–47, 50, 57, 65, 70, 73, 76, 79, 81, 85, 85n5, 95–102, 105–6, 109–12, 127, 135, 144, 150, 152
Campbell, Alastair, 19, 27
candidate endorsement, 13, 46, 81
candidate evaluations, 125
Capitol Hill, 110
Capra, Frank, 83, 109–10, 129, 132
care, 32, 34
Carpenters, the, 45
Carter, Jimmy, 45, 76, 85
Carter, Rosalynn, 96
Cartland, Barbara, 87
Casablanca, 62
celebrity, 11, 70, 75, 77, 82, 84, 87–88, 91–95, 99, 102, 103n5, 146; culture, 17, 72, 75–76, 88, 91, 93–95, 101; politician, 17, 69–86, 146; politics, 4, 17, 29, 94, 99, 102, 143; press, 76–78, 83, 90–94
censorship, 5, 37, 40–41, 43–44
character, 67, 107–9, 137, 139
charisma, 72, 76, 125
Choose or Lose, 44
citizenship, 1, 3, 4, 7–9, 10, 15, 17–18, 24, 39–40, 43, 46–47, 50–53, 56, 61, 64, 66–67, 107, 109, 123–41, 144–47, 149, 151; civil, 7; corporate, 8; cultural, 6, 8–9; political, 7, 9–10, 15, 17, 39, 43, 51, 61, 66, 151; sexual, 8; social, 8

City Hall, 113
civic education, 15
civic performance, 17, 56, 124, 144
civic virtues, 15, 63, 149
civil rights movement, 8, 50
Clapton, Eric, 49
Clark, Wesley, 80, 84
Clinton, Bill, 20, 25–26, 29–31, 45, 74, 84, 95, 100–102, 109, 111, 128–29
Clinton, Hillary, 17, 88, 93, 95–96, 99–103, 105–6, 146
Cobain, Kurt, 40
cognition, 63–64
cognitive miser, 69
"comeback kid," 30
communism, 49
community building, 62
competence, 72, 125, 129
"Concert for New York," 38
Condit, Gary, 25
conservatism, 12
Conservatives, British. *See* British Conservatives
conspiracy, 17, 107–9, 115–18, 120, 135, 137–38, 146
Cooke, Alex, 85n1, 110
cooking, 22
Cooper, Alice, 40
copyright, 39–40
corruption, 6, 26, 83, 87, 111, 113
couch potatoes, 55
counterculture, 8
country and western, 48, 52n6
Crossroad, 20
Crouse, Timothy, 109
cultural climate, 3
cultural mainstreaming, 14
cultural policy, 39, 51
cultural studies, 10
culture of conspiracy, 107
Cutler, R. J., 57

Dave, 109, 111–13, 128, 130–31, 134–38, 148
Day after the Revolution, 47
daytime soap, 23, 61

representation: in crisis, 6; as
   delegation, 3, 4, 59, 144; as
   portrayal, 12, 17, 23, 76, 93, 110, 112,
   114, 123, 127–28, 139; as
   resemblance, 3
Republican Party, 43, 45, 101–2,
   118–19, 126–27
Republican thought, 6, 147
research methodology, 18n1, 35n1
rhetoric, 4, 71–72, 75, 102
Richard III, 115
Roberts, Julia, 112, 139
Robin Hood, 107–8
"Rock against . . . ," 49, 52n7
Rock the Vote, 44
Rolling Stones, 41
romance novels, 55
Rousseau, Jean-Jacques, 88
running mate, 22

satire, 6, 10, 114, 132
Saunders, Clarissa, 110, 112
scandal, 25–26, 30, 43, 76–78, 96,
   99–102, 103n7, 108, 116, 138, 146
Schwarzenegger, Arnold, 1, 70, 84–85,
   110
self-regulation, 37
Shakespeare, William, 21, 115
Sharpton, Al, 81, 84
Sheen, Martin, 33, 118
"Shoot the Dog," 38, 47
Sinatra, Frank, 45
situated analysis, 4
Smith, Adam, 88
soap opera, 4, 15–16, 19–35, 51, 53–54,
   62, 72, 118, 143–44; generic features
   of, 23; as metaphor, 15, 24–35;
   narrative, 16–17, 21–23, 30–31,
   33–34, 56, 144
social capital, 62–63, 68n8
social cohesion, 62
Social Democrats, 18n2, 29, 76, 85n5
sociology, 10
Sophists, 71
sound-bite society, 2
Spice Girls, 45
Spin City, 116

spin doctor, 10, 15, 29, 31, 71, 110, 115,
   132
Springsteen, Bruce, 38, 45
stage, 72, 74–80, 82–83, 91, 95–96, 115,
   125
star system, 93
stars, 16, 20, 45, 53, 60–62, 64, 70,
   81–82, 84, 93–94, 107, 120
Star Trek, 62
Story, 76
subjectivity, 63
suede, 46
supermarket tabloids, 107
Sutherland, Kiefer, 116
symbols, 21–22, 35n1, 48, 87, 110
syntagma, 67, 145

talk show, 4, 20, 57, 70, 72, 75, 78–79,
   85n8, 90, 99
tariff barriers, 40
taste communities, 24
telegenic, 60, 71
television, 1–4, 10–21, 30, 32, 54–55,
   67, 67n4, 70–72, 76–78, 93, 99, 102,
   105, 113, 118, 128, 131, 133, 143;
   culture, 21, 67n2, 70; epistemology
   of, 12–13; ideology of, 12–13;
   influence, 11, 14; journalism, 11,
   109, 151; malaise, 11–16, 123;
   minimalism, 12; phenomenology
   of, 12–13
Thatcher, Margaret, 47, 84–85, 94, 114
Thatcherism, 45–46
theatre, 21–22, 72
"Things Can Only Get Better," 45
Third Way politics, 6, 29
Toledo, Alejandro, 26
Tories, British. *See* British Tories
trade restrictions, 40

U2, 1, 46
un-American messages, 41
undecided voters. *See* floating voters
Usenet, 61
U.S. government, 27, 49; immigration
   law, 40; presidential elections 2004,
   44, 57, 70, 72

About the Author

Liesbet van Zoonen is professor of media and popular culture at the University of Amsterdam. She graduated cum laude on an analysis of media coverage of the Dutch women's movement and has since then published widely on gender and media. Her book *Feminist Media Studies* (1994) is used in curricula around the world. Her current work focuses on the manifold articulations of popular culture, identity, and citizenship, for which her research center, Centre for Popular Culture, has received grants from the Dutch Science Foundation, the media industry, and the Dutch government.